IN
DEFENSE
OF THE
AMERICAN PUBLIC SCHOOL

EDITED BY

Arthur J. Newman

University of Florida

Distributed by
McCutchan Publishing Corporation
2526 Grove Street, Berkeley, California 94704

Copyright © 1978
Schenkman Publishing Company
Casebound edition distributed by McCutchan Publishing Corporation

ISBN: 0-8211-1307-0
Library of Congress Catalog Card Number: 78-19570

Printed in the United States of America

Contents

Introduction

"*America is in headlong retreat from its commitment to education. Political confusion and economic uncertainty have shaken the people's faith in education as the key to financial and social success....At stake is nothing less than the survival of American democracy.*"

—*Fred Hechinger*

Criticism of the American public school system has abounded since its inception. Nor should this surprise us. Many reasons account for the school's popularity as a clay pigeon. Certainly, few social institutions so intimately and pervasively affect so many of our nation's youth. Moreover, the school is the one agency of government which is at once highly visible, comprehensible (or so goes the popular image), and easily accessible. Many of those who are politically disenchanted naturally single out the school as a scapegoat.

Both in intensity and frequency, criticism of our public schools has increased greatly since the end of World War II. Many factors, not the least of which is the increased ease of reaching millions through the mass media, account for this ever-increasing critical tempo.

During the decade of the fifties, the schools were viewed by many as thinly disguised purveyors of international Communism. Like all American institutions, the public schools were attacked during the fervor of the mid sixties. Labels like "racist," "imperialistic," "mindless," and "irrelevant" glibly rolled off the tongues of many self-appointed educational experts. The Bicentennial era witnessed no silencing of the critics. Among the favorite indictments of the mid seventies is the alleged failure of public schools to adequately teach fundamental academic skills.

Whether all or some of these criticisms are justified or not, it is incumbent upon practicing and aspiring educators—as well concerned lay persons—to assess them intelligently and responsibly. Only as the professional educator becomes habituated to examining critically the

1

criticisms to which his institution has been (and continues to be) subjected is he or she in a position to (a) lend support to warranted attacks and (b) fend off those which are unfounded.

Except for the demagogue and/or the simpleton, it is exceedingly difficult to assess the validity of many of these attacks. Only through a process of imaginative reflection can we conclude that a particular onslaught is warranted, somewhat warranted, or clearly unfounded. However arduous the process, we are obliged to accept the challenge. To do otherwise would be to put ourselves in the wholly untenable position of not being able to respond effectively to attacks on our professional behavior.

If we are responsibly to support or reject particular public school attacks, we must, first of all, be sensitive to the social climate prevailing at the time a certain criticism is articulated. For example, an appreciation of the frequently abusive attacks of the mid sixties obliges us to relate them to the tense sociopolitical ferment which characterized this period of our history. Secondly, we must ask ourselves if the criticisms we are endeavoring to understand constitute a reasonable statement of the school's alleged wrongdoings. Thirdly, we should run the profile our analysis yields through our moral filter. In this regard, we must ask ourselves whether the critical attack we are examining meshes with our deeply held moral convictions. To recur to our example, were many of the harsh criticisms of the mid and late sixties pursued in a manner consistent with our interpretation of democratic behavior? Was the content of these criticisms consistent with our understanding of acceptable social policy?

This book is designed to aid the student in refining his assessment of contemporary attacks on public schools in an intelligent and responsible manner. It draws upon material which will help the reader adopt the critical perspectives discussed above. Many different types of material, reflecting a variety of evidentiary procedures, are presented, including thoughtful essays, empirical studies, anthropological impressions, and personal accounts.

Like all edited books of readings, this one reflects the biases of the compiler. It clearly reflects an idea regarded as heretical in many circles, the idea that the American public school is not nearly so inadequate as many contemporary critics would have us believe. Although, as the readings point out, the schools have quite admittedly suffered from some glaring weaknesses—especially in the area of extending equality of educational opportunity to minority group youngsters—their overall record of performance is not one about which we should hang our heads in shame. Intellectual honesty obliges us to acknowledge clearly and unequivocally our schools' grievous errors. This same sense of integrity compels us to celebrate their myriad strengths.

Recent critics appear to have been hellbent on besmirching and castigating our public schools. The Illiches, the Holts, the Silbermans, the Kohls, and the Kozols do indeed render us a notable public service by exposing some of our schools' shortcomings. However, as is so often the case, they and many other critics have become so caught up in their zealous assaults that they communicate a largely distorted public school image. Or, if not distorted, the profiles suggested by these critics have focused upon but one portion of a rich landscape, thereby communicating a clear, but nonetheless truncated and spurious image.

Unlike most such books of reading and/or texts, this volume attempts to correct this image. Such a "foil" is needed in the interest of presenting a fair and accurate picture of our school system. This point has been driven home to me by many undergraduate and graduate students I have taught in courses variously catalogued as Social Foundations of Education, Social Issues in Education, Sociology of Education, and the like. Throughout the decades of the sixties and seventies many of my probing students in Indiana, New Jersey, Saskatchewan, and Florida have asked me again and again: "Isn't there something positive you can say about the U. S. (or Canadian) public schools?" Too frequently my response has been one of fumbling, bumbling, stuttering and embarrassment. Hopefully, this volume will serve as a partial response to those many inspired teachers-to-be and their counterparts of today who aspire to enter our noble profession.

This book makes no pretense at being comprehensive in scope. Many glaring issues are not treated. For example, little mention is made of the richly compelling problem of the public schools' treatment of American females. Nor do I present analyses of religion and education, peace studies, and other exciting studies. They are no less significant than those included, but my choices were limited by the time and resources at my disposal.

Except in a tangential way the book does not relate to what is perhaps the most important expectation of the public school experience. I refer to the value orientations which the schools are charged to enhance. No apology is made for what some will regard as a glaring omission. A note of explanation will hopefully illuminate the reasons for not including much data which relate to this "affective" domain. It would be belaboring the obvious to explain why the research design and measurement problems involved in describing and evaluating student value dispositions are exceedingly intricate and complex. While numerous studies have been conducted on localized student populations, few have been attempted which treat the national population examined in this book. Hopefully, future studies will deal with this area of inquiry. At this time, however, the pickings are slim indeed.

It is my ardent wish that this book will help fill the academic vacuum resulting from focusing upon our public schools' weaknesses to the virtual neglect of their strengths. It is hoped that this book will spur others to engage in the process of criticizing the critics. Out of this enterprise might emerge a balanced picture of the American public schools. Nothing less will suffice.

SECTION ONE

The Charge to the Public Schools

The adage that hope springs eternal can be said to symbolize the aspirations which prominent Americans have had for public education. While the schools have always had their detractors, the political consensus of the American republic has been characterized by an unwavering commitment to the process of public education.

The continuity of the succession of proponents of American education is remarkable. Distinguished spokespersons throughout our history have articulated all-but-unbounded faith in the American public schools' capacity for facilitating the development of responsible, contributing citizens. This is well illustrated by the selections given here.

Our earliest "reading" (1685) reflects what might be regarded as the keystone of public education: Public education (in Colonial days restricted to the elementary level) should be provided in all settled locales for all children, regardless of social class.

One hundred years later, Thomas Jefferson suggested that there existed a strong, indisputable relationship between an educated citizenry and the ongoing welfare of a democratic society. Another highly significant note struck by Jefferson was his insistence that the public school should permit and encourage talented youngsters—regardless of social class—to develop their potential to the fullest. This pool of highly educated youth would hopefully provide the nation with leadership of the highest caliber. The core notion that the public schools should function as a vehicle for achieving status—as distinguished from saddling a young person with a given status ascribed at birth—has been a hallmark of our educational system.[1]

---

1. Most deplorably, of course, the institution of slavery thrived during Jefferson's life time and the public school privilege was not extended to hundreds of thousands of Afro-Americans until the contemporary era. Moreover, a multitude of young people of other minority groups have been denied equality of educational opportunity, i.e., have been victimized by an essentially caste-like system.

The next selection, by Dr. Benjamin Rush, echoes many of the convictions expressed by Jefferson. Public education (on the elementary level) should be extended to all, regardless of social class. *All* citizens have a responsibility to lend financial and moral support to the schooling enterprise. Another noteworthy conviction of Rush's—one which has become an integral part of American public education—is that the scholastic, liberal arts core of the curriculum should be complemented with a program in the useful arts. No better manifestation of this orientation can be cited than our land-grant universities which emerged in the late nineteenth-century.

Our fourth reading illustrates how the convictions of people like Jefferson and Rush were captured in a formal, legal document. The state of New Hampshire—like many of her newly-emerged sister states— acknowledged formally that the commonweal of the new nation was tied inextricably to an intelligent, responsible electorate.

The writings of Horace Mann constitute perhaps the most eloquent, cogent expression of the faith invested in the American public school system. Mann's forceful declaration that every child, as a matter of natural right, is entitled to an efficient, effective schooling experience stands as a classic. Like Jefferson before him, he insists that we are all bound together in a social context, a situation which both extends certain precious rights to all and exacts certain obligations from all. It is, indeed, uncanny that Mann, writing over 130 years ago, articulates the same contention (children's natural rights) which undergirds recent attempts (in states like New Jersey) to fund our public schools in a manner which guarantees to all youngsters a solid, wholesome educational experience.

Some twenty-six years after Mann wrote his brilliant essay, the Michigan Supreme Court, in the landmark *Kalamazoo* case, ruled that tax-supported public education should be extended to all youth through their adolescent years. This decision is highly significant for it spurred other states to provide free, universal secondary education to their youngsters, a process which became increasingly institutionalized by the turn of the century.

Our last reading, by the renowned philosopher and educator, John Dewey, is representative of the faith which twentieth-century America has invested in public schooling. Dewey, like Jefferson and Rush, insists that our society's ongoing vitality inheres, in large measure, in providing the American people with effective, viable schooling opportunities.

1
The Colonial Posture

Thomas Budd (1685)

1. Now, it might be well if a law were made by the governours and general assemblies of Pennsilvania and New Jersey, that all persons inhabiting the said Provinces to put their children seven years to the publick school, or longer, if the parents please.

2. That schools be provided in all towns and cities, and persons of known honesty, skill, and understanding be yearly chosen by the governour and general assembly, to teach and instruct boys and girls in all the most useful arts and sciences, that they in their useful capacities may be capable to read and to write true English and Latine and other useful speeches and languages, and fair writing, arithmetick, and book-keeping; and the boys to be taught and instructed in some mystery or trade the making of mathematical instruments, joynery, turnery, the making of clocks and watches, weaving, shoe making, or any other useful trade or mystery that school is capable of teaching; and the girls to be taught and instructed in spinning of flax and wool, and knitting of gloves and stockings, sewing, and making of sorts of needle-work, and the making of straw-work, as hats, baskets, etc., or any other useful art of mystery that the school is capable of teaching.

3. That the scholars to be kept in the morning two hours at reading, writing, book keeping, etc., and other two hours at the work in that art, mystery, or trade that he or she most delighteth in, and let them have two hours to dine and for recreation and in the afternoon two hours at work at their several employments.

4. The seventh day of the week the scholars may come to the school only in the forenoon, and at a certain hour in the afternoon let a meeting be kept by the school masters and their scholars, where, after good instruction and

Reprinted from U. S. Bureau of Education Circular of Information No. 1, 1899. Contributions to American Educational History #23. *History of Education in New Jersey* by David Murray (Washington, D. C., U. S. Printing Office, 1899), pp. 17-18.

admonition is given by the masters to their scholars, and thanks returned to the Lord for his mercies and blessings that are daily received from him, then let a strict examination by the masters of the conversation of the scholars in the past week, and let reproof, admonition, and correction be given to the offenders according to the quantity and quality of their faults.

5. Let the like meetings be kept by the school-mistresses and the girls apart from the boys. By strictly observing this good order, our children will be hindered from running into that excess of riot and wickedness that youth is incident to, and that will be a comfort to their tender parents.

6. Let one thousand acres of land be given and laid out in a good place to every publick school that shall be set up, and the rent or income of it to go towards defraying the charge of the school.

7. And to the end that the children of the poor people and the children of the Indians may have the like good learning with the children of the rich people, let them be maintained free of charge to their parents, out of the profits of the school arising by the work of the scholars, by which the poor and the Indians, as well as the rich, will have their children taught; and the remainder of the profits, if any be, to be disposed of in building of school-houses and improvements to the thousand acres of land which belongs to the school.

2
Ongoing Democracy and the Schools
Thomas Jefferson (1782)

Another object of the revisal is, to diffuse knowledge more generally through the mass of the people. This bill proposes to lay off every county into small districts of five or six miles square, called hundreds and in each of them to establish a school for teaching, reading, writing, and arithmetic. The tutor to be supported by the hundred, and every person in it entitled to send their children three years gratis, and as much longer as they please, paying for it. These schools to be under a visitor who is annually to chuse the boy of best genius in the school, of those whose parents are too poor to give them further education, and to send him forward to one of the grammar schools, of which twenty are proposed to be erected in different parts of the country, for teaching Greek, Latin, geography, and the higher branches of numerical arithmetic. Of the boys thus sent in any one year, trial is to be made at the grammar schools one or two years, and the best genius of the whole selected, and continued six years, and the residue dismissed. By this means twenty of the best geniuses will be raked from the rubbish annually, and be instructed, at the public expense, so far as the grammar schools go. At the end of six years instruction, one half are to be discontinued (from among whom the grammar schools will probably be supplied with future masters); and the other half, who are to be chosen for the superiority of their parts and disposition, are to be sent and continued three years in the study of such sciences as they shall chuse, at William and Mary college, the plan of which is proposed to be enlarged, as will be hereafter explained, and extended to all the useful sciences. The ultimate result of the whole scheme of education would be the teaching all the children of the State reading, writing, and common arithmetic; turning out ten annually, of superior genius, well taught in Greek, Latin, geography, and the higher branches of arithmetic; turning out ten others annually, of

Reprinted from Paul Leicester Ford (ed.), *The Works of Thomas Jefferson*, (N.Y.: G. P. Putnam, 1904), IV, pp. 60-65.

genius who, to those branches of learning, shall have added such of the sciences as their genius shall have led them to; the furnishing to the wealthier part of the people convenient schools at which their children may be educated at their own expense.—The general objects of this law are to provide an education adapted to the years, to the capacity, and the condition of every one, and directed to their freedom and happiness. Specific details were not proper for the law. These must be the business of the visitors entrusted with its execution. The first stage of this education being the schools of the hundreds, wherein the great mass of people will receive instruction, the principal foundations of future order will be laid here. Instead, therefore, of putting the Bible and Testament into the hands of the children at an age when their judgments are not sufficiently matured for religious inquiries, their memories may here be stored with the most useful facts from Grecian, Roman, European, and American history. The first elements of morality too may be instilled into their minds; such as, when further developed as their judgments advance in strength, may teach them how to work out their own greatest happiness, by shewing them that it does not depend on the condition of life in which chance has placed them, but is always the result of a good conscience, good health, occupation, and freedom in all just pursuits.—

Those whom either the wealth of their parents or the adoption of the state shall destine to higher degrees of learning, will go on to the grammar schools, which constitute the next stage, there to be instruction in the languages. The learning Greek and Latin, I am told, is going into disuse in Europe. I know not what their manners and occupations may call for: but it would be very ill-judged in us to follow their example in this instance. There is a certain period of life, say from eight to fifteen or sixteen years of age, when the mind like the body is not yet firm enough for laborious and close operations. If applied to such, it falls an early victim of premature exertion; exhibiting, indeed, at first, in these young and tender subjects, the flattering appearance of their being men while they are yet children, but ending in reducing them to be children when they should be men. The memory is then most susceptible and tenacious of impressions; and the learning of languages being chiefly a work of memory, it seems precisely fitted to the powers of this period, which is long enough too for acquiring the most useful languages, ancient and modern. I do not pretend that language is science. It is only an instrument for the attainment of science. But that time is not lost which is employed in providing tools for future operations; more especially as in this case the books put into the hands of youth for this purpose may be such as will at the same time impress their minds with useful facts and good principles. If this period be suffered to pass in idleness, the mind becomes lethargic and impotent, as would the body it inhabits if unexercised during the same time. The sympathy between body and mind during their rise, progress and decline, is too strict and obvious to endanger our being misled while we reason from the one to the other.—As soon as they are of sufficient age, it is supposed they will be sent on from the grammar schools to the university, which constitutes our third and last stage, there to study those sciences which may be adapted to their views.—By that part of our plan which prescribes the selection of the youths of genius from among the classes of the poor, we hope to avail the state of those talents which nature has sown as liberally among the poor as the rich, but which perish without use, if not sought for and cultivated.— But of all the views of this law none is more important, none more legitimate, than that of rendering the people the safe, as they are the ultimate guardians of their own liberty. For this purpose the reading in the first stage, where *they* will receive their whole education, is proposed, as has been said, to be chiefly historical. History, by apprising them of the past, will enable them to judge of the future; it will avail them of the experience of other times and other nations; it will enable them to know ambition under every disguise it may assume; and knowing it, to defeat its views. In every government on earth is some trace of human weakness, some germ of corruption and degeneracy, which cunning will discover, and wickedness insensibly open, cultivate, and improve. Every government degenerates when trusted to the rulers of the people alone. The people themselves therefore are its only safe depositories. And to rend even them safe, their minds must be improved to a certain degree. This indeed is not all that is necessary, though it be essentially necessary. An amendment of our constitution must here come in aid of the public education. The influence over government must be shared among all the people. If every individual which composes their mass participates of the ultimate authority, the government will be safe; because the corrupting of the whole mass will exceed any private resources of wealth and public ones cannot be provided but by levies on the people. In this case every man would have to pay his own price. The government of Great Britain has been corrupted, because but one man in ten has a right to vote for members of parliament. The sellers of the government, therefore, get nine-tenths of their price clear. It has been thought that corruption is restrained by confining the right of suffrage to a few of the wealthier of the people; but it would be more effectually restrained by an extension of that right to such numbers as would bid defiance to the means of corruption.

3
The Schools Are Everyone's Concern
Benjamin Rush (1786)

Before I proceed to the subject of this essay, I shall point out, in a few words, the influence and advantages of learning upon mankind.

I. It is friendly to religion, inasmuch as it assists in removing prejudice, superstition and enthusiasm, in promoting just notions of the Deity, and in enlarging our knowledge of his works.

II. It is favourable to liberty. Freedom can exist only in the society of knowledge. Without learning, men are incapable of knowing their rights, and where learning is confined to a few people, liberty can be neither equal nor universal.

III. It promotes just ideas of law and government. "When the clouds of ignorance are dispelled (says the Marquis of Beccaria) by the radiance of knowledge, power trembles, but the authority of laws remains immovable."

IV. It is friendly to manners. Learning in all countries, promotes civilization, and the pleasures of society and conversation.

V. It promotes agriculture, the great basis of national wealth and happiness. Agriculture is as much a science as hydraulics, or optics, and has been equally indebted to the experiements and researches of learned men. The highly cultivated state, and the immense profits of the farms in England, are derived wholly from the patronage which agriculture has received in that country, from learned men and learned societies.

VI. Manufactures of all kinds owe their perfection chiefly to learning— hence the nations of Europe advance in manufactures, knowledge, and commerce, only in proportion as they cultivate the arts and sciences.

For the purpose of diffusing knowledge through every part of the state, I beg leave to propose the following simple plan.

I. Let there be one university in the state, and let this be established in the

Reprinted from Benjamin Rush, *Essays, Literary, Moral and Philosophical* (Philadelphia: Bradford, 1798), pp. 1-6.

capital. Let law, physic, divinity, the law of nature and nations, economy, &c. be taught in it by public lectures in the winter season, after the manner of the European universities, and let the professors receive such salaries from the state as will enable them to deliver their lectures at a moderate price.

II. Let there be four colleges. One in Philadelphia, one at Carlisle, a third, for the benefit of our German fellow citizens, at Lancaster, and a fourth, some years hence at Pittsburgh. In these colleges, let young men be instructed in mathematics and in the higher branches of science, in the same manner that they are now taught in our American colleges. After they have received a testimonial from one of these colleges, let them, if they can afford it, complete their studies by spending a season or two in attending the lectures in the university. I prefer four colleges in the state to one or two, for there is a certain size of colleges as there is of towns and armies, that is most favourable to morals and good government. Oxford and Cambridge in England are the seats of dissipation, while the more numerous, and less crowded universities and colleges in Scotland, are remarkable for the order, diligence, and decent behaviour of their students.

III. Let there be free schools established in every township, or in districts consisting of one hundred families. In these schools let children be taught to read and write the English and German languages, and the use of figures. Such of them as have parents that can afford to send them from home, and are disposed to extend their educations, may remove their children from the free school to one of the colleges.

By this plan the whole state will be tied together by one system of education. The university will in time furnish masters for the colleges, and the colleges will furnish masters for the free schools, while the free schools, in their turns, will supply the colleges and the university with scholars, students and pupils. The same systems of grammar, oratory and philosophy, will be taught in very part of the state, and the literary features of Pennsylvania will thus designate one great, and equally enlightened family.

But, how shall we bear the expense of these literary institutions?—I answer—These institutions will *lessen* our taxes. They will enlighten us in the great business of finance—they will teach us to increase the ability of the state to support government, by increasing the profits of agriculture, and by promoting manufactures. They will teach us all the modern improvements and advantages of inland navigation. They will defend us from hasty and expensive experiments in government, by unfolding to us the experience and folly of past ages, and thus, instead of adding to our taxes and debts, they will furnish us with the true secret of lessening and discharging both of them.

But, shall the estates of orphans, bachelors and persons who have no children, be taxed to pay for the support of schools from which they can derive no benefit? I answer in the affirmative, to the first part of the objection, and I deny the truth of the latter part of it. Every member of the community is interested in the propagation of virtue and knowledge in the state. But I will go further, and add, it will be true economy in individual to support public schools. The bachelor will in time save his tax for this purpose, by being able to sleep with fewer bolts and locks to his doors—the estates of orphans will in time be benefited, by being protected from the ravages of unprincipled and idle boys, and the children of wealthy parents will be less tempted, by bad company, to extravagance. Fewer pillories and whipping posts, and smaller gaols, with their usual expenses and taxes, will be necessary when our youth are properly educated, than at present; I believe it could be proved, that the expense of confining, trying and executing criminals, amount every year, in most of the countries, to more money than would be sufficient to maintain all the schools that would be necessary in each county. The confessions of these criminals generally show us, that their vices and punishments are the fatal consequences of the want of a proper education in early life.

I submit these detached hints to the consideration of the legislature and of the citizens of Pennsylvania. The plan for the free schools is taken chiefly from the plans which have long been used with success in Scotland, and in the eastern states[1] of America, where the influence of learning, in promoting religion, morals, manners and good government, has never been exceeded in any country.

The manner in which these schools should be supported and governed—the modes of determining the characters and qualifications of schoolmasters, and the arrangement of families in each district, so that children of the same religious sect and nation, may be educated as much as possible together, will form a proper part of a law for the establishment of schools, and therefore does not come within the limits of this plan.

---

1. There are 600 of these schools in the small state of Connecticut, which at this time have in them 25,000 scholars.

4
The New Hampshire State Constitution
Section 83 (1784 and 1792)

Knowledge and learning generally diffused through a community being essential to the preservation of a free government, spreading the opportunities and advantages of education through the various parts of the country being highly conducive to promote this end, it shall be the duty of the legislatures and magistrates, in all future periods of this government, to cherish the interest of literature and the sciences, and all seminaries and public schools; to encourage private and public institutions, rewards and immunities for the promotion of agriculture, arts, sciences, commerce, trade, manufactures, and natural history of the country; to countenance and inculcate the principles of humanity and general benevolence, public and private charity, industry and economy, honesty and punctuality, sincerity, sobriety, and all social affections and generous sentiments among the people.

Reprinted from Benjamin Perley Poore, *The Federal and State Constitutions, Colonial Charters, and Other Organic Laws of the United States*, 2 Vols. (Washington: Government Printing Office, 1878).

5
The Education of Free Men

Horace Mann (1846)

I believe in the existence of a great, immutable principle of natural law, or natural ethics,—a principle of divine origin, clearly legible in the ways of Providence as those ways are manifested in the order of nature and in the history of the race,—which proves the *absolute right* of every human being that comes into the world to an education; and which, of course, proves the correlative duty of every government to see that the means of that education are provided for all.

In regard to the application of this principle of natural law,—that is, in regard to the extent of the education to be provided for all, at the public expense,—some differences of opinion may fairly exist, under different political organizations; but under a republican government, it seems clear that the minimum of this education can never be less than such as is sufficient to qualify each citizen for the civil and social duties he will be called to discharge;—such an education as teaches the individual the great laws of bodily health; as qualifies for the fulfilment of parental duties; as is indispensable for the civil functions of a witness or a juror; as is necessary for the voter in municipal affairs; and finally, for the faithful and conscientious discharge of all those duties which devolve upon the inheritor of a portion of the sovereignty of this great republic.

The will of God, as conspicuously manifested in the order of nature, and in the relations which he has established among men, places the *right* of every child that is born into the world to such a degree of education as will enable him, and, as far as possible, will predispose him, to perform all domestic, social, civil and moral duties upon the same clear ground of natural law and equity, as it places a child's *right*, upon his first coming into the world to distend his lungs with a portion of the common air, or to open his eyes to the common light, or to receive that shelter, protection and

Reprinted from Lawrence A. Cremin, (ed.), *The Republic and the School* (New York: Teachers College Press, 1957) pp. 63-77.

nourishment which are necessary to the continuance of his bodily existence. And so far is it from being a wrong or a hardship, to demand of the possessors of property their respective shares for the prosecution of this divinely-ordained work, that they themselves are guilty of the most far-reaching injustice, who seek to resist or to evade the contribution. The complainers are the wrong-doers. The cry, "Stop thief," comes from the thief himself.

But sometimes, the rich farmer, the opulent manufacturer, or the capitalist, when sorely pressed with his legal and moral obligation, to contribute a portion of his means for the education of the young, replies,— either in form or in spirit;—"My lands, my machinery, my gold and my silver, are mine; may not I do what I will with my own?" There is one supposable case, and only one, where this argument would have plausibility. If it were made by an isolated, solitary being,—a being having no relations to a community around him, having no ancestors to whom he had been indebted for ninety-nine parts in every hundred of all he possesses, and expecting to leave no posterity after him,—it might not be easy to answer it. If there were but one family in this western hemisphere, and one only in the eastern hemisphere, and these two families bore no civil and social relations to each other, and were to be the first and last of the whole race, it might be difficult, except on very high and almost transcendental grounds, for either one of them to show good cause why the other should contribute to help to educate children not his own. And perhaps the force of such an appeal would be still further diminished, if the nearest neighbor of a single family upon our planet were as far from the earth as Uranus or Sirius. In self-defence, or in selfishness, one might say to the other, "What are your fortunes to me? You can neither benefit nor molest me. Let us each keep to our own side of the planetary spaces." But is this the relation which any man amongst us sustains to his fellows? In the midst of a populous community to which he is bound by innumerable ties, having had his own fortune and condition almost predetermined and foreordained by his predecessors, and being about to exert upon his successors as commanding an influence as had been exerted upon himself, the objector can no longer shrink into his individuality, and disclaim connection and relationship with the world. He cannot deny that there are thousands around him on whom he acts, and who are continually reacting upon him. The earth is much too small, or the race is far too numerous, to allow us to be hermits, and therefore we cannot adopt either the philosophy or the morals of hermits. All have derived benefits from their ancestors, and all are bound, as by an oath, to transmit those benefits, even in an improved condition, to posterity. We may as well attempt to escape from our own personal identity, as to shake off the three-fold relation which we bear to others,—the relation of an associate with our contemporaries; of a beneficiary of our ancestors; of a guardian to those who, in the sublime order of Providence, are to follow us. Out of these relations, manifest duties are evolved. The society of which we necessarily constitute a part, must be preserved; and, in order to preserve it, we must not look merely to what one individual or family needs, but to what the whole community needs; not merely to what one generation needs, but to the wants of a succession of generations. To draw conclusions without considering these facts, is to leave out the most important part of the premises.

If the previous argument began with sound premises and has been logically conducted, then it has established this position;—that a vast portion of the present wealth of the world either consists in, or has been immediately derived from,those great natural substances and powers of the earth, which were bestowed by the Creator, alike on all mankind; or from the discoveries, inventions, labors and improvements of our ancestors, which were alike designed for the common benefit of all their descendants. The question now arises, *at what time,* is this wealth to be transferred from a preceding to a succeeding genration? At what point are the latter to take possession of, or to derive benefit from it, or at what time, are the former to surrender it in their behalf? Is each existing generation, and each individual of an existing generation, to hold fast to his possessions until death relaxes his grasp; or is something of the right to be acknowledged, and something of the benefit to be yielded beforehand? It seems too obvious for argument, that the latter is the only alternative. If the incoming generation have no rights until the outgoing generation have actually retired, then is every individual that enters the world liable to perish on the day he is born. According to the very constitution of things, each individual must obtain sustenance and succor, as soon as his eyes open to the light, or his lungs are inflated by the air. His wants cannot be delayed until he himself can supply them. If the demands of his nature are ever to be answered, they must be answered years before he can make any personal provision for them, either by the performance of labor, or by any exploits of skill. The infant must be fed, before he can earn his bread; he must be clothed before he can prepare garments; he must be protected from the elements before he can erect a dwelling; and it is just as clear that he must be instructed before he can engage a tutor. A course contrary to this, would be the destruction of your young, that we might withhold their rightful inheritance. Carried to its extreme, it would be the act of Herod, seeking in a general massacre, the life of one who was supposed to endanger his power. Here, then, the claims of the succeeding generation, not only upon the affection and the care, but upon the *property* of the second generation as full and complete a right to the incomes and profit of the world, as he has given to the first; and to the third generation as full and complete a right as he has given to the second, and so on while the world stands; it necessarily follows that children must come into a partial and qualified possession of these rights, by the paramount law of nature, as soon as they are born. No human enactments can abolish or countervail this paramount and supreme law; and all those positive and often arbitrary enactments of the civil code, by which, for the encouragement of industry and frugality, the possessor of property is permitted to control it for a limited period after his decease, must be construed and executed in subservience to this sovereign and irrepealable ordinance of nature.

Nor is this transfer always, or even generally, to be made *in kind;* but according to the needs of the recipient. The recognition of this principle is universal. A guardian or trustee may possess lands, while the ward, or owner under the trust, may need money; or the former may have money, while the latter need raiment or shelter. The form of the estate must be changed, if need be, and adapted to the wants of the receiver.

The claim of a child, then, to a portion of preexistent property begins with the first breath he draws. The new-born infant must have sustenance and shelter and care. If the natural parents are removed, or parental ability fails,—in a word, if parents either cannot or will not supply the infant's wants, then society at large,—the government,—having assumed to itself the ultimate control of all property,—is bound to step in and fill the parent's place. To deny this to any child would be equivalent to a sentence of death,—a capital execution of the innocent,—at which every soul shudders! It would be a more cruel form of infanticide than any which is practised in China or in Africa.

But to preserve the animal life of a child only, and there to stop, would be,—not the bestowment of a blessing or the performance of a duty,—but the infliction of a fearful curse. A child has interests far higher than those of mere physical existence. Better that the wants of the natural life should be neglected. If a child has any claim to bread to keep him from perishing, he has a far higher claim to knowledge to preserve him from error and its fearful retinue of calamities. If a child has any claim to shelter to protect him from the destroying elements, he has a far higher claim to be rescued from the infamy and perdition of vice and crime.

All moralists agree, nay, all moralists maintain, that a man is as responsible for his omissions as for his commissions;—that he is as guilty of the wrong which he could have prevented, but did not, as for that which his own hand has perpetrated. They then, who knowingly withhold sustenance from a new-born child, and he dies, are guilty of infanticide. And, by the same reasoning, they who refuse to enlighten the intellect of the rising generation, are guilty of degrading the human race! They who refuse to train up children in the way they should go, are training up incendiaries and madmen to destroy property and life, and to invade and pollute the sanctuaries of society! In a word, if the mind is as real and substantive a part of human existence as the body, then mental attributes during the periods of childhood, demand provision at least as imperatively as bodily appetites. The time when these respective obligations attach, corresponds with the periods when the nurture, whether physical or mental, is needed. As the right of sustenance is of equal date with birth, so the right to intellectual and moral training begins, at least as early as when children are ordinarily sent to school. At that time, then, by the irrepealable law of nature, every child succeeds to so much more of the property of the community as is necessary for his education. He is to receive this, not in the form of lands, or of gold and silver, but in the form of knowledge and a training to good habits. This is one of the steps in the transfer of the property of the present to a succeeding generation. Human sagacity may be at fault in fixing the amount of property to be transferred, or the time when the transfer should be made, to a dollar or to an hour; but certainly, in a republican government, the obligation of the predecessors, and the right of the successors, extend to and embrace the means of such an amount of education as will prepare each individual to perform all the duties which devolve upon him as a man and a citizen. It may go further than this point; certainly, it cannot fall short of it.

Under our political organization, the places and the processes where this transfer is to be provided for, and its amount determined, are the district school meeting, the town meeting, legislative halls, and conventions for establishing or revising the fundamental laws of the State. If it be not done there, society is false to its high trusts; and any community, whether national or state, that ventures to organize a government, or to administer a government already organized, without making provision for the free education of all its children, dares the certain vengeance of Heaven; and, in the squalid forms of poverty and destitution, in the scourges of violence and misrule, in the heart-destroying corruptions of licentiousness and debauchery, and in political profligacy and legalized perfidy,—in all the blended and mutually aggravated crimes of civilizations and of barbarism, will be sure to feel the terrible retributions of its delinquency.

6
The Kalamazoo Decision

Michigan State Supreme Court (1874)

The bill in this case is filed to restrain the collection of such portion of the school taxes assessed against complainants for the year 1872, as have been voted for the support of the high school in that village, and for the payment of the salary of the superintendent. While, nominally, this is the end sought to be attained by the bill, the real purpose of the bill is wider and vastly more comprehensive than this brief statement would indicate, inasmuch as it seeks a judicial determination of the right of school authorities, in what are called union school districts of the state, to levy taxes upon the general public for the support of what in this state are known as high schools, and to make free by such taxation the instruction of children in other languages than the English.

The more general question which the record presents we shall endeavor to state in our own language, but so as to make it stand out distinctly as a naked question of law, disconnected from all considerations of policy or expediency, in which light alone we are at liberty to consider it. It is, as we understand it, that there is no authority in this state to make the high schools free by taxation levied on the people at large. The argument is that while there may be no constitutional provision expressly prohibiting such taxation, the general course of legislation in the state and the general understanding of the people have been such as to require us to regard the instruction in the classics and in the living modern languages in these schools as in the nature not of practical and therefore necessary instruction for the benefit of the people at large, but rather as accomplishments for the few, to be sought after in the main by those best able to pay for them, and to be paid for by those who seek them, and not by general tax. And not only has this been the general state policy, but this higher learning of itself, when supplied by the state, is so far a matter of private concern to those who receive it that the courts ought to declare it incompetent to supply it wholly at the public expense. This is in substance, as we understand it, the position of the complainants in this suit.

21

When this doctrine was broached to us, we must confess to no little suprise that the legislation and policy of our state were appealed to against the right of the state to furnish a liberal education to the youth of the state in schools brought within the reach of all classes. We supposed it had always been understood in this state that education, not merely in the rudiments, but in an enlarged sense, was regarded as an important practical advantage to be supplied at their option to rich and poor alike, and not as something pertaining merely to culture and accomplishment to be brought as such within the reach of those whose accumulated wealth enabled them to pay for it. As this, however, is now so seriously disputed, it may be necessary, perhaps to take a brief survey of the legislation and general course, not only of the state, but of the antecedent territory, on the subject....

(Included here is a review of the educational history of the State, from the Ordinance of 1787 to the new state constitution of 1850.)

The instrument (the constitution of 1850) submitted by the convention to the people and adopted by them provided for the establishment of free schools in every school district for at least three months in each year, and for the university. By the aid of these we have every reason to believe the people expected a complete collegiate education might be obtained.... The inference seems irresistible that the people expected the tendency towards the establishment of high schools in the primary-school districts would continue until every locality capable of supporting one was supplied. And this inference is strengthened by the fact that a considerable number of our union schools date their establishment from the year 1850 and the two or three years following.

If these facts do not demonstrate clearly and conclusively a general state policy, beginning in 1817 and continuing until after the adoption of the present constitution, in the direction of free schools in which education, and at their option the elements of classical education, might be brought within the reach of all the children of the state, then, as it seems to us, nothing can demonstrate it. We might follow the subject further and show that the subsequent legislation has all concurred with this policy, but it would be a waste of time and labor. We content ourselves with the statement that neither in our state policy, in our constitution, or in our laws, do we find the primary-school districts restricted in the branches of knowledge which their officers may cause to be taught, or the grade of instruction that may be given, if their voters consent in regular form to bear the expense and raise the taxes for the purpose.

7

On Education

John Dewey (1897)

I Believe that

—education is the fundamental method of social progress and reform.

—all reforms which rest simply upon the enactment of law, or the threatening of certain penalties, or upon changes in mechanical or outward arrangements, are transitory and futile.

—education is a regulation of the process of coming to share in the social consciousness; and that the adjustment of individual activity on the basis of this social consciousness is the only sure method of social reconstruction.

—this conception has due regard for both the individualistic and socialistic ideals. It is duly individual because it recognizes the formation of a certain character as the only genuine basis of right living. It is socialistic because it recognizes that this right character is not to be formed by merely individual precept, example, or exhortation, but rather by the influence of a certain form of institutional or community life upon the individual, and that the social organism through the school, as its organ, may determine ethical results.

—in the ideal school we have the reconciliation of the individualistic and the institutional ideals.

—the community's duty to education is, therefore, its paramount moral duty. By law and punishment, by social agitation and discussion, society can regulate and form itself in a more or less haphazard and chance way. But through education society can formulate its own purposes, can organize its own means and resources, and thus shape itself with definiteness and economy in the direction in which it wishes to move.

Reprinted from *John Dewey on Education: Selected Writings*, edited by Reginald D. Archambault, courtesy of Random House, Inc., pp. 437-439.

—when society once recognizes the possibilities in this direction, and the obligations which these possibilities impose, it is impossible to conceive of the resources of time, attention, and money which will be put at the disposal of the educator.

—it is the business of every one interested in education to insist upon the school as the primary and most effective interest of social progress and reform in order that society may be awakened to realize what the school stands for, and aroused to the necessity of endowing the educator with sufficient equipment properly to perform his task.

—education thus conceived marks the most perfect and intimate union of science and art conceivable in human experience.

—the art of thus giving shape to human powers and adapting them to social service is the supreme art; one calling into its service the best of artists; that no insight, sympathy, tact, executive power, is too great for such service.

—with the growth of psychological service, giving added insight into individual structure and laws of growth; and with growth of social science, adding to our knowledge of the right organization of individuals, all scientific resources can be utilized for the purposes of education.

—when science and art thus join hands the most commanding motive for human action will be reached, the most genuine springs of human conduct aroused, and the best service that human nature is capable of guaranteed.

—every teacher should realize the dignity of his calling; that he is a social servant set apart for the maintenance of proper social order and the securing of the right social growth.

—in this way the teacher always is the prophet of the true God and the usherer-in of the true kingdom of God.

The Always-Abundant Criticism

Like all ideals, those which have characterized American public schooling have, at best, only been approximated. Performance has always fallen short of the expectations which were articulated in Section One. This section samples some of the disenchantment which has been generated by the disparity between the ideal and the real. We should not be surprised by the school's popularity as a target of attack. Indeed, we should be terribly surprised were we to discover an absence of such critical reaction. In a society which prides itself on being democratic, we should expect public school criticism to abound.

The readings in this section reveal that at least for the past "four score and ten" years, objects of public school attacks have been remarkably similar. This is particularly the case as regards such recurring themes as the concern for stressing "the fundamentals." The "lets get back to the three R's" clarion call is a firmly entrenched American tradition!

Just as contemporary public school criticisms range from the rational and the responsible to the carping and the capricious, so do the criticisms of the past. As today, critics of the past could be counted among the schools' sympathetic supporters or among their vicious detractors. In 1883 as well as 1978, some critics had a keen wit about them; others were (and are) apparently humorless.

Our first selection, written in 1883 by Dr. J. M. Rice, has a most familiar ring to it. In attributing school ineffectiveness (in this case, Baltimore elementary schools) to citizen apathy, political interference, inadequate supervision, and teacher incompetence, Rice reflects some of the apparently-perennial causes of our (alleged) public school affliction.

The next two selections suggest some of the critical concerns which predominated during the decade of the twenties. These criticisms, expressed in every geographic area of the country, could just as plausibly have been written in the 1970s! Of course, then as now, some of the attacks were warranted; others were without foundation.

Our fourth selection, written during World War II, is quite noteworthy in pointing up that public school criticism flourishes during times of national emergency. (The reaction to alleged public school failings during the "Sputnik" era of the 1950s is another case in point.) As professor Betts suggests, admitted public school shortcomings might well be the product of a public insufficiently committed to educational excellence.

Our last reading reflects some of the criticisms which abounded during the 1950s. The vigorous defense advanced by Mr. Saul could well be drawn upon by contemporary public school advocates who are attempting to ward off some of the more vicious attacks of the late seventies.

8
The Public Schools of Baltimore
J.M. Rice (1883)

As in New York, so in Baltimore, we find a school system that represents mechanical education almost in its purity. Indeed, all things considered, the schools of Baltimore compare unfavorably even with those of New York. While the schools of New York are in the main mechanical, at least this much can be said in their favor,—namely, that none but trained teachers are now appointed. In Baltimore, on the other hand, it is only in exceptional instances that trained teachers are added to the corps.

A characteristic feature of the schools of Baltimore lies in the fact that in the lower primary grades an amount of time entirely beyond the needs of the case is devoted to the study of arithmetic, and in its most abstract form. Among the first of the lessons that I witnessed in that city was a recitation in arithmetic in an "advanced first grade" (actually the second school year). The description of this lesson will indicate in what a soul-inspiring manner from one fourth to one third of the time is spent in the average Baltimore primary school during the first two years of school life.

On entering the class-room a large blackboard entirely covered with problems in addition, in endless variety, struck my eye. First there were columns such as—

$$1 + 1 = \qquad 1 + 2 =$$
$$2 + 1 = \qquad 2 + 2 =$$
$$3 + 1 = \qquad 3 + 2 =$$

running down to $10+1=$ and $10+2=$, respectively.

Then there were columns of mixed figures, four lines deep, five lines deep, and ten lines deep; next, examples in horizontal lines, such as $3+6+8+4=$, and columns where each succeeding figure was 5 greater than the one before: thus 1, 6, 11, 16, 2, 7, 12, 17; and so on.

From *The Public School System of the United States* (New York: The Century Co., 1893), pp. 55-64. Reprinted by Arno Press, Inc., 1970.

"We are just adding," the teacher said to me. "I am very particular with their adding. I devote from one and a half to one and three quarter hours a day to this subject; and I will tell you," she continued, growing quite enthusiastic, "my pupils can add!"

She then faced the class and said, "Start that column over again."

A little boy (apparently the leader of the orchestra) now began to tap on the blackboard with a stick, beating time upon the figures, while the class sang in perfect rhythm: "1 and 1 are 2; 2 and 1 are 3; 3 and 1 are 4," and so on until the column was completed; next they began with 2 and 1, 2 and 2, etc. (When later they came to 5 and 8 are 13, 5 and 9 are 14 the rhythm was retained, but the effect was changed.) Next came a column of 2s, the children adding "2 and 2 are 4; 4 and 2 are 6," and so on.

The teacher here said to me, "Now I shall let them add that column mentally," Upon receiving such an order, the children cried out, "2, 4, 6, 8, 10."

I discovered, therefore, that this teacher's idea of the difference between written and mental arithmetic was simply that in mental arithmetic the " and (2) are" is left out. Thus, 2, 4, 6, 8, 10 is mental arithmetic, while 2 and 2 are 4, 4 and 2 are 6 is the other kind.

When the children had reached the bottom of the last column in sight, I thought that they had finished. But here I was mistaken. The board had two faces, and turned on pivots. In an instant it was swung around, and then I discovered that the other side of the board was also completely covered with columns in addition.

When this exercise was finished the children had some reading. The reading was fully as mechanical as the arithmetic. It amounted simply to calling off words. Not only was there no expression, but there was not even an inflection, or a pause at a comma or a period. Nor did the teacher ever correct mispronounced words, or make any attempt to teach the pupils how to read. Before the children began to read the designated lesson, there was a ludicrously mechanical introduction, including the calling off of the words placed at the top of the page, thus:

"Page 56, Lesson XVIII., The Dog and the Rat. Dog, Rat, Catch, Room, Run, Smell, Wag, Jump." And then came the story:

Besides reading and arithmetic, there is, in this grade, oral spelling, a subject which is by no means neglected. This exercise is carried on both individually and in concert. The children also have instruction in penmanship. The remainder of the time is occupied as follows: Drawing twenty minutes twice a week, an object-lesson of thirty minutes once a week, and music fifteen minutes daily.

Now, as to the modifications of the above methods in the various schools, I found but few. In arithmetic this was mainly confined to the skill with which the children at the board wielded the baton while pointing to the figures and beating time. In some cases this procedure was extremely complicated and still more ludicrous. Reading-lessons, such as the one described above, I found in abundance, and the results were, as might be expected, miserable. In one class I found that the children did use inflections while reading. They religiously raised their voices two tones at commas and dropped them four tones at periods.

I asked one of the primary principals whether she believed in the professional training of teachers.

"I do *not*," she answered emphatically. "I speak from experience. A graduate of the Maryland Normal School once taught under me, and she wasn't as good a teacher as those who came from the High School."

One of the primary teachers said to me: "I formerly taught in the higher grades, but I had an attack of nervous prostration some time ago, and the doctor recommended rest. So I now teach in the primary, because teaching primary children does not tax the mind."

I had occasion to attend a number of geography lessons. Such a thing as teaching geography from pictures, from the molding-board and the like, was, as far as I could discover, unknown in Baltimore. It was all text-book work, and the words in the book were studied *verbatim*. In the highest primary grade, where geography is begun, the children learn how to rattle off definitions quite marvelously. I heard in one class the recitation of geographical definitions and of the boundaries of States in concert. In the grammar-schools, text-books were used in studying geography. The teachers, in most instances, opened their text-books at the page containing the subject of the day's lesson, and asked—or rather read aloud— the questions printed upon the page; and in reply the children endeavored to recite, word for word, the text-book answers to these questions. I met one principal who was quite enthusiastic, but as she was hampered in her work by lack of professional training, the teaching throughout her school did not differ much from that of other schools. She informed me, while speaking of natural-science work, that physics was studied quite thoroughly in the schools of Baltimore.

"Do the children experiment for themselves," I asked, "or do the teachers perform the experiments?"

"Oh, we have no experiments," she said. "We learn our physics from books. The city supplies us with no apparatus. We are at liberty to experiment if we desire. A friend of mind, a principal, informed me that she tried an experiment once, but it was a failure, and she vowed that she would never dream of making another one."

In one class where they were having physiology, in answer to the question, "What is the effect of alcohol on the system?" I heard a ten-year-old cry out at the top of his voice, and at the rate of a hundred miles an hour, "It—dwarfs—the—body,—mind,—and—soul,—weakens—the—heart,—and—enfeebles—the—memory."

"And what are the effects of tobacco?" asked the teacher.

In answer to this, one boy called off, in rapid succession, more diseases than are known to most physicians.

"What brings on these diseases, excessive or moderate smoking?"

"Moderate smoking," was the prompt reply.

Now, what do these illustrations mean? Simply that I did not succeed in discovering any evidence that the science of education had as yet found its way into the public schools of Baltimore. Is the pedagogical law requiring that the time and energies of the child be used to the best possible advantage taken into account when an hour and a half are devoted daily for two years to addition, and perhaps to a little subtraction; or when, in teaching children to read, two years or more are required to obtain results which (as the schools of a number of cities prove) might be attained in six months or less? Or is the law that the study of things must precede the study of words regarded when objective work is almost entirely neglected, and the sciences of physics and physiology are learned practically from books alone? What is there of a scientific nature in the teaching of geography—that study which can be made the means of opening channels of interest in so many directions—when the instruction dwindles down to little, if any, more than hearing the children recite the words they have learned *verbatim* from a text-book? Is the fundamental law of pedagogy not absolutely ignored when all interest is crushed out of the process of learning, and what can be less interesting to little children than the computation of abstract numbers by the hour, or calling off words in a meaningless way from a reading-book? Is there anything less interesting and more burdensome than learning text-books by heart, and especially when the words convey little meaning to the learner? And, finally, what is there in the teaching above-described which could not be undertaken by any one able to read, write, and cipher?

The causes of this deplorable condition of affairs in Baltimore are not difficult to discover.

First. *The citizens* of Baltimore glory in the fact that their schools are among the best in the country; or, as the more modest claim, second to none but those of Boston. And if things are perfect or nearly so, why interfere?

Secondly. *The Board of Education* of Baltimore is a purely political organization, its members being elected, one for each ward, by the members of the Common Council. But while each member of the school-board is officially elected by a majority vote of the Common Council, he is—so far as I have been able to learn—practically appointed by the member of the Common Council from his own ward,—that is, he is nominated by him, and the nomination rarely fails to receive the official confirmation. The Board of Education of the city of Baltimore is, therefore, a product of the ward politicians.

Thirdly. *The supervision is by far too meager.* While the city has some twelve hundred public-school teachers, the supervisory staff consists of only two members. With six hundred teachers in his own charge a superintendent is able to do very little toward raising their standard. Besides, the schools of Baltimore have not even supervising principals, each principal having charge of a class of his own which he teaches during the entire school period.

Fourthly. *The schools of Baltimore are almost entirely in the hands of untrained teachers.* Of those now in the system, some are high-school graduates, others have had no high-school education, and but comparatively few have ever received any professional training whatever. Further, political influence appears to play a much greater part in their appointment than merit. Although they are officially appointed by a majority vote of the Board of Education, the power to appoint teachers lies practically in the hands of local committees, consisting of two members, who have special charge of the schools of the two wards which they represent. These members nominate the teachers for the schools in their own wards, and the Board of Education simply confirms their nomination. Now, as each member of the school-board depends for his appointment on the councilman from his ward, it may readily be perceived to what extent the appointment of Baltimore's teachers lies in the hands of its ward politicians. The teacher is at first appointed on probation, the probational period being ninety days. Should her services during this time prove satisfactory, she receives a permanent license, which entitles her to teach for ten years. But, unfortunately, the supervisory staff is so small that each school can be visited but seldom by its members, and the ninety days' probation may elapse before either one of them gets a single chance to see the teacher at work in her class-room. This does not, however, deprive her of the right of receiving her permanent license when the probational period has expired. The discharge of teachers for negligence or incompetency is an almost unheard-of affair. There was one teacher who remained at home every time it rained, and yet she was not removed.

In consideration of these conditions—the schools practically in the hands of ward politicians, the teachers untrained and the supervision far too scanty—it is but natural that the schools of Baltimore should be as they are.

The causes of the evils are so manifest that the rememdies actually suggest themselves. They consist in taking the schools out of the domain of politics, in employing more adequately prepared teachers, and in rendering the supervision more thorough. As the plan of school government that I suggested for the improvement of the schools of New York city has for its object the eradication of evils similar to those found in the schools of Baltimore, it consequently applies to the schools of the latter city as well as it does to those of New York. Under a management of some such nature the schools of Baltimore would undoubtedly, within a very few years, present an entirely different aspect. Until a material change is effected, those attending the schools of that city will be doomed to a miserable childhood.

9
Criticism of Education

American Educational Digest (1922)

Education in a Democracy. As a matter of plain fact, the Ottumwa (Iowa) Courier declares, our American system of education is largely a hodge-podge of various European systems, and it contains, therefore, one essential fault which goes to the essential difference between government and society in the old world and the new. In Europe, education is designed to create an aristocracy and to cater to the "upper classes." It presumes that every worthwhile citizen will pursue education to the end of the university course, and its purpose from kindergarten days is founded on that theory, the writer states.

> Here in American there should be an entirely different principle underlying all our educational undertakings. We do not recognize aristocracy, save the aristocracy of individual performance. Our educational system should recognize always the fact that the boy or girl who does not go through the university is entitled to the utmost information and training that can be obtained up to the point where the individual student "drops out" of school and takes up the serious job of making a living.

As far as is humanly possible, the writer believes, our educational system should be so constituted that any day, from the beginning of the grade schools to the end of the university course, can be commencement day for any student.

Indicting the Schools. State Superintendent of Public Instruction E. C. Brooks, North Carolina, is of the opinion that defects in the administration of public funds are serious symptoms of the fact that local governments are going to be unable to meet the larger demands of the people. He says that society must look deeper into county government for the source of the

Reprinted from "Criticism of Education," *American Educational Digest,* Vol. 42, Aug.-Sept., 1922, pp. 22-33, and Oct., 1922, pp. 62-63.

trouble, and declares that schools and colleges are to blame for much of the ignorance prevailing today in regard to local government. Here are some of his comments:

> We teach in our schools the rise and fall of the Greek City States, the rise and fall of the Roman Empire, the rise of the English Constitution, the adoption of the Declaration of Independence, and the creation of the Federal and State Constitution. We have textbooks on civics that could be used as well in California as in North Carolina, when civics should deal with government at home, the whole county functioning as a unit. We do not teach the youth of today how to determine a well-governed community. Our colleges have not yet attacked this problem. We may rightly ask the question—Do our teachers know what constitutes good government?

Mr. Brooks believes that, generally speaking, there is not an organized body of laws guaranteeing the proper unification of county government and defining the functions of each department. He says that a student must look through the entire mass of public or local acts and the task is so great that few will undertake it. He believes, too, that defects in local government affect the public school system, especially in detrimental ways. "County Unit" organization, in Mr. Brook's opinion, is the way out.

The Vocational School. There are many occupations open where training is required, but for the untrained the chances are so few because the supply is so large, says the Marion (Ohio) Tribune. To the young man or woman with sufficient financial backing to get a college course, and the time to take it, the lack may not seem so great. But there is the other great class—those who must get to work at as early an age as possible. Parents have struggled and borne the burden as long as they can. Now the children must take a part of it from their shoulders—what of them? Are they to be left untrained, to be hewers of wood and drawers of water—to still further congest the market for common labor? Their only chance lies in the vocational school. They can manage, at the early teen age to spare two years for training in some calling. The schools can and should supply it. This is practical education.

What or How to Teach. The Exponent, published by the State Normal School, Aberdeen, S. D., says that many of the students who attended the summer session complained that the work offered did not prepare them for the state examinations. The Exponent goes on to say:

> Their argument was that too much time and emphasis have been put upon methods of teaching to the neglect of the "worth while" subject matter. All, will agree that these people should have secured a lasting grasp of the subject matter in the grades or in the high school. But they did not, and it remains for normal schools to make the best of existing

conditions. Apparently the question is clear, but the solution is debatable. Do these dissatisfied people base their complaint on the older theory of the necessary importance of the academic over the professional, or are we actually coming to stress method to the sad neglect of content?

Radicalism in Colleges. Is not the spirit of opposition-crushing censorship more inimical to a republican government than the teaching of Socialism? Such is the question raised by Jane R. Mayer in a letter to The New York World. The writer goes on to say:

> Can government improve otherwise than through broad, intelligent, open-eyed criticism? We are used to minorities which grow into majorities only to weaken again into minorities. Why such terror of a Socialistic minority? Why such terror of the mere word when some of Socialism's cardinal principles, such as government ownership of utilities, are matters of past and present experience? Should the conservatives' worst fears be realized and Socialism become our form of government, if it be not successful or be less so than our republican government, it will be soon superseded by some other. And our knowledge of government will be increased so that some day we may reach the ideal. The worst evil is stagnation, another word for retrogression.

"Moreover," the writer asserts, "the strongest anti-socialist should be the very one to desire Socialism explained, if it be an evil doctrine. The many radical youths who develop into conservative men would reach a stronger and more permanent radicalism if their first encounter with it should come later in life."

Favors Fewer Frills. The Rawlins, Wy., Republican quotes the Lander Journal to the effect that there is entirely too much time given to teaching toe dancing and similar accomplishments and not nearly enough to arithmetic and spelling. A lot of teachers seem to think that because comptometers and calculating machines are being more largely used in business than heretofore, arithmetic is not a necessary study any more and a lot of them seem to have believed for a long time that there would soon be a typewriter invented capable of spelling correctly almost anything fed to it by a gum-chewing flapper. A little of this fancy stuff may be all right but it can never take the place of sound old-fashioned education.

Schools that Stifle Thought. That was a startling but pertinent question propounded at the National Education Association by Dr. J. Mace Andress, observes the Atlanta Journal. "Is the school of today," he asked, "unconsciously an agency in promoting mental disability? In its mad rush for a mastery of facts is it neglecting the development of wholesome attitudes toward school work and life?" Whatever else needs to be omitted from an education, two things unquestionably are essential—power to think and love of truth, the Journal observes. If these be neglected or stifled by the mass of subjects presented, the rest will be but rubbish. To arouse and foster these has been the aim of good teaching, from the happiest schools of today back to the golden times of Hellas when master and pupil talked together in the market place or sauntered through templed groves.

Freshmen Lack English Preparation. Large numbers of students are slipping through high school totally ignorant of the simple facts of English grammar, according to Professor E. R. Barrett, head of the English department in the Kansas Norman School at Emporia, says the News Letter. A noun test given to freshmen in that school revealed figures upon which Professor Barrett bases his criticism. Out of 335 test papers, involving 159 ordinary nouns, only one word was not missed on any paper; five words were missed but once; the noun "use" was missed 229 times; the word "athletic" was called a noun 170 times; the noun "gentlemen" failed of a mark 211 times; and of those examined nine students missed over 200 nouns each. Since a freshman class is rather a selected group of high school graduates, and since a noun test reveals the most elementary knowledge of sentence structure, it appears that students enter college without getting, somewhere along the line, the practical drill in technique for intelligent expression in correct English, Professor Barrett concludes.

Eliminating Vacations. As for cutting out vacations, or making them any shorter than they now are, we are going to vote "nay" as long as there is breath in our body, vows the Arkansas Democrat. And further. If the efficiency experts do not quit trying to take so much joy out of the life of the youngsters with their efficiency theories, based on dry-as-dust statistics and psychological and philosophical arguments, we predict that somebody is going to start a little investigation of the efficiency experts themselves. We have more than a slight suspicion that the experts aren't nearly so efficient themselves as they are trying to look as they hand out theories about how the world should be run, says the Democrat.

The Essentials of Education. The tendency in the educational world in the last few years, says the Sandusky, Ohio, Journal, has been very decidedly toward the practical. The Journal goes on to say that school courses have been revised, always with the idea of fitting the student for some practical work in life. There has been a modification of requirements and manual training, domestic science and commerical courses have been substituted for language and higher mathematics. The cry has been that our schools have turned out boys and girls unfitted for any practical work in life. "Of what use is Latin or algebra to a boy or girl who expects to work in an office or store or factory?" is a question that has been asked repeatedly. The answer has been a great reduction of the time given to these studies. It must be said, from actual experience, that this modification of studies has not resulted in any material improvement in the writing and use of our own language. High school students spell and write no better than they did years ago—probably there has been deterioration—and it seems that a smattering of the "practical" is not sufficient to qualify a youth for work. Perhaps it is because of a realization of this weakness or failure, and other important developments, that we now note the first signs of a "a swing back."

No Preparation for Creative Work. Professor Dallas Lore Sharp in a recent lecture criticized the prevailing school curriculum because of its failure to prepare for creative work. We get power from it, he said, but no preparation for poetry, sermon or song. There is no chance to loaf and invite the soul as the poet must. It makes for power and leadership but not for poetry. Originality requires contact with nature, which is the source book of all writers, Professor Sharp declared. He condemned the kindergarten and urged bringing the child close to nature during his earlier years so that when he goes to school he has learned the memorable things from the lips of the winds and tides and stars. "We are not a happy-hearted people," Professor Sharp asserted. "We do not believe in poetry and music but in money and power. We take all our poets and prophets and prepare them for life by so underestimating the nobler things that they emerge from the process workers and money makers, and the parents are responsible."

The Financial Side. A prominent Iowa educator says that an education increases the average person's earning power $40,000, relates Austin Haines in the Des Moines News. He says:

> Sounds good but doesn't mean much. Depends altogether on the definition of "an education." I do not believe that the average boy who goes through high school, college and postgraduate courses will cash in on the investment. Take the amount invested in the 6 or 8 years above the high school. Capitalize it at 7 per cent for the balance of his life. Then do the same for the money he missed during those years— and the average boy will be a financial loser in the end. But think of the satisfaction, you say. That's another thing. We are talking in financial terms.

Education Is More Than Information. The mistaking of mere information for education is criticised by Dr. Chas. Aubrey Eaton, who points out that an educated man is a man who is master of his own powers. He may know little of book learning and yet be wise in manhood and the secrets of great living. Dr. Eaton continues:

We have a wonderful system of education running from the kindergarten to the university. But it is weak at one vital point. It overstresses information. It mistakes information for education. It is strong on eating, but poor on digestion. We need an education that makes each man master of his own powers, that kindles his ambition, gives him an objective in life, coordinates his powers of mind and heart and body, cultivates loyalty and co-operation, makes work a sacrament and thrift a joy—in a word, an education that makes manhood—wherever it is applied.

This is the only way, Dr. Eaton believes, that we can meet America's greatest need. Dr. John J. Tigert has emphasized a similar need in his plea that the "old-fashioned virtues" should not be overlooked. And Dr. Winship has called attention to the keen minds of "illiterates" in the Kentucky mountains. Certain kinds of information are important but they are by no means the whole of education.

The Student's Objective. A Boston teacher, discussing the attitude of the average young student towards his work and future activities, says that entering college today is a serious matter. He says that parents, who are sure that their son has mechanical ability, can not see anything beyond the present except the objective in the distance. They fail to realize the importance of the ground to be covered between the present and the future for which all concerned are planning. This well known teacher says:

Today I have an appointment with a boy who says that he is preparing for entrance to a well known college. One would not guess that he was at all serious in this preparation by the looks of his report card. Yesterday I interviewed his parents. Perhaps I should say that they interviewed me because they requested an interview as a result of the report sent home. These parents are fine people and they heartily wish to do everying possible for their son. They are, as a matter of fact, doing more for the boy than he is doing for them or for himself in that they are doing all that they can and he is not.

Now it is a perfectly natural thing for these parents to expect me to do something to make this boy do better work. As teachers, we have this proposition to face constantly. "Can't you do something to make my son or my daughter do better work?" says the parent, and the teacher says that he will try. But after fifteen years of teaching experience I am becoming more and more convinced that until the time arrives in the experience of every boy that he will himself accept the responsibility of attaining his objective, his teachers can do little. So today when this boy comes in to see me, I shall not threaten him or in any way punish him because he is not working up to his capacity, but I shall try to make him see that the attainment of the goal, which he seeks to pull himself up to is very much his own particular job.

Guarding the Three R's. A writer in the Omaha World Herald believes that the public schools are not holding fast in their work to the fundamentals. He says:

> Recently, in not a far distant city, a woman of more than average teaching experience returned home after a day's end spent in making reports of data on the latest pedagogic theories of mental measurements and such like. To her father, with decades of educational work in the past, she said, "If they continue in the next five years, as they have in the last five to require additional reports about this and that experiement and test devised and dreamed out by theorists, I shall have no time left for the common branches in my grade (the third); there will be no time left for reading, spelling, numbers, local geography, or stories from literature and history.

About the same time, in our own city, a grammar grade teacher of marked success was asked her opinion as to the benefits to her pupils from the recent novelties in tests and measurements, and she said, "Now that I am leaving the profession to become a wife, I feel free to speak without any feeling of disloyalty to my former superiors. I am sure my room has suffered during the past two years from lack of attention to the fundamentals of an elementary education. Too much time has been consumed in theoretical experiments and reports thereon." When asked whether there were any benefits returned back to her school by a summarization of these reports by the authorities to whom she reported, she replied that she had received none.

Concrete instances should remind us all, including school authorities, of the great primary purpose for which the common public school was established and for which it is liberally supported, namely, the education of American youth in the common branches. This should not be a superficial knowledge, but a mastery of those essentials to an intelligent citizenship.

The supervisors of special subjects, such as music, art, physical culture, penmanship, kindergartens, etc., jealously stand guard over their several subjects, making comparisons between rooms and buildings and doing all things possible and legitimate to create rivalry, interest and emulation. In case of lack of co-operation anywhere, report is made along the line from principal to the superintendent's office, where a card file is sometimes kept bearing the legend, "Supervisor's Reports of Teachers." This is in plain sight to all callers. All these influences are potent and give the teacher a strong urge to keep up her work in the special branches.

But what about the work in the common branches? Who jealously stands guard over the pupils' progress in the three "R's?"

Restricted Educational Opportunities. There is today a growing tendency throughout the country to restrict the educational opportunity to young men and women of wealth, an exchange declares. Requirements for beginning the study of medicine have been raised, and the expense of going through college has become so much greater that it is already prohibitive for thousands of bright students. The poor boys are therefore being driven away from the colleges into other activities which offer bigger prizes at smaller sacrifice, according to this critic.

Graduation Exercises Protested. In a recent statement, Peter J. Brady, New York, chairman of the committee on education of the State Federation of Labor, said: Many parents and children regard graduation from the 8B grade as the end of education, and this impression is heightened by elaborate public ceremonies when some trustee or prominent citizen attempts to advise the graduates on the brilliant careers opened to them. There should be no break in the continuity of advancement to the higher grades and graduation exercises should be held only on completion of the fourth year in high school. Foppish or overdressed children are a source of destruction in the class room, and wherever such a practice can be discouraged it will help to produce a better feeling among pupils and be an aid to their parents, who sometimes go without the necessities of life in order that their children may be as extravagantly dressed as other children.

Congressman Opposes Sterling-Towner Bill. A feature of the address given recently at Charleston, South Carolina, by Congressman W. Turner Logan was his criticism of the Sterling-Towner bill, according to the Charleston Post. He opposed the measure as a dangerous encroachment upon the rights and liberty of a community and declared that federal control of education would lead, ultimately, to the placing of white and colored school children in the same classrooms. It would mean, he claimed, that educational affairs would be conducted under orders from Washington, in spite of the apparent harmlessness of the legislation. Furthermore, Mr. Logan declared, the bill calls for an expenditure of $200,000,000, a burden which the people of the South do not want placed on them now. He quoted Elihu Root, Senator Tom Watson, Congressman Garrett, and others, who oppose the bill.

Promoting Pupils. The Sierra Educational News quotes Dr. Judd as summarizing the causes which operate when there is no basis for classification other than the teacher's opinion. Sometimes a school allows a pupil to move up a grade or class, although it is known that he has not done the work below, because the parents of the child have influence and it is not safe to antagonize them. Pressure of numbers in the lower grades or classes, a teacher's anxiety to unload the backward or disorderly pupil by passing him are other causes for promotion. Sometimes the calendar controls. The long vacation time arrives and pupils are declared to have completed the work whether they have or not. Sometimes it is argued that the backward pupil is larger than the other children and should be sent to the upper grade room where the seats are larger.

What Is the Matter with the Church? The Capital News observes that it is always much easier to say of anything "this is wrong" than to say of the same thing "this is the way it should be done." Destructive criticism is easy. Constructive criticism is difficult. It is simple enough to ask "what is the matter with the church?" or "what is the trouble with religion?" and as simple to answer, "it is old fashioned" or "it isn't modern enough" or "it lacks courage" or some other complaint which makes no suggestion. Of course, there is nothing the "matter" with religion. The belief in a Supreme Deity, and worship of that Deity is an ingrained human fundamental. The "matter" is not with the religion, but with the means taken to spread, to teach, to use that religion. And the "matter," to many people who try to think constructively, is that those in authority in the churches place too much emphasis upon the mechanics of religion and not enough on the spiritual things of that religion. Church fathers, elders, deacons, and dignitaries meet and spend precious time discussing what words to leave in, and what to take from, the ritual; they waste time and effort trying to decide whether this ban shall be removed and that one put on, while people hunger to be taught of God.

What Ails the School? Commenting upon the fact that while a public school was burning in New York City some five hundred pupils gathered near by and danced with glee at the prospect of a long vacation, Richard Spillane declares that such an incident is a powerful indictment of the public school system of some of our cities. Regardless of an inclination of the young to find interest, if not pleasure, in destruction, the writer sees in this a tragic lack of the school to appeal to the child. And he reminds us that in 1918, the latest year for which complete statistics are available, the appropriation for public education in the United States was $763,688,089. There were 10,349,488 boys and 10,504,050 girls in the public schools. The army of teachers numbered 650,709. And there were 142,768 men and 11,345 women being educated in colleges, universities and schools of technology. Before the world war the expenditure of the city of New York on public education was more than four times greater than that of all Russia. The wastage in the schools is great, the writer believes. For example, the average number of school days in the whole United States in a year is 160.7, and the average attendance, 119.8 days. Viewed as a business enterprise, it is questionable whether the public school is functioning properly. What is the trouble? The writer recalls the criticism regarding the rigidity of the school system, also the opinion that too little attention is given to essential branches of education and too much to non-essentials. While the Gary plan has been successful in Gary and other places, the general testimony is that it is not so well fitted for large cities. But whatever the point of view, the writer insists, it is clear that something is radically wrong when pupils dance and shout and consider the burning of their school a release from thralldom. A manufacturer turning out poor material would lose his market, "but the school goes on regardless of its output, without much attention from those who pay the bills or those most concerned."

10
Criticism of Education

American Educational Digest (1928)

School Costs

"EXORBITANT expenditures" or "throwing money away" is the taxpayer's first reaction to the rising cost of the public school system. Usually the condemnation is of two types, that censuring the so-called frills of education and that objecting to the whole fabric. Garrett P. Serviss in the *New Orleans States,* is among the former. He objects to the superficiality of the vocational courses, which are unwise in method, extravagant in expenses, and ineffective in results, and says:

> Ambitious boards of education, many of whom know as much about the principles of education as they do about the Einstein theory, are harassing the taxpayers all over the country with demands to countersign growing bonds, in order that addition may be made to a "smattering" curriculum. The neglect of the taxpayer makes the tax spender bold and the tax eater insolent.

But that the forces of propaganda are not always with the school and against the taxpayer's immediate bank account is indicated by the struggle for better schools in Alabama. The *Mobile Register* says:

> It is amazing that there should be men and interests who are willing to see Alabama continue to occupy the next to the bottom place among all the states in the amount of money expended for education. They are content to retain the one room, dilapidated shacks which are now the sole educational dependence of so many communities. They evidently want Alabama boys and girls to live in an ox-wagon age while the rest of the world rushes by in automobiles.

Hartford, Connecticut, also has its financial problems, according to the *Hartford Times,* which declares:

> There is something peculiar in the situation that caused Mayor Stevens

Reprinted from "Criticism of Education," *American Educational Digest,* Vol. 47, Feb, 1928, pp. 257-259, 415-416.

to call a joint meeting of the board of education and the high school committee to consider reduction of school costs without sacrifice of efficiency. Hartford, it has been discovered, spends more for its educational facilities than Bridgeport or New Haven. It may be true that Hartford not only spends more but gets more, and that is the question Mayor Stevens wishes settled.

The cost of education is an interesting problem in other communities as well. The *Elizabeth (N. J.) Journal* says:

> The annual cost of education per pupil in New Jersey is $110, and the problem of each board of education is apparent—to make each dollar of the taxpayer's money yield 100 percent return. The state is interested and vitally affected. Upon this training depends the future of society.

Perhaps the present cost is not the final apex. The casual observer may be forgiven an assumption or two from the trend stressed by the *Washington Times,* which says:

> The Board of education is to seek legislation that will make textbooks and supplies free to high school pupils in the public schools. Thousands of bright boys and girls are forced from the schoolroom because they are unable to meet the cost of books and supplies in addition to the increasing expenditure required for clothing. Our public schools cannot be even partially closed to ambitious and talented young people. Free books and supplies will help to lower the economic barrier, reducing the inequality of opportunity.

There seems little room for doubt concerning the high cost of education. The problems remain: What causes this high figure? and is education worth its cost? The *Durham (N.C.) Herald* answers the first question, saying:

> There are quite a few people who believe that there is too much new fangled work done in the schools, and perhaps there is cause for complaint. But changed conditions have almost forced the schools, often against the will of the school authorities, to put into the system these new courses of instruction. The responsibility for this state of affairs rests with the parents, who are not giving the children the home training that is necessary and are, thereby, forcing the schools to assume home duties. The moral development of youth demands character training, study in ethics, and religious instructions. Discipline has disappeared from the home and respect for law and order must come from the schools which must also safeguard the neglected health. Talents, once the concern of parents, are now a matter for school discovery and development. Childhood's personal problems are more and more rarely taken to the busy parent, more and more frequently they come to the ear of the school adviser. The home can no longer provide vocational training, and so the school must assume this additional burden. High school pupils are no longer a select, college destined group. The curriculum must be extended to fit the individual needs, not the needs of the college. A share of the teacher's time must be spent in keeping educationally abreast of the times, preventing a side occupation and compelling a living wage from

the public funds alone. The schools have become the "shock absorbers" of society, the stabilizers of thought, conduct, and action, and that good shock absorbers come high any motorist can testify.

Does education at such a tremendous cost pay? The *Los Angeles Times* thinks that it does, saying:

President Franklin S. Harris, of Brigham Young University, showed, before an industrial conference, that the rise of individual income since 1870 tripled simultaneously with the tripling of the number of persons seeking higher education. Even for manual laborers, education pays. A study of several thousand factory workers showed that their earning power was directly proportional to the number of years that they attended school, the greatest difference being between those who had only one year and those who had none. One year of schooling gave the laborer 16 percent advantage over the totally unschooled. From *Who's Who,* President Harris found that aside from engineers, who are almost invariably college men, over one half of the industrial men achieving distinction were college trained. It was found that a college man rises to a foremanship in approximately one-third of the time the average non-college man foreman attains his office. It takes the non-college man five times as long to attain a superintendency of a factory as it does the college man. In earning power the contrast is striking. The average untrained man earns $45,000 from fourteen to sixty years of age, the high school graduate, $78,000 from eighteen to sixty, and the college or technical school graduate $150,000 from twenty-two to sixty.

Education seems to be an excellent investment from a monetary standpoint. But character is the matter of prime importance, and while it has often been doubted whether cultivation of the intellect does make for "goodness" of character, the statement seems broadly true, in the opinion of the *Detroit News,* which says:

During one term of court 433 liquor law violaters were convicted. Only fifty-eight of them had advanced beyond the eighth grade and only two were high school graduates. Whether education insures a sufficient income to make lawbreaking unattractive, or whether there are moral scruples against bootlegging in the educated person has not been proved. The point is that the parent who does not wish his son to become an outlaw should keep him in school as long as possible, because, in spite of the high cost and the malignment, education does seem to pay in even more than dollars and cents.

Educational Conflict

That there is usually right on both sides of an argument, and educational differences are probably not exceptional, is the opinion of the *Salem (Mass.) News.* Differentiating between the contentions of the radicals and conservatives in education, the *News* says:

The aggressive group want the individual abilities of the child set free.

They disapprove of competition, they favor cooperation. There is much that is good in their stand. A boy can be diverted from improper conduct by cooperation in other interests where punishment and attempted compulsion would be certain to fail. But the conservatives are not without their virtues. There must be some system in courses of study. The pupil must learn to attend to some disagreeable things and to do some uninteresting work. He cannot dodge the hard tasks of life, and should not be allowed to form the habit of side-stepping issues in school.

Another Revolt of Youth

Ankle-length skirts worn by the principal are given as one of the causes for an Oregon high school strike. The accusation of "too old-fashioned" has other foundation, probably comments the *New York Sun,* but these are not enumerated. The debate has become so bitter that the state superintendent of public instruction has been called upon to intervene. Analyzing the situation, the *Sun* says:

> The case is interesting in its indication of the emancipation of youth. Differing from other youths merely in the cool manner in which these pupils assert their desires, the present reproach of old-fashioned is a mere repetition of the charge of every generation against the preceding one. And no doubt the youngsters are often right, because without these upheavals, there would form such a cake of custom that actual progress might be entirely curtailed. But those who belong among the elders have constitutional objections to being rushed into racoon coats and hair oil over night, and that also is well, for the equilibrium must come from them. There are, however, some among the elders who will understand the grievance of these pupils. Conservatism has its place but also its limitations. Moralists to the contrary, the world is still convinced that the apparel often does proclaim the man, and the person who would wield influence must beware of indifference to appearance. It is natural for youth to respect smartness of costume as indicative of alertness of mind. Perhaps it is not necessary to be an animated fashionplate, but there are compromises that the dignity of age can make and that youth will accept with respect. The implements of corporal punishment are gone. Moral influence is all that is left, and it cannot afford to restrict its influence by dowdy attire.

Education — What for?

The comparative value of an education for a life or for a living was the meat broiled over many a heated discussion long before the classic arguments between Socrates and the more ambitious Xantippe were written. In various guises and phases of educational controversy the problem constantly reasserts itself, often irrelevantly and impertinently. That its vigor is undiminished is proved by the round of editorials that followed a certain famed address given at Boston. Commenting upon its content, the *Brockton (Mass.) Times* says:

> Educators do not take kindly nor appreciately to the criticism President Lowell of Harvard University made of the schools. Either they do not understand it, or they prefer to avoid the issue. Dr. Lowell did not mention training for colleges as the objective of the high schools. What he did complain of was the inability of the college freshman to think. So much is undertaken in the high school and nothing is done. If, in the opinion of superintendents and school boards, pupils should be fitted for professions or trades in the public schools there is need for special schools for that purpose. The high schools cannot and should not try to do everything. All that educational institutions can hope to do is to form the mind, to train the intellect to grasp what is offered in the way of instruction or experience.

The *Scranton (Pa.) Times* sees another reason or two why the school curriculums are so overloaded that they do not function efficiently, bringing criticism of men like Dr. Lowell upon their heads. The *Times* explains:

> Not only are educators realizing the justice of the objection against too many "extras," but the public at large is beginning to understand that these fads and fancies are piling up expenses. Too many parents are shifting responsibilities upon the schools; too many things are being taught in the schools that were never intended for public education.

Revolt against apparent evils in the elective system and advocation of a return to the classics as a dominant feature in college education are not novel reactions, comments the *Boston Transcript* which predicts more attention to the classics in the future, saying:

> In a recent address Professor Rand of Harvard University said that the four years of college life should be consecrated to the attainment of a liberal or aristocratic education; aristocratic because it aims at the best. It is a vocational program in the art of life. The real question will be in the introduction and establishment of the ideals of Professor Rand into institutions already in part committed to different policies. His basic idea that the best culture and thought of the past are leading and imperative elements in the process of making life higher and finer can scarcely be gainsaid.

The chief quarrel that the *Wheeling (W. Va.) News* has with Dr. Lowell is one of point of view. Fearing that he would cater to the intelligent and the fortunate only, leaving the great majority to fall by the wayside, the *News* says:

> The public schools probably have a great many faults. But their error seems to be more in paying too much rather than too little attention to the "more intelligent." Sound public policy would seem to dictate a

course to equip all with the best possible foundation, both those who carry on into college and those who must leave the system early and make their way in the world.

The *Des Moines Capital* sees definite progress in the general availability of the schools. The ground gained has taken hard labor and painful struggle, and it must not be foolishly lost by radical changes, ill-considered. "It is hoped," the *Capital* says, "that President Lowell's address will not cause attention to turn too much to curriculums, causing a telescoping of courses and a narrowing of the school aims and ideals." A view taken by many others is that of the *Flint (Mich.) Journal,* which says:

> The eight percent of school children that enter college have crowded the institutions of higher learning to the doors. Manifestly, then, higher education is not for the masses. But the lower education is and should be. Manual training, technical courses, domestic science, and other innovations are helping secondary education come into its own.

Another defender of the public schools as the proper training field for all the activities of ordinary life is the *Rochester (N. Y.) Times-Union* which asks:

> What are the youngsters taught today? In addition to the three R's and their variants, sewing, cooking, singing, music, hygiene, nutrition, home economics, and similar subjects are offered. Free dental care, free nutrition advice, and the visiting teacher are included, in the very useful business of making better citizens as well as better scholars. Civilized society makes certain demands of its members, and if the home cannot or will not give instruction to meet these demands the schools must do so.

A pithy paragraph from the *Pittsburgh Press* includes the statement that parents are being given advice, and good advice, by their children educated in the public schools. These young people are being taught in a short time the facts that the older generation learned through bitter pain and experience. The *Press* goes on to say:

> Dentifrice and Diogenes are not bad companions. The combinations of academic and practical knowledge make not only for keen minds but for virile bodies and brains stimulated through health. There is no guarantee that every child will become a Tunney or a Huxley, but the modern brand of education affords an opportunity for self-help, and America is fortunate to have a school system which recognizes this fact.

Supt. W. F. Webster, of Minneapolis, considers vocational training in the public schools of such import that he is planning to spend his last year before retirement almost entirely upon that phase of education. Superintendent Webster says:

> We must organize, in the school, courses that will give the child the

education he needs to fit him for his goal. High school courses must be far more flexible,—must prepare the boys and girls to earn their livelihood when they leave school and go to work.

Supt. Carleton W. Washburne, Winnetka, Illinois, contends that children must be equipped to go out and compete, as they will have to compete, with other men and women for a living. Society must be studied in order that school administrators may know just what subjects, knowledges, and skills the child must have. Referring to the popular utilitarian objective in education, the *Memphis (Tenn.) Appeal* says:

> Education that fails to fit a man to live and work in harmony with his generation is worthless, but there is as yet no definite proof that so-called vocational education, to the exclusion of classical principles that have come down from the past, is more effective in that respect than a thorough comprehension of the fundamentals of mathematics and language. The utility of education is its paramount factor, but it is not the exclusive objective, nor is there any assurance that its highest utility is to be attained by abandonment of the conventional objectives of the Middle Ages.

Declaring that zeal for education through institutional machinery should not over-run the basic principle that the purpose of education is to train the pupil to think logically and to acquire the power of self-mastery, the *Atlanta Constitution* says:

> The confusion in public thinking, in schools, and in government is chargeable to the too great eagerness to train men and women to make money rather than for character and competent citizenship. Wisdom and civism have been sacrificed to the material idols of easier work and higher wages. Vocational training is of high value to young people but it is of highest value to make them understand that no vocation can prosper under bad citizenship and loose government. Technical schools are essential in a technical age, but not even the greatest expert can work and thrive in a country governed by the ignorant and corrupt. So, without abating a degree of our zeal for broader education, let us make sure that we do not neglect the thought power and the character and citizenship of our children.

College Knocks

The popular inclination is to "knock" cleverly the various sections of the school system, especially its higher reaches, for the purpose of registering palpable hits rather than of arriving at any serious conlcusions. Commenting further upon the situation, the *Chicago Journal* says:

> Any serious discussion of the institutions of higher education generally touches one or more of three problems involved, the intellectual and social waste, the monetary cost, and the problem of democratic opportunity. Hundreds of thousands of students are admitted into college, twenty percent of whom drop out during the first year and

twenty percent more before the end of the second year. Only one half of the remaining sixty percent will receive diplomas. Those who drop out will not receive anything like full value for the time and money invested by them or the college. There is a question, also, whether most of these students should have been allowed to finish if they had wished it. They usually become valuable members of a community, but not being students by inclination, their college hours are wasted time. Probably the tendency of the next decade will be toward more and more exacting selection of college material, and more and more toward having the students, or their parents, share the rising costs of college maintenance. Democratic or not, that seems to be the trend. Meanwhile the knocks at higher education go cleverly and plentifully on.

The Sawdust Trail on the Campus

The Godlessness of American college students has enlivened many a dull sewing or whittling circle. Whether there is any special foundation for the stigmatization or not was the purpose of a recent meeting at Princeton, where educators and students from over sixty Eastern and Middle Western colleges gathered for a three-day discussion. Commenting upon the results of the meeting, the *Independent* says:

> The undergraduates are probably hitting neither the sawdust trail nor the road to perdition but are blithely going their own sweet way, without much consideration of either destination. Dr. Ernest H. Wilkins, president of Oberlin College, stated that in a representative group of 1000 undergraduates, 800 were passive toward religion, 100 were agnostics or atheists, and the remainder were "religiously minded." Churchmen may be alarmed at these figures but not educators. It is natural that eight out of ten men at the ages of sixteen to twenty-two should be more interested in the pursuits of youth than in theology. One out of every ten is not an alarming percent of agnostics. The remarkable thing is that one of the ten young men has actually settled in his belief before maturity. Pres. Clarence C. Little, University of Michigan, took a sound position. He said that even though the younger generation refuses to bow blindly to any authority, they are living spiritual lives of their own. They are not Godless; perhaps they are even nearer the truth of religion than are their elders. If the facts of the situation were known, the complaint against Godless students would cease to have conversational value. Undergraduates are probably no more religious and no more Godless than any other slice of the community.

Self-Education

True higher education cannot result from a mere mechanical process of absorption; it is only attainable through hard mental activity, and under the direction of able instructors. Dr. A. Lawrence Lowell expresses his views in the *Forum*, saying:

Almost the whole field of education is debatable ground and for that reason an argument for self-education must not exclude other factors, but must endeavor to place correct emphasis upon a frequently slighted element of education, personal effort. Self-education means a desire to learn and self-directed attention, with personal inquiry. No man is truly educated until he has acquired the power of self-direction in seeking knowledge and in discerning its import. No subject is mastered by any student until he has made it his own. All higher education in its true and best form is self-education under guidance, and its main object should be the laying of a broad foundation for thought in the whole of the student's later life. But in America the indifferent who are disinclined to use their brain are common. Compulsory methods are discarded somewhere in the public schools, and in the colleges the only recourse seems to be the artificial creation of a voluntary effort, a paradoxical avoidance of a paradox. In other words, the aim is to make work easy. Yet it is well-known that to arouse strong interest, the problem or the subject must not be easy at all, but hard, for it is only by strenuous mental exertion that power is developed. Eastern colleges are trying to stimulate enduring interest by making the mastery of a subject a visible objective. This is accomplished by demanding an examination upon graduation hat is not just a review of the course of instruction but includes the results of personal research. The system has stimualted many undergraduates to keen interest because the work is their own. The result is self-education.

11
What Shall We Do About Reading Today?

Emmett A. Betts (1942)

And now it is reported that the Army has found it necessary to teach *some* of the draftees how to read. Because of this situation, both outright accusations and subtle inferences are made about the educational program in these United States. When the going gets tough and rough, it is possible for unintelligent appraisals to be made of education because of the "High Expense of Army Illiteracy." It takes a war to bring these things to national attention. Under the strain of a national and international crisis, strong educational leadership is essential to maintain progress.

After visiting the Aberdeen, Maryland, training center, Eleanor Roosevelt reported the cost of training a draftee to read is approximately $175 per month. It is interesting to note that, according to this report, the Army believes it can get the best results with classes of not more than 10 to 12 students. One of these students had only four months of schooling, another was foreign born, some came from sections of the country where educational opportunities were meager, and so on. In short, the First Lady's report emphasized the lack of educational opportunity rather than the questionable quality of instruction. There was, however, the questionable inference that all individuals can acquire essential language abilities in the primary grades.

In a democracy, the people get the kind of schools they want. One of the many functions of an educator is to point the way to ever better schools. If the people want many public and private institutions for the preparation of teachers regardless of the quality of the work or the teacher supply and demand, the people get them. If the people want better school plants and better instruction, they make their will known at the polls and they get what they want. In a democracy, the quantity and quality of educational

From Emmett A. Betts, "What Shall We Do About Reading Today?," *The Elementary English Review,* XIX, No. 7, 1942, pp. 225-226. Copyright © 1942 by the National Council of Teachers of English. Reprinted by permission of the publisher.

opportunity is a product of what people want, and what they want is to no small degree conditioned by the educational leadership they have elected to follow.

Very soon strong pressure will be felt by elementary school teachers to intensify instruction in certain areas, such as reading. This pressure will be brought to bear by non-educators who have found a deficiency but who may offer no other solution than a "stronger prescription." Years of fruitful researches on learning may be cast aside in order to "do something about reading instruction in wartime." To prevent this wastage, educators must be prepared to bring to bear a considerable accumulation of information that permits an adequate resolving of this problem.

12
I'll Stick Up for the Schools

Walter Biddle Saul (1950)

On January thirty-first of this year six young men came before a
Philadelphia judge to be sentenced for theft. Four of the criminals were
under twenty, and the defense lawyer asked for mercy because of their
youth. According to the newspaper report, the judge's tart reply was,
"We're not going to play nursemaids any more. We sweat and spend hard-
earned money to educate them and then they turn to crime. Apparently the
high schools have been failures. I'm sick and tired of running luxurious
schools which merely give them more proficiency for criminality."

I can understand the judge's exasperation, but as president of the
Philadelphia Board of Education, I'm sick and tired of hearing the public
schools flayed by critics who apparently know nothing about them. As a
matter of fact, these particular criminals had among them a total of less
than three years in Philadelphia high schools, but that's not the point. Like
all too many critics, the judge in this case simply ignored the fact that in
America we have a system under which every child, irrespective of his
background and mental capacity, must attend school. As long as society
has criminals at all, therefore, they will necessarily be products of some
school; and since the majority of children attend public schools, it should
not prove so very startling that some of these turn to crime.

If this attack on the public schools were an isolated example, it would
hardly be worth reporting. But in recent years such attacks have appeared
with growing frequency. Everybody, it seems, has some shocking
revelation to make about the nation's free-education system; to me, the
really shocking revelation is that most of the critics simply don't know
what's going on in the schools. How people can be apathetic about an
institution to which they entrust their children—and which, in

Reprinted by permission from *The Saturday Evening Post,* Vol. 222, No. 42, April 15, 1950,
pp. 22-23, 65-66, 70, 73-74.

Philadelphia, spends more than $50,000,000 of their money annually—is something I find hard to understand.

It's quite true that a good deal of the criticism is justified in some cases, and perhaps some of it in all cases; as a human institution, the public-education system isn't likely to be perfect. Honest, well-informed critics can be enormously helpful. But nobody benefits from vilification leveled indiscriminately at the whole system by critics who are apparently further behind the times than they accuse the schools of being. And it's high time that somebody spoke up in defence of a system which, by and large, is doing a magnificent job. Because the Philadelphia schools are the ones I know best—first as a pupil, later as a teacher, and for the past twenty years as a member of the Board of Education—I shall use them as my example, but I doubt if the problems that arise in Philadelphia are very different from those faced by other large-city public schools or, indeed, by any other public school.

One major group of critics accuses the schools of blind devotion to antiquated curriculums, of preparing children not for life, but for college—when, in fact, only about 10 per cent of them will ever go to college at all, and less than half of these will complete four years. The students, these critics assert, would benefit far more from an ability to run a turret lathe or a typewriter than from any amount of dexterity at setting up quadratic equations or construing Latin or translating: "This is the book of the sister of my friend" into French.

For a good many students—probably for most of them—this is quite true, and educators have recognized the fact for several years. In Philadelphia, for instance, pupils spend six years in elementary school, where they take a broad standard course of studies, and another six in high school, where their activities are increasingly focused on specialized fields determined by their abilities, interests and ambitions. During the first two years of junior high, the student continues a general curriculum—English, mathematics, social studies, art, music, home economics, industrial arts and regularly scheduled extracurricular activities. During the last year the courses become somewhat more specialized, chiefly through the addition of a different required major subject for each of the different curriculums—academic, commercial, industrial and home economics.

The tendency, however, is away from specialization in junior high and toward more exploratory courses, such as general mathematics, general science, foreign-language introductory courses and shop courses that include not only wood, metal and electrical work but ceramics, textiles, photography and other fields as well. For these are the years of a child's development, during which differences in mental capacity, native intelligence and background begin to emerge in some recognizable pattern;

and the curriculums are designed to help the individual find out what type of further schooling will be best for him. Tests of his aptitudes and interests, the record of his past achievements in different subjects, and the advice of teachers and counselors—all play a part in helping the student decide.

Of these, probably the most important is a teacher's experience with each pupil. In most seventh- and eighth- and many ninth-grade classes, one teacher has the same children during a daily multiple period—a period equal in length to two, three or four normal single periods, and combining a number of subjects, such as English, social studies, general mathematics and general science. In these periods, wherever possible, all the different subjects covered in the class are brought to bear on some central problem. Perhaps the greatest single advantage of this is that, although the multiple-period teachers are qualified to—and do—continue regular drill work in the individual subjects, the program takes pupils out of the textbook vacuum and puts them to work on readily understood problems of everyday life. And, of course, it gives teachers a much better understanding of the individual students than they could get in a single daily period.

Almost equally valuable to the student is the counseling service, a program adopted in 1942 to cope with problems running all the way from what to do about the little first-grader who suddenly begins to kick everyone within reach, to arbitrating between the high-school student who wants to be a mechanic and his father, who insists the boy take a commercial course. At present, 221 men and women, specially trained as counselors and paid on the same scale as classroom teachers, are assigned to the schools on a full-time basis by the Division of Pupil Personnel and Counseling. Last year they held nearly half a million conferences, a fifth of which concerned educational or vocational guidance for junior-high students.

With teacher and counselor, each student goes over the various senior-high-school curriculums, learns what each will involve during the next three years and where each will lead him. Then he decides whether to go to one of the sixteen other high schools, to choose a more specialized curriculum in one of the senior high schools or to attend one of the three vocational-technical schools. Besides the academic, college-preparatory course, the senior high schools offer curriculums in home economics, vocational art, building construction and eight other specialized fields. The vocational-technical schools offer forty-one different curriculums, including such widely diversified specialties as baking, industrial chemistry and radio servicing.

In addition to these courses, about 1500 secondary-school students are engaged in one of the three special programs that combine school work with on-the-job training. In Distributive Education, students attend classes

fifteen hours a week and work in a local store fifteen hours, with the classroom subjects designed to anticipate and review the problems met in retailing. A not inconsiderable feature of the program is that the students are paid for their work, at the prevailing wage for their jobs. This makes it possible for many to continue their education when financial reasons might otherwise compel them to leave school—legally, students may do so at sixteen to take any approved job or at fifteen for domestic service or farm work. Yet statistics prove that high-school graduates on an average earn about 35 per cent more than elementary-school graduates.

A second work-school program gives senior commercial students experience as general office workers, file clerks, typists or stenographers by arranging the course so that they work and attend school on alternate weeks. Two students are assigned to each full-time office job, one working while the other is in school, and reversing their roles every week. One rather striking indication of the program's effectiveness is the fact that the companies employing these students on an every-other-week basis recently hired 77 per cent of them when they graduated.

The third work-school program is broader. It is open to both junior- and senior-high-school students and covers almost any approved job. Designed primarily to encourage students who need to earn money to continue their education, it arranges to give a student his major subjects in the morning and eliminates minor subjects so that he is free to work for the entire afternoon. Teachers and counselors check on the student's work outside the school, and, if it is satisfactory, give him credit for it, in place of the missed minor subjects. Classroom work, meanwhile, is co-ordinated with on-the-job work, and students graduate with a very high likelihood of permanent employment.

The facts, then, are these: critics accuse us of being so hamstrung by the college-prep tradition that we are teaching most of our students nothing to prepare them for realistic participation in life; yet the record shows that about 65 per cent of our pupils have used their high-school years to prepare for their life work, and many have already started on productive careers before they graduate.

Another large group of critics takes precisely the opposite viewpoint: that we no longer satisfactorily prepare our students for college at all. These critics, too, simply haven't bothered to examine the facts. They assert that the modern high-school graduate doesn't rate as high educationally as did the average graduate of forty or fifty years ago, which is quite true, and claim that that proves their point, which is quite false. Back in my youth, only about one out of every ten children went to high school; and when they were unable to handle the more or less rugged curriculum, they were unceremoniously dropped. Today, better than 60 per cent of the boys and girls of high-school age are enrolled, and most of the other 40 per cent are absent because they are employed, not because they couldn't keep up with their studies.

Should we answer these critics by reducing the compulsory-attendance age, making it possible to eliminate slow students and thus maintain a high average of educational achievement? I have heard this seriously proposed, but then the question arises: what would these children do if they were dropped from school? Go to work? In 1939 unemployment throughout the nation was three times greater among youth under twenty-one than among the adult working population. From 1943 to 1947 there was a 62 per cent decline in the number of youths of sixteen and seventeen employed full time. And today there are not enough jobs for the sixteen-and seventeen-year-olds who want to leave school for work, much less for children of fourteen and fifteen.

It seems fairly clear that if these young people weren't able to attend school they would be idle most of the time. In Philadelphia alone there would be a 50,000-child group of potential delinquents if all but 10 per cent of the children aged 14 and over left school. Quite apart from this consideration, however, I happen to think that compulsory education is an experiment of which this country should be extremely proud.

The pertinent question is not: What is the average achievement level? but: What is the achievement level of the graduates who correspond to the select group of forty or fifty years ago? In short, how well are we preparing the "college material" for college? At present some 35 per cent of our high school students are taking the academic curriculum. Of these, about 15 per cent will go to college, and another 10 per cent to some other kind of postgraduate training, while most of the remaining 10 per cent are taking the academic curruculum because they haven't settled on any specialized field of work. And, of course, some of those who aim at college just don't meet the requirements.

Since there is no absolute yardstick against which we can measure the students of half a century ago and those of today, we can only compare the record of our current high-school graduates with that of the current graduates of private and parochial schools. This was done not long ago, in a survey of the freshman classes of several colleges over a period of fifteen years; the average achievement level of Philadelphia high-school graduates proved to be substantially above that of all other freshman in those colleges during that period.

In May 1945, 2000 young men from Pennsylvania, New Jersey, Delaware and Maryland were qualified by examination for the Army Specialized Training Reserve Program. Of these 110 were graduates of Central High, our academic boys' high school. In the Phi Beta Kappa elections at the University of Pennsylvania two years ago, twenty-eight boys and five girls were chosen. Seventeen of the boys and four of the girls were from Philadelphia public schools.

Last winter the president of Central High received a letter from the Massachusetts Institute of Technology, which read in part:

> ...The composite record made at the Institute by graduates of Central High School in recent years has been such as to permit the Committee on Admission to waive the usual entrance test requirements for any of your graduates who graduate in the highest fifth of the class and whom you recommend to us for admission on this basis.

On the whole, it seems fairly clear that the high schools of today are preparing their college material for college at least as well as they did fifty years ago, unless we take the position that the over-all level of educational achievement has declined during the years—something that oldsters are fond of saying, but have never yet been able to demonstrate.

There remains one sizable body of critics who condemn us for not requiring certain "traditional" studies. These detractors point out that many young people don't realize today what subjects they may later feel the lack of—that, for instance, a student who drops mathematics without taking algebra and geometry may later find himself held back from promotion to a better-paying job just because he hasn't had these subjects.

This is perfectly true. Unfortunately, it is seldom possible to say definitely what studies a pupil may or may not need in later life, and there simply isn't time to teach everything. Our policy, therefore, has been to give every student at least the tools of living—reading, writing, a reasonable amount of arithmetic and a reasonable ability of expression; to train each student to live with his fellow men, giving him sufficient knowledge of the social studies—history, geography and civics—to enable him to take his place as a useful member of society; and, over and above these, to give each student as broad an education and as much education as he is able to attain.

In the high schools, since we cannot positively predict a student's future scholastic needs, we have to rely on practical experience to indicate the subjects with the greatest likelihood of usefulness. If a student shows ability and interest in a career that requires mathematics, he takes mathematics as part of his course; this is so, for instance, in all but three of the forty-one vocational-technical curriculums, as well as in the academic course. But if a student is specializing in something like child care, there are a good many subjects which seem more likely to be needed.

This does not mean that we simply select the subjects with the highest probability of usefulness and let it go at that. Because we realize that our graduates may at any time feel the need of some course they missed in school, and equally because many adults want to enlarge their education for reasons of either business or pleasure, we feel that we'd be doing only half a job if we didn't make courses available to men and women of post-high-school age.

At present about 42,000 students are enrolled in better than eighty adult extension classes—for a total of more than 2,000,000 student hours annually. There are evening classes for workers who wish to complete a high-school education. There are recreational and hobby programs, since experience proves that intelligent use of leisure time is not a natural attribute, but must be taught. There are vocational-training courses and a course in English and citizenship for new Americans. Around 1500 pupils of varying ages are currently taking this course.

New courses are added whenever there seems to be a need for them. An example of this is the practical-nurses' training program. Because of the critical shortage of graduate nurses, there has been an urgent need for more practical nurses; and, with the co-operation of local hospitals, we were able to organize a one-year training program for women between the ages of eighteen and fifty who wished to enter this profession. They spend three months in school, where trained nurses and home-economics instructors teach nutrition, preparation and care of the patient, nursing procedure and home management. For the nine remaining months, students are given practical training in Philadelphia hospitals. When they receive their certificates they are not only well qualified but virtually assured of a position.

They are also, in a sense, our answer to the critics who would have us require more of the old-time traditional subjects. Nursing was something these women didn't take in their regular schooling; the chances are that few of them had even seriously thought about nursing as a career. Yet the time came when they did decide they wanted such a course, and the schools were ready for them. They are equally ready for students who, in later life, find they need courses in the traditional subjects. Still other critics of the public education system take exception to the way we teach more than to what we teach—to policies affecting the individual student rather than the student body. One of the chief problems the modern public-school system faces is a result of the great difference in ability and intelligence between the top and bottom students of any given age. By law, they are entitled to equal opportunities, but no statute can impose equality of intellect. When all the children of a community are required to attend school from the ages of eight to seventeen, the question inevitably arises of what to do with the student who fails to learn the study material of his grade. Should he be made to repeat the course until he passes or should he be promoted regardless, so as not to drop him behind his age group? The answer, of course, is: it depends.

When a teacher's observations indicate that a certain student is capable of learning the class material and has failed to pass because of either laziness, inattentiveness or prolonged absence from school, that student is held back. Surveys have shown that this happens to about 18 per cent of the students at least once. However, if a teacher judges the student incapable of benefiting from another year in the same class, he is not held back. If he were, it would be theoretically possible to find a near-moron attending first grade in company with six-year-old boys and girls until he reached the age of seventeen and the law no longer required him to go to school.

Depending on the nature and extent of the pupil's difficulty, one of several things may be done. If he is seriously retarded mentally—with an I.Q. in the neighborhood of 65, say—he will be put in a special class for backward children; last October we had more than 6500 such children in 355 classes designed to teach at least self-respect, self-control and the habit of assuming responsibilities. Children of higher intelligence who are still such slow learners that they clearly can't profit from the standard courses are assigned to classes which teach them as much of the three R's as they can handle and, beyond that, concentrate on giving them a general educational background for modern life. These classes include training in civic responsibility, human relations and American history, occupational guidance, development of good health habits and an insight into moral and aesthetic values.

If, on the other hand, the pupil's difficulty is relatively slight, even though enough to prevent his benefiting from another year in the same grade, he will be promoted with his regular class, but given special help. Any one of three different devices may be used to give this help. The first is a system of parallel classes, which divides the students taking the same term work in the same subject into two groups; one is accelerated and enriched for the benefit of the brighter students, while the other sticks to the minimum requirements. The second device gives students of different ability different types of work within the same general field: while the slower boys are taking a general shop course, for instance, the quicker ones are learning more advanced skills in a special shop course. The third device is the varying of class assignments to match the students' particular abilities. When the whole class is engaged in working on some general problem such as how to set up a budget for a family of five, the brighter students do the more exacting work and the slower ones do the routine work. Each makes a real contribution, and each benefits from the others' as well as from his own. When the problem is finished, each has learned more than he could have in the same time alone—a valuable lesson in social living.

In addition to these devices, many students are helped to an amazing degree by special work in reading. We have found pupils of pre-primer reading ability in junior high school, and some of second- and third-grade ability in the senior highs; and, since nearly all classroom study requires an ability to read intelligently, these students were seriously handicapped. As one boy in a remedial-reading class put it, "Reading is just about the basis of everything." Other students have volunteered the information that they were able to do better work in the social studies, science and mathematics after taking a remedial-reading course. Not long ago a chronic truant, a boy who had been involved in several major disciplinary incidents, was put in a remedial-reading class. His teacher discovered that he had been ashamed about his inability to read as well as his classmates. When the special class showed him not only that there were others as badly off as he but that something could be done about it, he made rapid improvement, and has attended school regularly ever since.

No less important is the program for educating the physically handicapped. There are currently some 175 deaf children, ranging in age from four to seventeen, being given special help at the Willis and Elizabeth Martin Orthpedic Day School. Most of these boys and girls were either born deaf or became so during their first two years, and therefore never learned to talk. It usually takes about five years for them to acquire enough speech and language understanding to participate in the courses of study for normal children, and upon graduation from the equivalent of eighth grade, they either continue their education in a junior high school, enter a vocational school or leave to go to work.

Other children who pose a special problem are those who have to spend months or years of their lives in hospitals as a result of accidents or of such diseases as rheumatic fever and infantile paralysis. At present, we have eleven teachers in eight hospitals and nursing homes. Naturally, the program of study is extremely flexible. It must fit in with the hospital regime, and it must vary with the needs, desires and abilities of the individual children. This does not mean, however, that the children miss out entirely on the work they would have been taking in school. Recently a young serviceman who'd been a patient in one of the hospitals for four years came back to visit the children who are patients there now, and I think that what impressed them most was learning that, because of the instruction he'd been given while he was there, he'd been able to make up two of the four school years he missed.

Still other pupils suffer from defects that, although not requiring hospitalization, do keep them from school. There are approximately 200 such children in Philadelphia, representing grades from the beginning elementary level to the last year of senior high school. To teach them, we have twenty-five visiting teachers, and hope soon to have thirty. Naturally, the children don't get as many hours of schooling as they would in school, but the individual instruction seems to compensate for this.

Recently, one of a pair of twins fell seriously ill with rheumatic fever and was unable to enter school when her sister did. After she became convalescent, a visiting teacher worked with her three times a week, and the next year she entered second grade with her sister, and with the same skills that her sister had learned at school in first grade. In another case, two boys who had been stricken with infantile paralysis graduated from high school with their classmates because a visiting teacher had given them the same course of study they would have had in school.

Some children, both in hospitals and at home, are too ill to keep up with school work at all, and, naturally, the teachers don't try to make them follow the regular course. Each one represents a specific problem, and it is the teacher's job to help solve it, whether it is simply learning to read or to write a letter or to make artificial flowers. However small the achievement, it means real happiness to the children...and an educational system that measured achievement only in terms of tests and textbooks would be a pretty cold-blooded institution.

All in all, in one way or another, the Philadelphia public-school system serves some 215,000 children—about 8000 of whom are so seriously handicapped that they cannot attend regular classes—and more than 40,000 adults. It maintains some 260 separate school buildings and employs over 7000 full-time teachers to give pupils aiming at college an education at least as good as that given in private and parochial schools; to train in various vocations the students who want to enter the skilled and semiskilled occupations of business and industry as soon as they graduate; and to teach the slower-learning children at least the use of the fundamental tools of living and the privileges and duties of citizenship in a community and in the nation.

We are doing our best to accomplish these purposes. Naturally, there is room for improvement. We want to expand and improve the remedial-reading program. Classroom space has been far from adequate in many cases with some teachers forced to use rooms intended as shops, science rooms, even bicycle rooms; better materials are needed, for books designed to interest eight-year-old third-graders can't be expected to interest fourteen-year-olds of third-grade reading ability; above all, we need many more teachers specifically trained as remedial teachers.

In fact, the school system as a whole needs more teachers. There should be no more than twenty-five students to each teacher; today the average is thirty, with many classes running to forty or more. And unless we can add to our staff quickly, the situation is going to be far worse. This year, student enrollment is almost 6000 greater than it was in 1948, and estimates for 1952 indicate a further increase of about 10,000 over today's figure. With the present enrollment, if class size were reduced to twenty-five, we would need over 1400 more teachers; in 1952 we'd need 400 more. Leaving out all other considerations, this would cost over $7,000,000 a year more, at the present average classroom teacher's salary of $3800. If this seems high, I might mention two pertinent facts: first, raising the salary schedule of our present teaching staff to the level of that in cities of comparable size would cost nearly $3,000 more a year; second, $7,000,000 for Philadelphia's schools works out to be about six cents more a week for each resident—the price of a nickel candy bar.

Still, money is something that schools always seem to be asking for. Let's judge them on their present basis. Taken by and large, I firmly believe that the great majority of our public schools are doing, if not a perfect job, at least close to the best job possible with the facilities available. It is fashionable to find fault with the younger generation and to blame everything on the schools. It is true that the schools must—and should be proud to—accept much of the responsibility for the children they educate. But whenever I hear that our children are going to the dogs I am reminded of two statements that appeared in an editorial column a couple of years ago. One declared: "The children...have bad manners and contempt for authority; they show disrespect for their elders." The other read: "Our earth is degenerate in these latter days....Children no longer obey their parents." The first opinion was delivered by Socrates, the second by an Egyptian priest thousands of years before Christ.

The Schools' Record in Academic Achievement

It is not at all surprising that the area of academic achievement has been a particularly popular target of the contemporary school critic. There are several reasons for this, not the least of which is the relative ease with which academic skills can be measured. Among the most honored of American traditions is the comparing of local achievement test results with nationally standardized norms. Such a procedure admits of relative administrative ease and the results are fairly easy to interpret.

Another reason for the current popularity of assailing our schools for being "soft on the fundamentals" is that the mastery of such skills is regarded as essential for improving one's socioeconomic status. The desire to improve one's socioeconomic condition is especially intense, of course, among minority group parents and students. Many of the critics who represent these minority group concerns insist that the public school has traditionally short-changed downtrodden youngsters by failing to provide them with the necessary academic tools.

Yet another reason which partially accounts for the "let's get back to the three R's" plea is the relationship drawn between excellence in speech and writing on the one hand and a "liberated" disposition on the other. This discursive bias is a pronounced part of our Western cultural heritage.

One other prominent reason is quasi-political in nature. Rightly or wrongly, many critics have insisted that the "loose," "permissive," experimental orientation of public schools which has been prominent from roughly the mid sixties through the mid seventies has elevated the concern for wholesome emotional development to the virtual neglect of intellectual refinement. The "open classroom" approach is frequently singled out as being a main culprit.

Whatever the reasons which account for contemporary inclinations to attack schools for failing to provide students with essential academic skills, today's educator has an obligation to respond to the critics in a thoughtful, forthright manner. These responses must be rooted in evidence garnered from respectable historical and empirical interpretations; ideological rhetoric will not suffice.

In assessing the academic performance of the institution of American public education, it is helpful—indeed, crucial—to look at our schools from a *comparative* perspective. Unless we compare our schools' record with that attained by the schools of similar societies we run the risk of holding it up to an absolute standard of perfection. This latter process, while indeed fruitful insofar as it yields educational ideals for which we can constantly strive, can also be a grossly unfair procedure if untempered by comparative analysis.[1] As the first reading illustrates, given the all but insuperable mission the United States public school system has accepted, our record of achievement is not nearly so poor as some would have us believe.

The next reading provides us with some fairly sophisticated empirical conclusions which indicate that, in selected areas of academic achievement, the report card for our public schools is, indeed, rather mediocre. However, the same study indicates convincingly that in other significant areas our performance is highly encouraging. One of the most hopeful notes of this study is the significant increase in functional literacy among black youngsters.

The third selection relates to the recent decline in SAT scores. That these scores have declined is apparently beyond dispute. Whether public school shortcomings are exclusively responsible for this condition is a matter not so easily resolved as some contemporary critics insist.

That public school experience *can* have a dramatic impact upon academic performance is illustrated by the last selection in this chapter. Contrary to popular myth, increasing the amount of time a youngster spends in school appreciably affects his or her level of academic performance.

The readings in this chapter indicate that a balanced, judicious assessment of the American public schools' efforts to promote academic achievement will reveal that our record is in some respects mediocre; in others, fairly good; and, along some dimenstions, truly outstanding. When examined from a comparative perspective, our schools appear to be doing a creditable job, indeed. When looked at solely within the context of the American historical experience, it is apparent that the public school record, while admittedly not as solid as one might wish, is nonetheless quite impressive. More importantly, several significant achievement trends *do* engender a sense of cautious optimism. As the reading on the decline in the

---

1. I believe it was John Dewey who observed that the best is the worst enemy of the better.

SAT scores illustrates, the old bugaboo about the public school having failed to stress the fundamentals, is a simplistic assertion, wholly lacking in sophistication. Rather than wringing their hands in despair, those concerned with the relationship between public school capabilities and academic achievement have good reason to be hopeful.

13
Are Schools Better in Other Countries?

Grace and Fred M. Hechinger

All attempts to compare educational achievements are fraught with danger. What seems like success in one community may leave judges elsewhere, under different conditions, entirely unimpressed. Expectations and standards are culture-bound. And so, it is an act of considerable courage when academic researchers try to assess and compare the educational achievements, not of the schools of one city to those of schools in another city, but between literally thousands of children, teachers, and schools in 22 nations.

Yet, that is precisely what the International Association for the Evaluation of Educational Achievement (IEA) has attempted. Based in Stockholm and financed by foundations and agencies of governments, including the U.S. Office of Education, the research agency has surveyed educational achievement in science, literature, and reading comprehension. The nations taking part in the studies were Australia, Belgium, Chile, England, Finland, France, West Germany, Hungary, India, Iran, Ireland, Israel, Italy, Japan, the Netherlands, New Zealand, Poland, Romania, Scotland, Sweden, Thailand, and the United States.

Masses of data were collected in this, the biggest international education survey ever attempted. Some 258,000 students and 50,000 teachers in 9,700 schools participated—taking or administering tests, answering questions in interviews, or filling out questionnaires. Millions of items of information have been collected at a cost of $5 million. In addition to the volumes to be published on each of the subject areas, data banks in Chicago, Melbourne, New York, Stockholm, Tokyo, and one at Stanford University in California will store all the information for future use by researchers and scholars all over the world. While the experts are still sorting out the facts and debating possible conclusions, the temptation is to ask: "Who's ahead?

Grace and Fred M. Hechinger, "Are Schools Better in Other Countries?" reprinted by permission from *American Education,* Jan.-Feb., 1974, pp. 6-8.

Is it true that Johnny can't read, and is Hans reading any better? And what about the charges made by American sociologists that school really doesn't matter or doesn't work?"

Torsten Husen, the chairman of the IEA and a professor of education at the University of Stockholm, was well aware that the horse-race aspects of the study would most intrigue the press and the public. He recalls what he considers the "fiasco of 1964," when the IEA disclosed the findings of its first international survey—one relating to achievement in mathematics. The only part of the report to get any attention was that which showed that Japan was ahead of everybody or, in more parochial terms, "beat the United States."

Professor Husen considers this a simpleminded approach to complex problems. It ignores differences in the national, cultural, and social environments and priorities. It brushes aside such questions as: What proportion of the children actually go to school? What is expected of pupils in other areas of study? And what are the yardsticks of achievement in different countries?

"Our intention," says Professor Husen, "has been to avoid any sort of intellectual Olympics." The aim was rather to find answers that might be useful in reviewing, charting, or changing educational policies.

For the United States, any international comparison of educational achievement raises the enormously important question of whether the basic philosophy and the guiding principles of mass education really work—not just in theory, but in comparison with other nations.

Universal education in America has long been an article of faith. To generations of immigrants the promise of the land of unlimited opportunity was virtually synonymous with free access to free schools. There was no sorting out at age ten or eleven, as in Britain, Germany, and many other countries, of those who would or would not pursue an academically oriented course which, in turn, determined the child's future life and career. Education, universal and egalitarian, was, in Horace Mann's optimistic forecast, the cornerstone of a free, open, prosperous society.

Dream or reality? Conservative critics of American education have never fully accepted this egalitarian approach. They warned that this undifferentiated access to the public schools for all comers penalizes the gifted by lowering the level of achievement to a mediocre common denominator. They felt, as did Britain's Tories in the face of proposals for expanded educational opportunities, that more means worse.

When the high financial cost of educating everybody is considered in additon to such philosophical and ideological doubts, the question of how well the United States compares with other nations assumes an importance quite different from that of intellectual Olympics.

One of the study's crucial findings therefore is that, in reading comprehension, the top nine or ten percent of the American high school seniors performed better than the similar elite groups of all the other nations. This is clearly significant, particularly when it is viewed against the fact that many of the other countries in the sample remain highly selective—or restrictive. In other words, the cream of talent in the United States does as well as or better than the able students in educationally less egalitarian or more elitist countries.

"It is actually the selective system that pays a price in lost talent and social dislocation," says Professor Husen. To prove his point, he showed that in West Germany, which screens out "non-academic" children roughly at age ten, the top-achieving group among high school seniors also showed the "highest index of social bias." This means that these most successful students came almost exclusively from the privileged classes. At age 18, only one percent of children from lower-class (unskilled or semi-skilled workers') homes were found in German schools, compared with 14 percent in American schools.

In science, the American top group of high school seniors, it must be conceded, finished in only seventh place—not as spectacular a performance as that of the reading comprehension lead, but still a respectable performance. (The reason may well be that, compared with many European counterparts, American schools are quite lax in the amount of science required of their students. It is a laxity that has been frequently criticized most persuasively by James B. Conant, who tried in his high school reform proposals to stiffen the science requirements for the upper 15 percent of gifted students.)

The important and undeniable conclusion to be drawn from the IEA study is that mass education, American-style, while in no way hurting the academic achievement of the most talented young people, assures a constant infusion of new blood into the academic elite. This is crucial to any effort to keep society fluid and to allow rich and poor, workers' and professional people's children, long-term Americans and recent immigrants to rise to the top.

Such an open society does, of course, pay a price in terms of the total standing in any international competition. For example, in an assessment of the entire senior class, rather than just the top nine percent, the United States dropped from top rank to only 12th place. While such a "poor" showing may alarm all uninformed observers and may give rise to the charge that Johnny can't read, a realistic look should lead to quite a different conclusion.

The United States, which graduates by far the highest proportion—75 percent—of its school-age youths from high school, should quite naturally be expected to score near the bottom in a comparison with nations which, at that level, have already eliminated large numbers—in some instances, the majority—from their academic schools, and thus from the competition. While these American youngsters, by remaining in school, may bring the United States' total achievement scores down, at the same time they benefit from the additional years of education. In other words, their inclusion in the international test scores may superficially hurt the "image" of the United States, but far more important is the fact that the additional education opportunities they enjoy will not only help their own future careers but give to their country a much better pool of educated manpower. (This is precisely the reason why Professor Husen warned against the abuse of the IEA findings by those who turn the comparative studies into scholastic Olympics.)

Closely related to the IEA's findings is an issue that is currently arousing intense debate and controversy in the United States and abroad—the relationship between schooling and subsequent success and status in society. For example, the Stockholm report appears to challenge the widely publicized theories of the Harvard research team headed by Christopher Jencks which holds that schools have failed to reduce social and economic inequality.

The IEA survey admittedly did not concern itself directly with children's future income; but by clearly showing that open access to schooling allows children from poor and disadvantaged homes to rise to the level of the academic elite, it offers persuasive evidence that education does open the doors to economic success as well. And while the schools may not have achieved as much on that score as might have been wished, they have clearly done better in the United States than elsewhere.

At the same time, the IEA survey appears to confirm the claim—first published by James Coleman in 1966—that in the total pattern of achievement, home background is more important than anything the schools have so far been able to contribute. But Professor Husen nevertheless stresses that the schools do make a substantial difference and that there is a direct correlation between concentrated study and success. Or, as one of the Stockholm researchers put it: "Get them and stretch them"—open access and hard work is the winning combination.

Here, an item of some slight mystery enters the findings. An analysis of the schools' greater success in teaching science—which the Stockholm researchers call a "school-oriented" subject—than in teaching "home-oriented" reading raises questions about the educators' capacity to adapt their teaching methods and attitudes to children's needs. "The schools," says the report, "appear to do little to mobilize their resources for the improvement of reading beyone the early years."

The very fact that there is a clearly defined difference in the schools' success with "home-oriented" subjects—that is, those in which Coleman's theory is found to hold to a remarkable degree—and those "school-oriented" areas in which most of the work is being done by teachers, with the home making only a minimal contribution, suggests that educators could do a better all-around job if they reordered their own priorities. Or, to put it differently, the "mysteries" that make children learn science, mathematics, and other school-oriented subjects with relatively more success than they do home-oriented subjects could undoubtedly be more effectively identified and applied to the latter subjects as well.

That this is more than a wishful hypothesis is suggested by another IEA finding—confirmation of the charge made by women's liberation that girls are being traditionally and chronically shortchanged by the schools. Thus, the study found that, virtually without exception (and those exceptions were found to occur only in a few highly specialized schools), girls lag behind boys in interest and performance in science. The clue to the reason for that discrepancy is in the discovery that the gap grows wider the longer girls attend all-girl schools, where the teachers clearly act on the assumption that girls ought not to be bothered with such boy-oriented subjects. When girls attend coeducational schools, the study found, the gap narrows significantly.

It therefore seems evident that, whether the accepted doctrine is one of the "home-oriented" or the "boy-oriented" subject, the cause for low achievement is in large part to be sought in the schools'—and society's—lack of determination to overcome learning problems.

The IEA research ventured on the most slippery ground when it tried to get a reading not only of students' achievements but also of their attitudes. Such efforts, whether by way of questionnaire or interview, tend to be devalued by the fact that teachers and pupils everywhere usually know how to outguess their questioners, and to come up with the answers they feel are expected of them.

Too many subtle factors affect attitudes to allow them to be easily reduced to charts. For example, a surprising finding was that Swedish pupils scored rather high on "dislike" of school. (The U.S. sample, contrary to widespread American complaint, scored on the positive, "liking school" side of the chart.) A visit to a typical suburban school near Stockholm offered a reason for this attitude on the part of Swedish students. The facilities were superb—all-carpeted classrooms, super-modern laboratories, extensive student activities and meeting rooms, the latest in cafeteria equipment. But it was also evident that the students' activities and behavior were rigidly supervised and monitored. In contrast to American-style freedom enjoyed by Swedish youngsters only when they were outside the school, the academic atmosphere was stiff and regimented, and it seemed hardly surprising that such a discrepancy would lead to a relative dislike for school.

In other areas, however, the question of likes and dislikes did point to enough international agreement to make the answers useful and relevant to educational planners everywhere. Fourteen-year-olds in all countries, regardless of class or socioeconomic background, prefer humor, adventure, mysteries, sports, and romance in their reading. Upper secondary school students tend to read current events, history, and travel, as well as adventure and humor. (Incidentally, American students were more interested in symbolic meanings than were young people from any other countries.)

"The best students in most countries," the study found, "enjoy reading humor and comic strips in newspapers as well as folklore"—surely a blow to the more conventional, not to say stuffy, pedagogues.

"The implications of the IEA literature study are vast," concludes the report. "If teachers and schools can persuade students to see stories and think of them as their teachers do, the schools might not be so ineffective as some have suggested. A new look at the goals of schools and what schools *can* do could lead to a serious consideration of the curriculum in literature and mother tongue studies as a whole."

In summary, the virtue of the IEA studies is that they shatter much of the parochialism of both the conservative and the radical critics of American public education. The international comparisons provide a more rational perspective. The most vocal challengers of American public education, in keeping with the prevailing mood of self-criticism, make their judgments from an essentially provincial point of view. While they are entirely justified in exposing those policies and attitudes which have discriminated against the poor and against the minorities, they have tended to characterize such deficiencies as peculiarly American sins. A look at the schools of other industrialized nations—such as Germany, England and France, where stratification is still far more rigid—places the American achievement, with all its short comings, in a different light.

It is precisely because the IEA study has no preconceived notions about ideas which have long become articles of faith with American public school leaders that its findings tend to be reassuring. And central to those findings are two key points which have long been paramount with American public education philosophers: Schools *do* matter in keeping society fluid, and more *can* be better.

14
How Much Are Our
Young People Learning?

Stanley Ahmann

The Need for Assessing Achievement

Have you tried to balance your checkbook lately? If so, with what success? For most of us in our post-secondary school years this is (or should be) a monthly task, one which we probably view with mixed feelings. The cause of these feelings is easily identified: Balancing a checkbook is difficult even though it requires only simple addition and subtraction. Are you surprised to know that when a national sample of young adults (ages 26 to 35) received canceled checks, a bank statement, and a personal register in which checks had been recorded, barely 16 percent could reconcile the personal record with the bank record?

Now consider another everyday activity—voting. A typical ballot was given to 17-year-olds and young adults and, with it before them for careful study, five questions were asked about the voting options available. About 41 percent of the 17-year-olds and 44 percent of the young adults could answer these questions.

Finally, a small section of an ordinary television schedule was shown to young Americans of ages 9, 13, 17, and 26 to 35, and five questions were asked about the program selections available. When allowed generous time limits and ample opportunity to refer repeatedly to the printed schedule, approximately 11 percent of the 9-year-olds, 34 percent of the 13-year-olds, 53 percent of the 17-year-olds, and 62 percent of the young adults were able to answer the questions.

What is your reaction to these percentages? Do you find the success rates pleasing or disturbing? Are they consistent with your levels of expectation? In short, do these results suggest that our educational system is largely

Reprinted by permission from *How Much Are Our Young People Learning? The Story of the National Assessment,* by Stanley Ahmann, Phi Delta Kappan Educational Foundation, Bloomington, Ind., 1976, pp. 5-7, 9-12, 13-16, 21-22, 24-27.

succeeding or failing in these instances? These are important questions that deserve answers.

To be sure, the foregoing three examples provide only a few isolated bits of information about the achievements of American youth. Suppose that we had hundreds more, collectively representing all of the major learning areas of concern to schools. Actually many hundreds are available—the products of a major national achievement survey designed to obtain solid data about the principal outcomes of our education system—in other words, what students are learning. With those in hand, we are better able to understand our educational programs and formulate impressions about them.

Too frequently our opinions about the quality of American schooling are based only on rather vague general impressions from the past and a scattering of recent firsthand experiences. Useful as these are, they fail to provide a broad, strong basis for making the complex educational decisions we face. Now more than ever we need definitive information about the achievements of American youth. After careful study of such information, we should be better able to identify the strengths and weaknesses of our educational enterprise, then mount bold, innovative programs to improve it where necessary.

Traditionally, accreditation procedures have provided good information about the inputs and processes of education but little about the outcomes. In the last decade, assessments of student outcomes have been developed and implemented, which supplement the accreditation efforts very well. These are census-like surveys of levels of student achievement, emphasizing the students' intellectual changes that have occurred largely because of schooling. Typically they provide hard data about students as groups, not as individuals, and thereby familiarize us with the "big picture" of student change.

Methods of Assessing Student Achievement

Every day major national surveys are completed and their results disseminated to the public. Most prominent is the population census taken every ten years. Also highly visible are health statistics, concerning various diseases, unemployment data, the gross national product, and the consumer price index. These are closely watched, and decision makers respond to them. Economic data such as changes in unemployment levels, for example, can cause government units to adjust their estimates of tax income, public officials to modify their economic and social programs, and investors to increase their buying or selling of common stocks. The consumer price index is tied to a number of major labor contracts and retirement programs, and its major fluctuations can cause income shifts for many thousands of people.

In education we are now developing data of comparable importance through local, state, and national assessments. Their purpose is to determine levels of student achievement in major learning areas schools are concerned with, repeating the measurements every three to six years to discover changes. Needless to say, the direction and size of such changes are of vital interest to educational decision makers.

Although various assessments differ in notable ways, they often follow a general plan that is thoroughly tested. It has four basic steps:

1. Selecting learning areas and identifying their objectives.

2. Developing achievement test items to determine the degree to which these objectives are achieved.

3. Administering the test items to representative samples of students and gathering background data about them.

4. Analyzing the results and disseminating them to educators, board members, legislators and the public.

The National Assessment of Educational Progress: Goals and Methods

The largest, most informative assessment ever designed follows the general plan described very closely. It is the National Assessment of Educational Progress (NAEP), for which planning began in 1964. Its basic goal is to describe what young Americans know and can do. More specifically, it is designed 1) to obtain census-like data on the knowledges, skills, concepts, understandings, and attitudes possessed by young Americans in a variety of learning areas; and 2) to measure the growth or decline of these achievements that occurs over time.

To accomplish the foregoing, NAEP selected ten learning areas for assessment and formulated objectives and subobjectives for each with the help of committees of teachers, scholars, and concerned lay people. For an objective or subobjective to be useful in the assessment, there must be agreement that it is reflective of acceptable teaching goals, important for a young person in today's society, and meaningful to subject-matter specialists.

The learning areas selected include those receiving primary attention in the elementary and secondary schools (for example, the basic skills) and some of those receiving secondary emphasis (for example, music and art). The ten areas are:

Reading	Citizenship
Writing	Music
Mathematics	Art
Science	Literature
Social Studies	Career and Occupational Development

Four age groups were chosen for testing: 9-year-olds, 13-year-olds, 17-year-olds, and young adults (ages 26 to 35). The first three ages represent crucial points in one's educational career, while the last is at or beyond the terminal point of most formal education. Annually NAEP draws national samples of young Americans in most or all of these age groups, and measures their levels of achievement in one or more learning areas.

After the objectives and subobjectives are established in a learning area, test items are constructed to represent each of them. Some of these test items are unlike those found in the typical achievement tests used in schools. Varieties of materials, including motion pictures, graphs and tables, audio presentations, and narrative texts are used as the basis for the student's task. Furthermore, the type of student response required varies from checking a correct answer or providing lengthy written responses (such as writing an essay or giving reasons for an answer), to performing (such as using scientific apparatus, singing and playing instruments, and drawing a picture).

Levels of achievement in a learning area are determined by administering test items to young Americans selected in the national sample. No one is tested more than once, but some test items are used a second or third time when a learning area is reassessed.

In large measure, NAEP follows a systematic plan for assessing achievement levels in the ten learning areas. Those assessments completed are listed in Table 14-1.

Table 14-1
Assessments Completed by the
National Assessment of Educational Progress

Year	Learning Area
1969-70	Science, Writing, Citizenship
1970-71	Reading, Literature
1971-72	Music, Social Studies
1972-73	Mathematics, Science*
1973-74	Career and Occupational Development, Writing*
1974-75	Art, Reading*
1975-76	Citizenship/Social Studies*

*Second Assessment

Of crucial importance are the second assessments. The result of a thorough reexamination of the objectives, they involve reusing about one-half of the test items from the first assessment with a new sample of young Americans in most or all age groups. Now NAEP is measuring changes in levels of achievement.

Visualize, if you will, a third and fourth assessment, each following its predecessor by three to six years. By this means achievement trends over time can be known. National Assessment is very ambitious in its plans for future reassessments, preparing for succeeding assessments while it completes initial ones. Imagine the questions that can be answered, at least in part, by the data produced. For example:

1. Are the 9-year-olds living in the inner city developing their reading skills so rapidly that their achievement in this learning area will probably approach the national level within the next decade?

2. Is there any shift over time in terms of understanding and applying the First Amendment to the Constitution by young adults living in the Northeast as contrasted with those living in the Southeast?

3. Will young Americans living in rural areas continue to improve their skills in science at a rate that far exceeds that of the nation as a whole?

4. Are 17-year-old and young adult women raising their level of proficiency in consumer mathematics to a degree that will significantly reduce the gap between them and men of the same ages?

5. Will the direction and amount of change in levels of achievement in the basic skills be the same, for all practical purposes, as those in the general subject-matter areas (for example, science and social studies) or the fine arts (for example, music and art)?

6. If the levels of achievement in a learning area drop as time passes, what are the specific knowledges, understandings, skills, and attitudes with the greatest weaknesses and toward which special remedial programs can be directed.

In order for NAEP to answer questions such as these, it must maintain a high degree of productivity for a long period of time. Examining the highlights of its findings provides a good idea about the productivity needed.

Profiles of Student Achievement

Within each of the ten learning areas, National Assessment determines the percentages of the respondents at each age who can acceptably answer a question or successfully perform a task. The number of questions and tasks used in each assessment varies according to the learning area, ranging from 300 to more than 500. The primary manner of reporting National Assessment results is to report the percentage success and failure for various subgroups of students and young adults for each test item or groups of similar test items. Consequently, literally thousands of pieces of data are available about the performance level of American youth in the learning areas reported.

The percentages of acceptable and unacceptable responses for each test or cluster of reflated test items are reported by age groups, and, within each age group, by sex, geographic region, level of parental education, size and type of community, and race. Thus rough but useful profiles of student achievement are created. Table 14-2 presents a more detailed breakdown of the classifications used.

Major Findings: First Assessments by National Assessment

Summarizing the findings of the first assessment by National Assessment is most difficult. The following are a few of the highlights resulting from assessing nine learning areas—all the areas tested except art.

Table 14-2
Subgroups of the NAEP National
Sample Used for Reporting Results

Classification	Subgroups
Age level	9, 13, 17, 26 to 35 years
Sex	Male Female
Geographic region	Northeast Southeast Central West
Level of parental education	No high school Some high school Graduate from high school Post high school
Size and type of community	Inner city Affluent suburb Rural area Main big city Urban fringe Medium-size city Small city
Race	Black White

When each of the learning areas is considered as a composite, one finds a large degree of consistency within National Assessment findings from one learning area to another. This is to say that the differences in relative achievement among subgroups of the sample are largely consistent in direction even though they are not totally consistent in size. This can be illustrated by examining the achievement levels of some of these subgroups.

Regions of the country. The level of performance in the northeastern portion of the country is typically higher than in the other three regions in all nine learning areas reported. This is less noticeable in the young adult group than in other age groups. The lowest level of performance is consistently found in the southeastern region. It should be noted, however, that these differences are comparatively modest. For example, the Southeast is normally no more than 5 percent below the national average.

In the western region, the achievement of 9-year-olds is often below national levels, but by adulthood achievement is usually above national levels. All four age groups of young Americans in the central region typically perform at or slightly above national levels.

Size and type of community. Consider for a moment the performance of young Americans from the inner city, the rural areas, and the affluent suburbs. The first group typically achieves least well by a wide margin. These deficits are smaller, but still serious, for citizenship and music. The rural youth do somethwat better but still perform well below the national average. On the other hand, with the exception of young adults, their achievement levels in social studies and music are only slightly below the national average. Finally, the affluent suburb groups exceed the national average consistently by an important margin. This is most noticeable in mathematics.

Sex. Male-female differences in achievement vary. Female respondents generally achieve at higher levels than male respondents in many learning areas. The exceptions are science and mathematics, with little difference existing in citizenship and social studies. In some areas, the female superiority in achievement is more pronounced at the school ages than for young adults.

In science male respondents achieve at a consistently higher level, the advantage increasing with age. In mathematics the picture is mixed. Females have a better command of the computational aspects of arithmetic at age 13 but fail to achieve as well as men when young adults. In consumer mathematics, the level of achievement of males surpasses that of females at all ages, with the smallest difference at age 13 and increasingly larger differences at ages 17 and young adult.

Educational level of parents. The highest level of education of either parent of a respondent is classified into one of four categories: no high school, some high school, graduated from high school, and post high school training. The last category includes any kind of formal education following high school graduation.

It is clear from the NAEP data that the educational level of the parent of the respondent is also a vital factor in the student's level of achievement. Young Americans with parents who have only a grade school education perform least well of all. As the level of the parents' education increases to some high school, then to completion of high school, and ultimately to post high school education, the performance level of the respondent increases markedly and with striking consistency in all nine areas of achievement reported. Particularly vivid examples of this trend are found in the basic skills—mathematics, writing, and reading.

Race. Assessment data for whites and blacks only are reported by National Assessment. Achievement levels for blacks typically fall below the national average, while those for whites are above. This pattern is very pronounced in science, writing, reading, literature, social studies, and mathematics, less extreme but still notable in citizenship and music.

Major Findings: Changes in Levels of Achievement

The major findings from the first assessment by National Assessment are noteworthy in their own right. They display the strengths and weaknesses in achievements by American youth to a degree never before known. On the other hand, few reference points are available to be used when interpreting these data.

The results of the first assessment can be thought of as "bench marks." With these set up, one can now repeat a major part of the assessment three to six years later, and establish a second level of achievement that will reveal the direction of changes occurring and estimates of their sizes. This is invaluable information. The long-term trend of achievement is at least as meaningful for decision making as the levels indicated by the original assessments.

The full meaning of the word progress in the title "National Assessment of Educational Progress" is now before us. NAEP is repeatedly measuring the levels of achievement of young Americans, using about half of the test questions from the first assessment of each learning area. Great care is exercised to be sure that the test items used and the objectives on which they are based are still pertinent when reused three to six years later.

Measurements of changes in levels of achievement have been completed in three learning areas. They are science, writing, and reading, using the schedule shown in Table 14-2. In science and writing standard procedures were followed, though data are reported for school-age groups only. In reading, a "mini" assessment, much more limited than a regular reading assessment, was conducted. Although a complete reading assessment was conducted in 1970-71, only one age group (17-year olds in school) was retested in 1974, using a comparatively small part of the total number of test items. These questions were extracted from the original assessment because they seemed to measure functional literacy, that is, the essential knowledge and skills in reading required by everyone for effective functioning in society.

Note that the period of time for measuring change is as short as three years and not longer than five years. To the surprise of some, these are sufficiently lengthy periods of time to reveal changes of importance in these three learning areas. This fact alone reemphasizes the dynamic nature of education. Constant monitoring of its output is highly essential. The following results represent the beginning of this effort.

The National Picture

For 9-, 13-, and 17-year olds alike, achievement is dropping on most science test questions. This occurred with about two-thirds of the test items, while improved performance was observed on about one-third. This pattern is reasonably consistent in both the physical and biological science questions, and with all objectives.

On the average, the overall drop in science performance at each of the three age levels is about 2 percent—too large to be chance occurrence. The significance of this amount grows when we realize that it corresponds to a loss of about one-half year of learning experience in science.

Surprisingly, two important low-achieving groups do not follow the national trend: students in the Southeast and in rural areas actually improved their standing compared to the nation in the second assessment in science. In the Southeast, performance was the same or slightly improved in the second assessment as contrasted with the first, while all other regions fell, particularly the western region for ages 13 and 17. Students attending rural schools improved their overall science achievement by approximately 3 percent to 4 percent while the nation declined—a truly remarkable achievement. If these trends continue, these groups could reach the national levels of performance in less than a decade from the time of the second assessment.

On the other hand, it must be kept in mind that all other groups of school-age youth follow the national trend quite consistently. For both male and female, black and white, suburbanites and inner-city dwellers, achievement in science is slipping.

Changing Levels of Writing Achievement

Each of the two writing assessments consisted of a number of survey questions, multiple-choice questions, and essay tasks. In this way achievement in both general writing ability and writing mechanics (punctuation, capitalization, spelling, and word usage) are measured. The former is the more difficult to handle in a testing situation. The respondents are given a topic to write an essay about. In one instance, 9-year-olds were given 15 minutes to write a story about a picture of a jumping kangaroo, and 13- and 17-year olds were given 26 minutes to write a descriptive essay. They were not instructed to edit or rewrite their essays but were asked to do their best writing.

The essays provide two kinds of information. First, we can judge their overall quality, including such elements as word choice, creative style, expression of ideas, and depth of thought. Second, we can tabulate the mechanical errors like misspelled words, faulty punctuation, and poor grammar.

Comparing essays written in 1969-1970 with those written in 1973-74 reveals some unusual changes. Here are a few highlights for each age group:

Seventeen-year-olds.

1. The overall quality of the essays declined in five years, and the percentage of students writing good or excellent papers dropped from 85 percent to 78 percent.

2. Very good writers are as good as they were in 1969, and there are a few more of them. They are writing longer essays without losing coherence or increasing their error rates in areas such as punctuation, word choice, spelling, run-ons, fragments, and so on.

3. Poor writers are worse than they were. They are writing shorter, less stylistically sophisticated essays but are retaining about the same error rates in writing mechanics. More poor essays are incoherent than in 1969.

4. In general, most aspects of writing generally called mechanics and stressed heavily in elementary and junior high school English classes are being handled adequately by the vast majority of students, and deterioration in their use is not evident during the five-year-period.

Thirteen-year-olds.

1. The average essay written by 13-year-olds in 1973 is not as good as that written in 1969. Fewer essays are excellent.

2. There is a movement toward shorter, simpler expression. The essays were shorter in 1973; this is largely because they contained fewer phrases within sentences. Also, the vocabulary employed in 1973 was somewhat simpler.

3. A marked increase appeared, particularly among males, in rambling prose, which is somewhat unfocused writing containing more run-on sentences and more awkwardness than was evident in 1969. In other

words, the percentage of people adhering to the traditional conventions of written expression decreased.

4. The quality of the essays by both male and female writers dropped in four years, and the drop was greater for males. Thirteen-year-old females clearly surpass males in general writing ability.

Nine-year-olds.

1. The percentage of 9-year-olds writing good or excellent papers rose from 51 percent in 1970 to 57 percent in 1974.

2. Nine-year-olds are writing longer, somewhat more sophisticated essays, but they are losing some coherence in the process.

3. Most essays by 9-year-olds are virtually free of run-on sentences, agreement errors, comma errors, period errors, word choice errors, and structure work errors.

4. Very few 9-year-olds write fully developed paragraphs focusing on a topic sentence, and the percentage is decreasing. The most rapid decrease is among the high quality papers.

Changing Levels of Functional Literacy

In contrast to the first reading assessment conducted in 1970-71, the mini-assessment of functional literacy is much smaller and more focused. Only 17-year-olds enrolled in schools were retested, and about 25 percent of the test items used in the first test assessment were readministered in 1974. Furthermore, these questions were selected to present the formats of reading materials we frequently encounter in everyday life and with which we must be able to cope to function adequately. The reading materials employed are passages such as newspaper articles, stories, and poems; common reference materials used when one seeks information; and graphic materials such as signs, coupons, drawings, charts, maps and graphs. Included are questions about such things as a telephone bill, a traffic ticket, and an excerpt from an insurance policy.

When administered in 1971 as part of the complete reading assessment, the test questions for functional literacy proved to be easy for most 17-year-olds. This is reasonable since the questions represent a minimal level of proficiency in reading; mastery is desired. Did the level of success of 17-year-old students rise three years later? Yes, definitely.

All groups gained in functional reading skills, the average national level rising 2 percent. Importantly, groups who had the lowest levels of achievement on the first assessment gained most. In other words, substantial improvement was found for 17-year-old students who are male, black, live in the inner city, or have parents without a high school education. The average achievement of the last group jumped nearly 5 percent.

And, you might ask, what is happening to the two groups of American youth who bucked the downward trend in science achievement, namely, residents of the Southeast and of rural areas. The answer to this question is more encouraging news. Of the four regions of the country, 17-year-old students in the Southeast improved the most—almost 3 percent on the average. Those from rural areas raised their achievement level more than their peers living in other types of communities, registering a sharp gain of more than 4 percent. In total, it's a pleasant picture to contemplate.

15
Achievement-Test Score Declines

Annegret Harnischfeger and David E. Wiley

After two decades of educational reform and innovation, there is now emerging a strong movement toward restoration: Back to the fundaments of traditional schooling. This movement is nourished by resource cutbacks often resulting in instructional curtailment, but also by alarming news of achievement test score declines. The common view seems to be that if the declines are real, something is wrong with American Education, and that the way to correct this condition is curricular reconstruction: Back to Basics!

Some Facts About Test Score Changes

The apparent facts about achievement changes, as exhibited in the media, in research reports and on the occasion of conferences focusing on achievement measurement, curriculum and school administration, are the following. Since the mid-1960s, declines have occurred in these tests:

1. *Scholastic Aptitude Test.* SAT scores (11th and 12th grade) have dropped for males and females in both verbal and mathematical sections.

2. *American College Tests.* ACT scores (11th and 12th grade) have dropped in English, mathematics and social science for males and females.

3. *Minnesota Scholastic Aptitude Test.* High school junior test scores (11th grade) have declined.

4. *Iowa Tests of Educational Development.* ITED scores have declined in all areas for grades 9 through 12 in the State of Iowa.

5. *Iowa Tests of Basic Skills.* ITBS national norm data indicate drops in

Reprinted by permission from Annegret Harnischfeger and David E. Wiley, "The Marrow of Achievement Test Score Declines," *Educational Technology,* June 1976, pp. 5-14.

language, mathematics and reading. State of Iowa data from grades 5 through 8 show decline in all areas.

6. *Comprehensive Tests of Basic Skills.* CTBS national norm data show declines in mathematics and reading from grade 5 and language from grade 6 through 10.

7. *National Assessment of Educational Progress.* NAEP data show declines in science at each age level and in writing at ages 13 and 17.

No trends have been found in these:

1. ACT Science test (11th and 12th grade).

2. *Preliminary Scholastic Aptitude Test* (PSAT: 11th grade).

3. ITBS State of Iowa data for grade 4.

4. CTBS national norm data for grade 5 reading and language in grades 3 and 5.

Increases have been detected in these:

1. NAEP literacy for 17-year-olds and writing for 9-year-olds.

2. ITBS State of Iowa data for grade 3 in all areas.

3. CTBS national norm data for grades 2 and 4 in reading, language and mathematics, and grade 3 in reading and mathematics.

4. *Stanford-Binet.* Norming data between the 1930s and 1972 show a dramatic rise.

5. *Metropolitan Readiness Tests.* These scores have risen for pre-first-graders.

Generally, through the 1940s, 1950s and up to the mid-1960s, achievement test scores steadily increased. Since then, scores have been declining in all tested achievement areas for grades 5 through 12, with more dramatic drops occurring in recent years and being most evident for higher grades. The declines have been most pronounced in verbal tests and therein for college-bound females. There is no evidence for declines at younger ages and in lower grades (grades 1, 2, 3 and 4), but perhaps there are increases. It is noteworthy that today's first-graders enter school with more developed skills, as measured by readiness tests, than their counterparts of the mid-1960s.[1] Definitely, children now enter first grade with more knowledge of letter names and word meaning, and also more knowledge about numbers. Our analyses indicate that these findings are real, not artifacts, and that

---

1. Mitchell, B.C. "Changes Over an Eight- and a Nine-Year Period in the Readiness Level of Entering First-Grade Pupils." Paper presented at the Annual Meeting of the National Council on Measurement in Education, Chicago, April 1974.

they describe a national phenomenon.[2] And this great generality of the phenomenon draws our concern.

Some of the specifics of the declines provide provocative ground for more complex interpretations than those commonly advanced. The fact that achievements measured in higher grades have declined more than those measured in lower ones reflects differences in content tested as well as the ages of the test-takers. For example, large declines have generally been observed in most verbal-oriented tests, except those given in the lower and middle elementary grades. However, the latter primarily measure decoding, word-structure, basic vocabulary and simple comprehension skills, i.e., literacy, while the tests used in later grades are oriented toward comprehension and interpretation of more complex textual materials. The only increases in verbal skills that were found for higher grades (11th and 12th)[3] correspond to those simpler skills measured by standardized tests in elementary school. One straightforward interpretation would be that "basic" reading skills are increasing but more advanced ones are declining. As the grade-level discrepancy in achievement-score trend holds more generally, not merely for verbal-related skills, interpretation of those results must give heed to test content.

Have Compositions of the Tests or the Test-Takers Changed?

In evaluating the findings, our first explanatory attempt concerned the measurement instruments that showed the declining score trends. But we soon had to conclude that changes in scoring, scaling, testing conditions or test content could not explain the large achievement decreases. We did not pinpoint any content changes in tests. A limited formal assessment was made by longitudinally comparing categories of test items for one test (SAT) over time, but less formal assessments were performed for other tests. In general, test content changes might have to take responsibility for slight score changes, but they can definitely not explain the general phenomenon. Some non-content, technical changes in tests worked in the opposite direction. For example, we found that changes in two tests (SAT, PSAT) had resulted in scaling increases. Thus, accounting for these would even augment the magnitudes of achievement test score declines.

The other immediately obtruding possible *explicans* for the achievement score drops is change in the test-taking student population. And, in fact,

2. Harnischfeger, A. and D.E. Wiley. *Achievement Test Score Decline: Do We Need to Worry?* St. Louis, Mo.: CEMREL, Inc. 1975.

3. U.S. Department of Health, Education and Welfare, National Center for Education Statistics. *The Condition of Education.* Washington, D.C.: U.S. Government Printing Office, 1975.

Munday (1976)[4] in a report on college-bound students claims that the large score drops for college-bound females are due to the greater number of less skilled females now entering college. This actually might explain part of the more severe verbal score declines for females. Another achievement-relevant factor often advanced to explain the declines among the college-bound is the socioeconomic status of test takers. We need to explore the likelihood of a decrease in the socioeconomic level of those taking college entrance examinations. However, these changes, and those in the entering college population generally, cannot account for the decline.[5] The portion of college entrants coming from upper income families (over $15,000; constant 1973 dollars) increased 17 percent (from 41.3 to 48.2 percent) from 1967 to 1973, while those with lower income increased only about 8 percent (from 6.7 to 7.3 percent). Middle income families decreased their representation 14 percent (from 52.0 to 44.5 percent). Over-all, the median income of college students' families rose 8.9 percent (from $13,481 to $14,679). Thus, if scores of each socioeconomic group had remained constant, the average scores of all college entrants would have *increased* due to compositional effects, given the known relation between socioeconomic status and achievement.

Compositional changes of test-takers have been brought about in grades 5 through 12 by a sharp decrease in pupil dropout rate, which has been especially pronounced for higher grade levels. From 1950 to 1968 the pupil dropout rate fell from 50 to 25 percent.[6] Since then it has been stable. This fact implies that considerably greater numbers of pupils who a decade ago would have dropped out of school, and therefore not taken tests, are now in fact taking tests. These students typically are in the lower achievement ranges and might thus account for a part of the general achievement decline.

Another factor being held responsible for achievement score declines for 12th graders is the states' policy trends of easing early graduation. The argument is that these policies result in creaming off the high achievers. Actually, early high school graduation has increased nationwide from 2.2 percent (1971-72) to 7.7 percent (1973-74).[7] However, the data indicate that early graduating pupils represent most of the spectrum of high school pupils except the lowest ranges of achievement, and this has not changed.

---

4. Munday, L.A. *Declining Admissions Test Scores.* ACT Research Report No. 71. Iowa City, Iowa: American College Testing Program, 1976.

5. The Socioeconomic compositions of groups of, e.g., SAT-takers, has been almost identical to the corresponding college entrants.

6. High school dropouts per 1,000 students entering 5th grade.

7. Educational Research Service. "Early Graduation from High School: Policy and Practice." *ERS Report.* Arlington, Virginia: Educational Research Service, 1975.

Definitely, there is little overrepresentation of college entrants. Thus, the relatively large achievement score declines for 12th graders cannot be explained by a cream-off effect of early graduators.

Although slight portions of achievement score decreases might be attributable to factors inherent in test developments and to distributional changes of test takers, the extent of the decline, both with respect to magnitude and consistency, over the past 10 years demands further analysis in order to clarify possible implications for educational policy. Efforts must be made to strengthen conclusions about the extents, locations and types of declines.

We have avoided estimating precise amounts of decline or change. Characterizing precise magnitudes in achievement test score trends not only necessitates further research assessing drifts in scaling and composition changes of test takers, but also evaluating other, probably more potent, factors yet to be discussed. It further demands the assessment of content correspondences among instruments and the comparable scaling of content-similar tests.

We are not in the position of attaching quantitative labels to the various factors to which test score changes might be attributable. But we are able to assess grossly the likely potencies that some forces might have in explaining the achievement decline. Definitely, further research should analyze and attempt to attribute precise amounts of test score changes to relevant factors. However, that is merely one step in answering the more important questions of what skills do test scores represent and which of these have declined? E.g., does the large decline in verbal scales indicate less vocabulary or literature knowledge, or fewer conceptual skills? To evaluate and valuate achievement test scores, we will have to find the answers to this type of question.

So, if we conclude that only a minor amount of the test score decline can be attributed to changes in test construction (i.e., test content, scaling) and the composition of test takers, then most of the decline has to have been effected by changes in school, family and society.

The Role of the Schools

Naturally, achievement test score declines have, without any deliberation, been valued negatively, and blame has been immediately thrown on schools and teachers. But also television and societal changes, such as broken families, working mothers and drugs, have been cited as responsible.

The reported achievement declines are presently being taken to support or initiate diverse movements. A considerable number of schools and districts are moving "back to basics," and districts and and states are establishing minimal requirements for graduation from elementary and secondary schools. Groups claim on the same data basis either a necessity for more resources in education or, in opposition, try to justify resource cutbacks, claiming that the last decade's increased educational expenditure did not pay off. All of these actions and claims lack ground, as, so far, more expert and intensive attempts at attribution (or scapegoating) have failed. More thinking, analysis and research are required before grounded action or reasoned policies can be recommended. And we should be prepared in our process of research evaluation and valuation of the last decade's achievement score declines to find a multifaceted array of decline-relevant factors that is not easily translatable into action plans.

The likely potentiality and the relative ease of intervenability tempted us to first search for factors allowing the attribution of achievement decreases to the school. And therein, curricula, course taking, length of school year and day, absences, desegregation, teaching staff characteristics and attitudes toward learning seemed viable for assessing the meaning of the achievement declines.

Curriculum, one fundamental characteristic of education, is often ignored by those concerned with the interpretation of test scores: What is *learned* depends strongly on what is *taught*. Differences in educational quality or efficiency contribute to the rapidity with which children move through a curriculum, but when curricula are diverse, children will learn different things. Curricular diversity is thus reflected in the levels of achievement exhibited by tests. That is, one of the strongest contributors to the test-specific pupil achievement ought to be the curriculum. Curriculum in this sense refers to the content that is actually taught in the schools. It varies often within the school, from school to school and district to district, as well as, of course, over grade levels. Curricula vary in their goals and objectives, in teaching methods, in materials, in course and instructional organization, in sequencing and in timing of instruction.

Standardized tests are constructed so as to take many of these features into account. The item-selection process might hold one key to the understanding of test score declines. Typical resources for goal analysis involved in items-selection are state and local curricular guides and curricular materials. Items are developed from different curricula across the United States, and their norms are derived from national samples of pupils in the relevant age and grade ranges.

This item-selection process boldly assumes a match of guidelines, textbooks and other materials with actual teaching. It is worthwhile asking to what extent this has been or is the case. What we do know is that when basic curricula drastically change, as with the introduction of the "new math," tests fundamentally change so as to not result in "artificial" achievement declines in the test content aligned to former curricula.

Unfortunately, direct evidence of curricular changes in United States schools is difficult to discover. Neither federal agencies, responsible for educational data collection, nor interest groups (such as the NEA) have seen fit to regularly collect data on this important aspect of schooling. We actually do not know how closely tests match what is taught in the schools.

If we find that tests and curricular goals match less nowadays than a decade ago, then the relevance of the achievement test score decline would be restricted to the matching parts of tests and curricula. If, however, we discover that present curricula and tests address the same goals, then we ought to be able to detect other factors responsible for lowered achievements. It is mandatory therefore to assess the likely congruence of tests and instruction.

The view conveyed here distinguishes among curricular goals, implemented curricula and achievement test results. If tests are to be learned in the schools, then they must be interpreted in terms of their matches to the desired goals and to the educative activities taking place. Otherwise, they cannot enlighten us about the relation between teaching and learning.

Some gross, indirect evidence of curricular change, the nearest approximations to direct curricular evidence available, can be drawn from data for secondary-school course enrollments by subject area. The National Center for Education Statistics has available survey data on the average numbers of courses taken by secondary pupils in various curricular areas from 1948-49 to 1972-73.[8] The data are spotty in their coverage, intermediate school years being only 1960-61 and 1970-71. Generally, the average numbers of courses were constant for the two earliest years, higher in the 1970-71 sample, and dropped again by 1972-73. It is unclear when the decline in course taking began. The peak could have occurred during any of the school years between 1961 and 1971. However, there was clearly a large drop between 1970-71 and 1972-73. In this period, also during which achievement declines occurred, the average number of courses per pupil dropped by 13 percent. These gross numbers are difficult to interpret, however, because they do not indicate what kinds of courses were taken. Fortunately, refined data are available for 1970-71 and 1972-73, so we can discuss some of the details of more recent short-term curricular changes.[9]

Some large changes occurred over the two-year period in the

8. U.S. Dept. of Health, Education and Welfare, National Center for Education Statistics, *The Condition of Education.*

9. Gertler, D.B. and L.A. Barker. *Patterns of Course Offerings and Enrollments in Public Secondary Schools, 1970-71.* DHEW Publication No. (OE) 74-11400. Washington, D.C.: U.S. Government Printing Office; Osterndorf, L. *Summary of Offerings and Enrollments in Public Secondary Schools, 1972-73.* DHEW Publication No. (NCES) 76-150. Washington, D.C.: U.S. Government Printing Office, 1975.

proportions of pupils enrolled in each grade from 7 through 12 who were also taking general grade-specific English courses. The proportion of course-enrolled pupils decreased at every grade level. This drop is substantial, averaging about 15 percent over all grade levels. The over-all percentages of secondary pupils (grades 7-12) enrolled in other (neither general nor grade-specific) English courses has increased over the two-year period. However, these enrollment increases by no means balance the decreases in regular, general English courses.

The total proportion of all secondary pupils enrolled in regular courses declined from 88.7 percent to 75.2 percent, a drop of 15.2 percent,[10] while the enrollment in other courses only increased 5.2 percent (from .517 to .544 courses per pupil). A total drop of almost 8 percent in total English enrollments (from 1.405 to 1.296 courses per pupil) in a two-year period is a probable and startling cause of verbal score declines.

A similar picture emerges in foreign language enrollments. While junior high school enrollments have remained stable at 4.6 percent of total secondary course enrollments, there has been an enrollment decline of 7.5 percent in high school foreign languages (from .199 to .184 courses per pupil). The largest declines have occurred in French (-14 percent), with only marginally smaller drops in German (-13 percent) and Latin (-13 percent). Spanish enrollments, on the other hand, have slightly increased, by 2.6 percent (from .115 to .118). The decreases have been relatively greater (-25 percent) in less popular languages, total course enrollments dropping from .012 to .009 courses per pupil over this period. The most sizable drops have occurred in high school first-year language courses (-9 percent), followed by second-year course enrollments (-7.5 percent). Enrollments in more advanced courses have shown the smallest decline (-3 percent).

History enrollments have not shown any sizable drop (-0.6 percent), diminishing from .507 to .504 courses per pupil. However, they have redistributed markedly. Regular history course taking has declined 6 percent (from .438 to .412), with the largest drops occurring in U.S. History (-7 percent) and State History (-14.5 percent). World History has not substantially altered in popularity. By level, the greatest decrease in regular history enrollments took place in junior (-10 percent) rather than senior high school (-4 percent). Elective and specialized courses took up the slack from these declines, increasing by 33 percent (from .069 to .092 courses per pupil) over the two-year period.

---

10. The drop of 15.2 percent is calculated on the base of 88.7 percent in 1970-71, i.e., 0.152=75.2—88.7. This figure represents the relative drop in the proportion of those enrolled over the two-year period. This mode of calculating percentages is also used for the curricular areas which follow. Also note that these figures are actually number of courses per pupil. Only when pupils are not likely to take more than one course do we refer to percentages.

Mathematics enrollments show an interesting pattern of change. Remedial math taking increased by more than 80 percent (1.4 to 2.6 percent) while enrollments in general mathematics decreased 15 percent (41.1 to 34.8 percent). Traditional college preparatory mathematics (algebra, geometry, trigonometry) remained approximately constant (12.4 to 12.8 percent), drops in algebra being compensated by increases in more advanced areas. And other mathematics (mostly advanced) increased by about one-third from 2.8 to 3.7 percent. In aggregate, these changes imply that the total number of courses per pupil in mathematics decreased from 0.768 to 0.713, a total drop in enrollment of more than 7 percent in two years. Again, curricular change is a likely strong influence on tested achievements in mathematics.

With respect to natural science curricula, there has been a large drop in secondary enrollments in general science (-13 percent, from 25.2 to 21.9 percent), especially in senior high school, where the decline reached 30 percent (from 9.2 to 6.4 percent). In the specific sciences, enrollments in the regular first-year courses offered in high schools have suffered the most systematic deterioration (biology: -1 percent, from 14.8 to 14.6 percent; chemistry: -10 percent, from 6.0 to 5.4 percent; physics: -30 percent, from 3.3 to 2.3 percent), the decline increasing with more stringent mathematical prerequisites.

On the other hand, there has been an increase in total high school enrollments in the biological sciences (+15 percent, from 19.9 to 22.8 percent), but these increases have occurred solely through advanced and speciality courses (+61 percent, from 5.1 to 8.2 percent). In the physical sciences, advanced and specialized enrollments have remained essentially constant (-0.7 percent, from 14.9 to 14.8 percent), implying an over-all course enrollment drop in physical science of 7 percent.

Finally, the question arises: If there are such drops in academic course taking, have there been corresponding increases in more practical course enrollments? The answer to this appears to be a resounding NO! Courses for practical training (e.g., vocational, business, home economics) dropped more than 30 percent over the two-year period.

These data present a general picture of the developments which have taken place from 1970-71 to 1972-73 in American secondary curricula as they have been implemented in the schools:

1. There has been a general enrollment drop in academic courses.

2. This general decline has come about mostly because of substantial decreases in general course taking which have not been substantially replaced by increases in elective or speciality courses.

3. There has been a sizable drop in the proportions of pupils enrolling in

the traditional basic courses of the college preparatory curricula: algebra, first-year foreign language, chemistry and physics.

4. There have been no sizable declines in advanced college preparatory courses. It is not clear whether this was due to stable basic enrollments of those who traditionally take advanced work, or whether the enrollment drops in more basic courses had not yet reached advanced levels.

5. Additionally, there have been extreme drops in more practical courses giving preparation for employment and homemaking.

6. We lack information on what pupils' activities have changed *to*. Possible factors are: lowered instructional offerings and increasing work-study programs not accounted as courses.

These course enrollment declines parallel closely the test score decline patterns. Declines both in course enrollment and achievement scores are largest for English, followed by mathematics and natural sciences. The one test (ACT) that had stable science scores and the sharp decline in the national science assessment also parallel the stable enrollments for advanced science courses, taken by college-bound students, and the sharp decline in basic natural science course enrollments, intended for typical high school students.

What does the enrollment decline in basic secondary courses indicate? Definitely, pupils are taking fewer courses in most curricular areas. And the redistribution pattern of courses actually taken indicates a shift away from standard courses and traditional academic courses toward specialty and elective courses. These facts raise a host of questions: Are fewer secondary schools offering traditional courses? Or, are fewer pupils enrolling in offered courses? Or both? How are decisions made about enrollment and are the factors which strongly influence secondary pupils' choices different than they used to be? What makes Johnny take algebra? Has the lowered pay-off of college education extended its influence to secondary school? Have parents become less interested in their children's education?

In spite of all these unanswered questions, one clear inference is that typical students are less exposed to traditional basic courses. If, therefore, achievement tests centrally focus on these goals, typically addressed in basic courses, we would expect a score decline. Another viable question, however, concerns shifts in goal emphasis, i.e., the goals that students still are expected to reach as compared to those that now receive less stress. Total test scores do not reveal that selection process; only content-based item analyses would yield this highly important information.

Collaterally, we have detected some increase in elective courses. An important question is: Which goals of those courses are tests now representing? Elective course diversity is large, which makes test coverage of goals difficult. The extent to which such goals are reflected in current achievement tests warrants investigation. So, independent of the question of what goals *should* be attained, we have to analyze the match between goals addressed in school and goals tested. Any valuation of test score declines has to perform this analysis.

We would like to strongly emphasize this necessity by pointing to two results: (1) A study of curricular evaluations by Walker and Schaffarzick[11] indicates that when achievement tests are aligned to the goals of an innovative curriculum, it generally out-performed rival curricula. However, when more traditional tests are used, the traditional curricula, to which the new one was compared, produce higher scores. (2) A number of school districts startled by declining achievement test scores have taken immediate action toward back-to-basics, meaning restoration of traditional obligatory basic courses, often accompanied by revival of long-forgotten disciplinary rules, including dress codes. A sizable number of these districts and schools claim that they have reversed the declining achievement score trend.

We cited these occurrences to pinpoint the crucial character of the curriculum-test match and to caution the reader away from short-circuited inferences. So far, we only certified that some of what used to be learned is not learned any more. We neither know, at other than a general level, what it is that pupils are not learning any more, nor do we know what they might be learning that is not tested.

The back-to-basics movement clearly reflects curricular change. Sales of instructional equipment are dropping, while those of textbooks with more traditional content emphasis are rising. This development does not, however, merely reflect a change in curricular emphasis. The whole notion of "basic" skills or, more generally, "basic" education is fundamentally homogenizing. It implies that there is an underlying foundation of skills or learnings which precurse subsequent, more diverse learnings. Whether these are conceived as psychologically prerequisite or socially mandatory is irrelevant to their homogenizing character. Under either conception they are exhibited as a primary common component of the curriculum. Consequently, the greater the emphasis on (the more instructional time devoted to) such basics, the more similar are the educative experiences of individuals.

The back-to-basics movement counters one important characteristic of recent curricular trends: The increase in the diversity of offered and accepted experiences, at least in secondary school. This trend has exhibited

---

11. Walker, D.F. and J. Schaffarzick, "Comparing Curricula." *Review of Educational Research,* 1974, *44,* 83-111.

itself in (1) the increasing local diversity of curricula, (2) the augmented numbers of courses appealing to special groups and (3) the greater numbers of elective as opposed to "core" courses.

It is, of course, much easier to representatively assess the state of intended learnings when the curricula have a large common core of "basics" than when they have little commonality. If we have moved from an era when tests were developed against the background of strong consensus on goals, and consequent great similarity in the curricula widely offered, to an era of disagreement over goals and curricular diversity, but little change in test coverage, then achievement declines on standardized tests would naturally follow. In fact, it is hard to see, under these conditions, how scores could not drop.

Problematically, the back-to-basics movement seems to neglect the untested content in only focusing on skills that are commonly represented in most tests. Has the movement's re-emphasis on educational fundamentals been simplistically derived from test score declines, together with other dissatisfactions, such as increased societal permissiveness, or has it resulted from a thorough reconsideration of educational goals and the curriculum? For a thoughtful and engaged educator, it is at this time difficult to endorse the movement. What we need, and what the achievement score trends should provoke, is a reconsideration and debate over educational goals.

While secondary schools have undergone tremendous diversification— high school consolidation, career education, cultural and ethnic group considerations all have nourished this development—it is likely that elementary schools have more intensively concentrated on "basics." Enormous amounts of federal funds have been focused on reading, writing and arithmetic, especially in the lower elementary grades. And, actually, test scores up to grade 4 indicate rising rather than declining achievement. It is worth considering whether the focus on basics in those grades and the close match of tests and curricular goals are responsible for this achievement picture. The picture is further confused by the increase in pre-first grade readiness scores, cited above. We have little understanding of these issues, as we completely lack data that would enlighten the inside of elementary school.

Our ignorance about our schools is astounding, and this in a country where more data collection, assessment and evaluation are taking place than anywhere else. Besides the crude and simplified course enrollment data for secondary schools, no nationwide data on content of teaching and learning are available. We definitely should be more informed about school education, as this is the society's most important investment.

Although we do know that the length of the school year over the last decade has typically been about 180 days, we only suspect from scattered survey data that there must be large variation in the length of the school day. No nationwide statistics are available.

A factor that might be related to achievement test score trends is pupil absence rate, which has steadily increased over the past decade, resuling in smaller average amounts of schooling for pupils, but also burdening the teaching process considerably.

A factor to be positively valued, although it might be responsible for part of the *evident* test score declines, is pupil dropout rate (see 2) which, in 1968, stabilized at an all-time low (25 percent). Considerably more dropout-prone—and typically low achieving—pupils now continue schooling until graduation. We should not undervalue this as a possible cause of manifest test score decline, even though it may signal increases in general academic accomplishment.

Have pupils changed in their assessment of the importance of schooling to their future lives? If so, this could have important effects on how much and what they choose to learn and on how seriously they take those testing situations used to assess their accomplishments. Lower pupil motivation might follow from the now generally lower pay-off of education in our society. Data supporting an economic view of education are the lower college enrollment figures for students of middle income families (see previous section). But we might also conceive that pupil motivation for learning, especially for traditional academic areas, could decrease as a consequence of more general societal movements favoring emotional, religious, expressive and aesthetic issues over academic or predominantly cognitive aspects. Presently, we lack empirical evidence on motivational changes of pupils, although lowered motivation for school and learning is an often heard complaint from teachers and parents.

Pupil mobility or desegregation seem not to have any explanatory power, as regional and state differences contradict the widespread character of the declines.

Teaching staff characteristics such as experience and education are possible distal causes, but existing data do not reveal any evidence for their playing a relevant role in the current test score drops.

Also, for some of the factors connected to school reorganization in the past decade, such as continuing high school consolidation and the crowded state of elementary schools following the post-war baby-boom, we could not draw any straightforward conclusion of powerful determination of decreasing achievement test scores. This difficulty arises from the simultaneity of their accompaniment by massive funding increases and the inconsistency of their likely impact with grade-level differences in the decline.

The school, however important, is but one agent in educating and socializing children. It is prominent as its mission is defined as primarily educative and developmental, and does not include leisure work, or participation in societal efforts. Politically, the school is most relevant, as it can be used instrumentally both to support or counteract social trends and to achieve new societal goals.

Societal Changes

We must consider pupils' out-of-school experiences for two reasons: First, definitely, much learning relevant to academic achievement takes place outside of school and, therefore, we have to look for changes in these contributory experiences of children. Second, the syntony of school and non-school learning will determine if important achievements have been neglected or whether children are paralyzed by inconsistencies in their in- and out-of-school life. Efforts to avoid the latter can be seen in the school's taking charge of many issues that earlier were considered to be the family's responsibility, such as health and sex education, home economics, etc.

The effects of school extend into the pupil's out-of-school social life also as schools frame the opportunities for social activity and personal interaction. They determine the availability of friendships, and initiate most activities—including highly problematic ones such as drug and alcohol consumption—merely via the amount of time that peer groups are required to spend together.

The National Institute on Drug Abuse (NIDA) reports that 8- to 14-year-olds constitute the fastest growing group of drug users. It has been estimated that 20 percent of pupils older than 11 years have tried marijuana and that about 6 percent of high school seniors smoke it and/or drink alcohol daily.[12] Another indicator of non-compliance with societal norms is the recently reported and alarming increase in youth crime. Are youths indifferent to traditional societal values and achievement goals? We don't know. Certainly this issue needs clarification in understanding achievement test score declines.

Television is often assigned a core function in altering pupil experiences over the past 25 years. The main arguments are that it decreases the time that was otherwise devoted to homework and reading and that it impoverishes family interaction. We did not discover or retrieve any data enlightening this issue. The only evidence we found indicates that, in fact, set ownership and the amount of time that families spend viewing television has continually increased since 1950, including the period of the test score decline.[13] But to be of any evidential significance, we would need to know

12. Holden, C. Drug Abuse 1975: "The 'War' Is Past, the Problem Is as Big as Ever." *Science*, November 1975, *190(14)*, 638-641.

13. Bower, R.T. *Television and the Public*. New York: Holt, Rinehart, and Winston, 1973.

what and how long children of various ages view television. Is it likely (1) that the general visual and verbal stimulation of television and the existence of educative pre-school programs are responsible for the achivement increases in lower grades, and (2) that older children's television viewing has a contrary effect—keeping them from educationally important activities, such as reading or consultative interaction with adults? No data are available.

Clearly, the American family has undergone dramatic changes over the past 25 years (1945-1974).[14] Some educationally important indicators are:

1. the increase of labor force participation of married women with school-aged children, from 26 to 51 percent;

2. the increase of single parent families, from about 10 to almost 17 percent of all families;

3. the 50 percent drop in the proportion of extended families; and

4. the tripling of illegitmate children.

These trends seem startling, but as we are not able to concretely relate these societal factors to achievement, we limited ourselves to merely listing them. Composed and configured to a comprehensive and differential picture of changes in the American family, they might well demonstrate relevance for the explanation of declining test scores:

But there are still other family- and generation-specific factors that might relate to achievement declines. The pupil population of the last decade, now in secondary schools, is the baby-boom generation. This pupil generation did not only crowd schools, but also had an unusual family environment. Their parents typically married and had children at a considerably earlier age than parents in the periods before or after.[15] This implies, since income increases with age, that those children were, on the average, born into economically poorer environments. A hypothesis we have not yet been able to confirm concerns the likely higher proportion of children born during that time to lower as compared to middle classes. Both historic occurrences might contribute to present test score declines. But there is a third unique feature to that generation, relevant to achievement: childspacing. Children were also born relatively closer to each other in time. Research indicates that, in general, close spacing seems

---

14. Bronfenbrenner, U. The Next Generations of Americans. Paper presented for the Annual Meeting of the American Association of Advertising Agencies. Dorado, Puerto Rico, March 1975.

15. Whelpton, P.K., A.A. Campbell and J.E. Patterson, *Fertility and Family Planning in the United States*. Princeton, N.J.: Princeton University Press, 1966.

to have negative effects on achievement.[16] Reasons proposed to explain this finding circle around the decreased amount of individual parental attention or interaction that children receive when siblings are close in age. However, we lack direct evidence of the relation of these societal changes to achievement test score changes. We, therefore, have to remain very speculative about those potential causes of test score declines located in the society and more intimately in the family.

Implications of Score Declines: Some Cautions

Beyond doubt, beyond differences among and alterations in assessment instruments, or in test-takers' compositions, achievement scores have been declining for about a decade in all grades from grade 5 upwards. Score declines are more pronounced in higher grades and in recent years, and they are more severe for tests probing verbal rather than mathematics achievements. These are the facts and they describe a national phenomenon.

There is no sole and solitary cause for declining achievement test scores. Several factors have differentially contributed to the decline, and their precise assessment is hampered by complex interrelations. Our analysis served mostly to point toward some possibly productive research areas, giving priority to areas which are more tractable politically.

The factors discussed which mostly concern changes in the family and general society seem to be more distal to the decline issue, and most of them have little political potency. We, therefore, abstain from encouraging extensive research in those areas as a means of clarifying the relevance of political actions to the test score decline issue. These are more commonly located within the school context.

In the school arena, one important issue is the consequence for manifest achievement test score declines of the drastically lower pupil dropout rate. We need to know the extent to which distributional changes are due to the test participation of types of pupils who used to drop out before the mid-1960s. And we need to clarify the distributions of absences, over grades, for different types of pupils. This research is, in substance, closely related to the elucidation of possible changes in pupil's learning motivation.

We reported lowered test scores in diverse areas: English, writing, literature, vocabulary, reading, social studies, mathematics and natural

---

16. Breland, H.M. Birth Order, "Family Configuration and Verbal Achievement." *Child Development,* 1974, *45,* 1011-1019; Zajonc, R.B. "Family Configuration and Intelligence." *Science,* April 1976, *191* (16), 227 - 236.

sciences. These are traditional academic learning areas. What are the typical accomplishments in these areas that are assessed by standardized tests? And where are the deficiencies? Are they losses in knowledge, concept formation, abstraction, analytic skills...? Only thoughtful content analyses of tests can answer these important questions. We also need to ask whether pupils have gained in areas not assessed with typical standardized tests: Have they improved in effectiveness of public debate and speech? Have they gained in human understanding or aesthetic issues (art, music)? Have there been relevant curricular changes?

The trend in secondary education toward "special" and more expressive courses indicates that the traditional common academic base may not be readily accepted anymore, either by teachers or by pupils, as course offerings and enrollments hint. Maybe parts of traditional course contents are obsolete, and perhaps instead of attempting innovation of traditional curricula, which is a cumbersome and expensive process, the practical education community has been helping itself with new "special" courses, whose contents might be highly distinctive from school to school and not attended to by test developers.

For example, do the changes in history course-taking, moving from State and American history toward World history and special courses (including Black history), indicate a due revision of traditional history offerings? Does the move toward "special" courses in English, such as science fiction and media analysis, necessitate a reconsideration of what basic courses should contain? Are academic courses with stress on future long-term intellectual and economic benefits, especially in a time of lowered educational pay-offs, losing out to courses allowing more short-term satisfactions and immediate gratification? What are the changes in out-of-school learnings? And what do test developments pick up?

It seems that the call for "back to basics" is unfounded in that it is not based on thorough reconsiderations of what is and should be learned in school. Instead of rethinking educational goals and calling for matching, goal-unfolding assessment instruments, this movement seems to blindly adhere to an authority named "test," which is nothing but a means for assessing and evaluating actual educational goals.

Definitely, curricular changes are highly likely to be responsible for part of the test score decline. But we also need to clarify what lower academic course enrollments mean. Other systematic changes, including declines in vocational and music enrollments and increases in artistic ones, make the general pattern difficult to understand. Are these decreases indicators for shortened school days, or increased study halls which substitute for homework? If not, to what extent are these courses replaced—beyond the small increases in special offerings—by aesthetic or expressive activities, or vocational pursuits not categorized as courses, such as work-study programs or increases in part-time jobs?

We need to valuate losses and possible gains in pupils' knowledges and skills responsibly against a thoughtful vision of our, but mainly their, future. The recent test score declines should initiate a reconsideration of basic and advanced skills, skills necessary for a rounded life, consumption, employment, leisure and political action. The importance of achievement test score declines can not be meaningfully assessed—and thoughtful action can not be initiated—without a thorough consideration of these issues and questions.

16
Quantity of Schooling is Important

David E. Wiley and Annegret Harnischefeger

In the last few years, we have been inundated with repetitions of a new schooling myth. From the report on *Equality of Educational Opportunity* (Coleman *et al.*)[1] and the most recent reanalyses of its data (Mosteller and Moynihan)[2] to the Jencks *et al* book on *Inequality*[3] we have been flooded with reports of the lack of effect of schooling. These reports have discouraged professional educators and comforted those who would reduce the resources allocated to education. Moreover, recent teachers' strikes, response to the "energy" crisis, and budget cutbacks passed on as shorter school years and increased class sizes, all have decreased the amount of schooling and instruction for many pupils in this country. These curtailments did not produce any enraged outcry or concerted action from those who for so long have promoted quality and equality of education. It seems that those concerned have silently joined the chorus performing *De Nihilo Nihil.* What they do not realize is that they play a part in a new American tragedy.

Schooling does have effects and rather than asking if there are any effects of schooling, we should be asking how much of an effect schooling has. If we take a more appropriate stance towards assessing school effects and a fresh look at the above studies, then we not only conclude that schooling has large effects on pupils' achievements but also must take immediate steps to insure equality and quality of education. The drawbacks that

Reprinted by permission from David E. Wiley and Annegret Harnischefeger, "Explosion of A Myth: Quantity of Schooling and Exposure to Instruction, Major Educational Vehicles," *Educational Researcher, 81,* Vol. 3, No. 4, April, 1974, pp. 7-12.

1. Coleman, J.S. *et al. Equality of Education Opportunity.* Washington, D.C.: U.S. Government Printing Office, 1966.

2. Mosteller, F. and Moynihan, D.P. (Eds.) *On Equality of Educational Opportunity.* New York: Random House, 1972.

3. Jencks, C.S. *et al. Inequality: A Reassessment of the Effect of Family and Schooling in America.* New York: Basic Books, 1972.

currently result from cutting the amount of schooling are alarming, as we will show.

Quantity of Schooling

It is unwarranted to say that schooling has no effect. Certainly some children would learn to read even if they did not attend school, and certainly, the school is not effective in teaching reading to some children. However, this does not mean that children do not acquire appreciably better reading skills by attending school. Some children learn to read who would not learn to read if they did not attend school. Some children who would have learned to read anyway, read much more capably because of their schooling. The level of discussion however, still has not risen above the question: "Does schooling have an effect?"

It is the degree of schooling effect that is important for educational policy. For example, if it were found, after a large concentration of resources in reading instruction, that only small gains in levels of competency were attained, then we might be dissatisfied with the return on our investment in this area. In this case, we would perhaps want to understand why there was such a small effect so that we could modify the conditions of our investment, i.e., change the conditions of instruction or perhaps, we might wish to reduce our investment in this area, either so we could improve the yield of the system in another area, where we could produce more valued outcomes with the same amount of resources or invest our resources in non-educational endeavors. To facilitiate such educational decision making, we must be able to assess the extent of effect that is produced by a given amount of schooling. A distinct notion in this regard is the view of schooling, as well as its effect, as a quantitative rather than a qualitative phenomenon. We must not only begin to ask how much of an effect schooling has, we must also ask the more sophisticated question: What is the effect of a particular amount of schooling?

This question has been systematically disregarded. When Mosteller and Moynihan (p. 27), in their introduction to a singularly uninspiring set of reanalyses of the *Equality of Educational Opportunity* survey (EEOS) data, cite a *New York Times* story reporting a two-month loss in grade-equivalent reading achievement resulting from a two-month teacher strike, they considered this, for some opaque reason, a *qualitative* effect of "no schooling" rather than a *quantitative* reduction of the school year from nine to seven months.

It is obvious that if a child does not go to school at all, he will not directly benefit from schooling. If a child goes to school every day for a full school year, he will achieve his maximum benefit from that schooling, other circumstances being equal. It would also seem clear that if he attends school less than the full year, but more than not at all, the benefits he derives from schooling should be in between. That is, the quantity of schooling should be a major determinant of school outcomes.

Husen (1972)[4] has reviewed research findings with respect to the question: Does more schooling produce more achievement? Although he finds some ambiguity in the available data he concludes that an increase in the amount of schooling will not produce a proportionate increase in achievement. To us, his review seems not to support his rather refined conclusion of non-proportionality, since the studies he reviewed were neither originally designed nor reanalyzed to shed light on this issue.

Attendance, length of the school day, and length of the school year are important characteristics of schools to assess. The average number of hours of schooling for pupils in a particular school may be calculated by multiplying the Average Daily Attendance (ADA) by the number of hours in the school day by the number of days in the school year. If schooling is quantified in this simple way, we find large variations in the total number of hours of schooling per year (ranging, e.g., in the Detroit EEOS data from 710 to 1150 hours). Typical pupils in some schools receive fifty percent more schooling than pupils in other schools. There is an enormous variation in exposure to schooling. If this variation is not taken into account, the consequences of teacher and school characteristics for achievement will be obscured.

If we take this perspective and look back at preceding studies, it is quite obvious that attendance was generally considered a student-composition or background variable, and as such was placed in the wrong category.

For example, in the EEOS study, attendance (ADA) was categorized as a characteristic of the student-body composition. Later, Jencks (1972)[5] included ADA in his category of regional and community characteristics. Both investigations did not place ADA in any category representing exposure to schooling and even ignored it as an important moderator of the effects of school characteristics. Attendance is clearly influenced by the child's background and by his home and by the community in which he resides, but it is not a background variable; it is a mediating variable for outcomes.

An appropriate causal model of these elements would have three parts (Figure 16-1). The first would be an explanatory submodel for pupil attendance. This model (relating A to B) would contain explanatory variables reflecting the pupil's prior characteristics, characteristics of the community and perhaps allow for the possibility of an effect of the school

4. Husen, T. "Does More Time in School Make a Difference?" *Saturday Review*, April 29, 1972, 32-35

5. Jencks, C.S. The Coleman Report and the Conventional Wisdom. In: Mosteller, F. and Moynihan, D.P. (Eds.), *On Equality of Educational Opportunity*. New York: Random House, 1972.

itself. A second component-model (relating B, C, and D to E) would define exposure to schooling in terms of ADA and other aspects of the amount of instruction. A third sub-model (relating A and E to F) would explain pupil achievement in terms of home background, community characteristics, and exposure to schooling. These three models together constitute an explanatory system for achievement. The study discussed below was an attempt to partially explicate such a system using data from the EEOS.

A Potent Path for Policy

In a recent paper (Wiley, 1973)[6] we reported an analysis based on the presented model and on data from the Detroit Metropolitan Area sixth-grade sample of the EEOS. Three outcome measures were used: verbal ability, reading comprehension, and mathematics achievement. These particular variables should not be taken to mean that achievement, especially in the narrow meaning sometimes given to that term, is all or the most important part of what schooling has to offer. Schooling occupies a

Figure 16-1
Schooling Exposure and Achievement

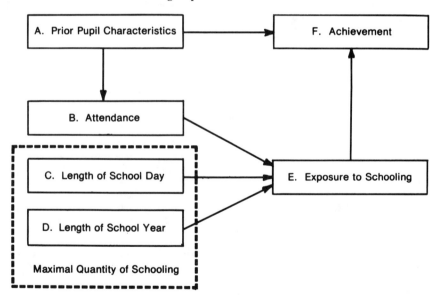

6. Wiley, D.E. "Another Hour, Another Day: Quantity of Schooling, a Potent Path for Policy." *Studies of Educative Processes, No. 3,* University of Chicago, July 1973. To be published in: Sewell, W.H., Hauser, R.M., and Featherman, D.L. (Eds), *Schooling and Achievement in American Society.* (In preparation).

major portion of the child's life in postindustrial societies and as such should have a major impact on the entire socialization process, including education in its broadest sense. Also, because of the major role it plays in childhood, attention must be given to its short-term effects and qualities as well as its long-term influences. For a more elegant exposition of these points see Jackson (1973).[7] This paper is restricted to an assessment of the impact of schooling using examples in the "achievement" category only, because of restrictions in the type and quality of data available.

Table 16-1
Quantity of Schooling and Achievement: Some Empirical Results

Achievement Test	Unstandardized Regression Coefficient*	Standard Error	Grade-Equivalence Conversions of 1 Score Point (Mos.)
1. Verbal Ability	9.58	3.35	1.93
2. Reading Comprehension	9.57	2.87	3.78
3. Mathematics Achievement	4.08	1.57	4.57

*The school-level model (N=40 schools) linked total test scores to the natural logarithm of average number of hours of schooling.

Table 16-2
Selected Statistics for Public
Elementary and Secondary Schools for Four States (1969/70)

State	Enrollment	Mean Length of School Year	ADA as Percent of Enrollment	Days Attended/ Pupil Enrolled	Expendi- ture*/Pu- pil ADA ($)	Total Expenditure* (Mil. $)
Vermont	101,262	172.6	96.6	166.6	934	101
	924,257	182.7	85.0	155.4	882	929
Iowa	660,409	180.0	94.5	170.2	890	650
Missouri	1,078,347	174.0	84.0	146.2	714	822

Note: The total expenditure figures vary somewhat from estimates that could be calculated from the figures on enrollment, ADA, and expenditure per pupil, because of differences in sources.
Source: Digest of Educational Statistics, 1972.
*Statistical Abstract of the United States, 1970.

7. Jackson, P.W. "After Apple-Picking," *Harvard Educational Review,* 1973, 43, 51-60.

Three background variables marked the pupils' prior characteristics: race, number of possessions in the child's home (out of a list of 9), and number of children living in the child's home. Exposure to schooling was expressed as the average number of hours of schooling in a particular school, defined above.

In a school-level regression analysis, we estimated the coefficients linking verbal, reading, and mathematics achievement to number of hours of instruction per year with adjustment for pupils' prior characteristics (Table 16-1). In terms of typical gains in achievement over a year's period, we concluded that in schools where students receive 24 percent more schooling, they will increase their average gain in reading comprehension by two-thirds and their gains in mathematics and verbal skills by more than one-third. These tremendous effects indicate that the amount of schooling a child receives is a highly relevant factor for his achievement.

An application of our model and results to simple average elementary and secondary school statistics of selected states (1969-70) further elucidates the significance of quantity of schooling for educational policy. In 1969-70, the average length of the school year in the United States ranged from 172.6 days in Vermont to 182.7 days in Maryland. Pupils in Maryland were offered 10.1 days or 5.9 percent more schooling than those in Vermont (Table 16-2). In view of the above model, this would indicate that in 1969-70, pupils in Vermont, on the average, gained 17.1 percent less in reading comprehension than similar pupils in Maryland. Studying the costs and benefits of a potentially higher reading comprehension gain in Vermont, we estimate that, under the assumption of proportionate cost increase, the additional costs, resulting from increasing the quantity of schooling in Vermont to that in Maryland, would be 52 dollars per pupil-year. For the whole state of Vermont, the six-percent increase in educational costs would amount to about six million dollars.

Attendance rates also vary widely. For example, if we compare Iowa, which has an everage 180-day school year and an ADA of 94.5 percent, with Missouri, which has an average 174-day school year and an ADA of 84.0 percent, we find that Iowa exposes its children, on the average, to 16.4 percent more schooling. With the same assumptions, this corresponds to a 45.8 percent higher reading comprehension gain in Iowa than in Missouri for similar pupils. If Missouri were to increase her attendance rate to those of Iowa, and if we assume, that increasing ADA costs as much proportionately as increasing the length of the school year, then Missouri would have to spend 117 collars more per pupil-year. Statewide, this would amount to about 135 million dollars per year.

The third factor, subject to policy manipulation, is the length of the school day. However, for this fundamental factor in exposure to schooling, no nationwide statistics are available. An approach to the policy potentiality of this factor can be drawn from Jencks' (1972, p. 76) reanalysis of the EEOS data. He reports the mean and standard deviation for both length of school year and length of school day for 684 Northern elementary schools for which he claims representativeness. These data imply that, in relative terms, the length of the school day varies considerably more than the length of the school year. From these data we might infer that, while almost no schools have school years six percent longer than the mean year length, there are a considerable number (about 16%) of schools with school days ten percent longer than the mean length. It may, therefore, be much easier to increase the length of the school day by a sizable percentage than to do so for the second year. This implies a greater potential policy impact from increasing the length of the school day.

Figure 16-2
Individual Instructional Exposure and Achievement

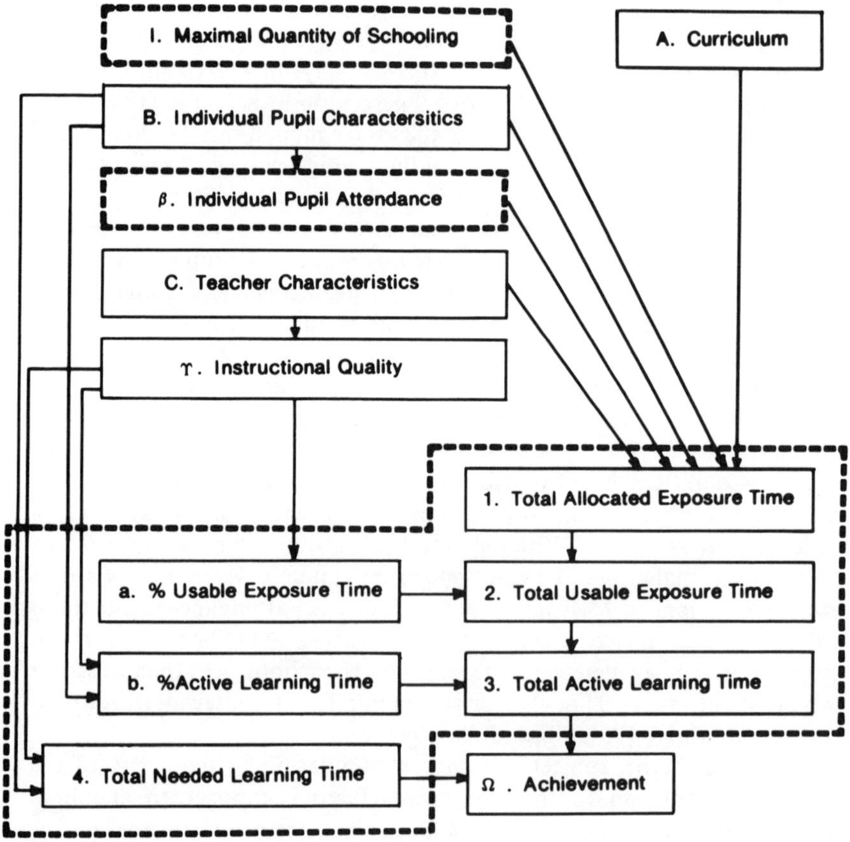

Our statewide exemplary figures are extremely crude, as they do not differentiate between elementary and secondary schools and among grades and because the general statistics were applied to a model, based on sixth-grade school data, collected in 1965 in one metropolitan area. But what these figures show, even if they are biased upwards, is the importance of the quantity-of-schooling dimension for educational policy. We were able to show that the amount of schooling a child receives has a tremendous effect on his achievement. We are, therefore, concerned about current events and policies resulting in decreases in the total amount of schooling.

The wide variation in quantity of schooling also implies large differences in educational opportunity. We will have to investigate whether those who need schooling most, get the smallest share. A recent study by Welch (1973),[8] using historical data, indicated that although differences in the amounts of schooling per year between Southern black schools and all schools have steeply decreased in this century, blacks in the fifties still received less schooling than whites. Investigation using more detailed and current figures should have high priority for determining more precisely the potential policy impact of exposure to schooling.

Refining the Model: Instructional Exposure and Achievement

The concept of quantity of schooling, defined above, is a rough one. Yet as we have seen, it is robust enough to explain a significant amount of achievement differences between schools. But the concept needs more refinement if we are to understand the dynamics by which schools influence achievement and consequently, if we are to allocate our educational resources most effectively and desirably on the basis of this understanding.

As early as 1963,[9] Carroll formulated a model of attractive clarity within which time played the major role for school learning. We will present a more refined model for the analysis of school effects that heavily relies on Carroll's time concepts. Our focus is on appropriately detailing a pupil's exposure to instruction, so that policy inferences are possible.

In Carroll's model, achievement has two determinants: *time needed for learning* and *time actually spent in learning*. The time an individual needs to learn a specific task or reach a particular goal is influenced by his

---

8. Welch, F. Black-White differences in Returns to Schooling. *The American Economic Review,* 1973, 53, 893-907.

9. Carroll, J.B. "A Model for School Learning." *Teachers College Record, 1963,64,* 723-33.
    Carroll, J.B. "Fitting a Model of School Learning to Aptitude and Achievement Data over Grade Levels." *Research Bulletin,* No. 51, Princeton, N.J.: Educational Testing Service, 1973.
    Carroll, J.B. "Notes for the Agenda Concerning the Study of French as a Foreign Language." Paper pepared for Workshop on Foreign Language, Harvard-IEA Conference on Educational Achievement, 1973b.

aptitude, his *ability to understand instruction* (which is itself influenced by "general intelligence" and "verbal ability"), and the *quality of instruction* to which he is exposed. The time an individual actually spends in learning is determined by the *time allocated to learning* the specific task and by the individual's *perseverance*.

We may summarize the impact of Carroll's two major variables in his functional equation:

$$\text{degree of learning} = f\left(\frac{\text{time actually spent}}{\text{time needed}}\right)$$

Carroll has unfolded what he considers to be the major determinants of time needed and has more recently tested some of these propositions (1973a,b).

Within the confines of the school, it is obvious that a pupil can not learn a task to which no time is allocated; that he can only partially learn a task when he is allocated less than the time he needs, that is, quantity of schooling for an individual, the time allocated to him for learning, must have a forceful impact on achievement. We consider it, therefore, important to elaborate the concept of quantity of schooling. The flow of our unfolding argument can be more easily followed from a pictorial model of school effects (Figure 16-2), within whose dotted lines our time concepts are graphically detailed.

Two of our previously defined factors (length of school year and length of school day) determine the maximum time available for the exposure of an individual pupil to school-based instruction. Within the limitations imposed by this maximal amount of time, the actual exposure of a pupil to instruction is determined by his attendance, the instructional programs, and by allocation decisions which occur within the classroom. These decisions are of three basic types:

— those concerning variations in instructional emphasis, possible within the general educational policies of the district and the school;

— those concerning the organization of teaching; and

— those concerned with the educational experiences of an individual pupil.

The factors which affect these decisions are primarily related to teaching strategies, which interact with teacher characteristics. They are also related to characteristics of the individual pupils receiving instruction. An example of the latter might be that some teachers allocate more instructional time to pupils who are achieving poorly, while other teachers may allocate more time to highly active pupils. These situations imply an interaction between teacher and pupil characteristics in the determination of allocated time.

The total time for a given instructional task which is actually allocated to an individual pupil (1.) and the time a pupil is actively engaged (3.) represent the bedrock of our exposure-to-instruction concept. To lay out the bed between the rocks, we first refer to Anderson (1973)[10] and Bloom (1973)[11] who improved Carroll's notion of active learning time by defining the ratio of Total Active Learning Time (3.) to Total Allocated Exposure Time (1.) as the percentage of "time on task" and inserted this latter concept as a mediating variable into Bloom's (1971)[12] model of school achievement. Thus, Anderson has unfolded Carroll's concept of "time spent." This is a conceptual advance, because the percentage of time a pupil is actively engaged in a task has different determinants than the total time allocated to or spent on a curricular task. Anderson was thus able to isolate the impacts of some of the psychological factors influencing the percentage of time a pupil is actively engaged in a learning task.

However, Anderson's concept requires further refinement, because the time a teacher assigns to a specific instructional topic (1.) has to be reduced by the amount of time the teacher uses for purposes such as disciplining pupils or organizing work groups. This sets realistic limits for a pupil's active engagement in a particular task. This time actually devoted to teaching (2.) is equal to the product of the Total Allocated Exposure Time (1.) and the proportion of that time which is instructionally usable (a.). The latter is a variable with distinctive causes, e.g., teaching efficiency and the prevalence of discipliniary problems. We define Percent Active Learning Time (b.) as the ratio of time spent in active learning (3.) to total *usable* time (2.) rather than to total allocated time (1.). The virtues of these detailed time concepts will emerge when we now relate them to other factors in school achievement.

Achievement (Ω) is directly determined by only two variables: total time needed by a pupil to learn a task (4) and total time a pupil actively spends on a given learning task (3). All the other variables' influences are mediated through these factors. On the basis of our refined model, we may now specify a pupil's achievement by the following equation: where

Achievement = f(WXY/Z)

  W is the total Allocated Exposure Time

  X is the percent of Active Learning Time, and

  Y is the percent of Usable Exposure Time

  Z is the total Needed Learning Time.

---

10. Anderson, I.W. *Time and School Learning.* Unpublished Ph.D. Dissertation. Department of Education, University of Chicago, 1973.

11. Bloom, B.S. *Time and Learning.* Thorndike Address, 81st Annual Convention of the American Psychological Association, Montreal, 1973.

12. Bloom, B.S. *Individual differences in School Achievement: A Vanishing Point?* Bloomington, Indiana: Phi Delta Kappa, 1971.

The remainder of the diagram is an attempt to specifiy those factors which influence the four main concepts determining achievement: Total Allocated Exposure Time (1), Percent Usable Exposure Time (a), Percent Active Learning Time (b), and Total Needed Learning Time (4). The extent to which each separately contributes to achievement is not clear. Conceptually, they are all equally important. Variations in achievement in the actual classroom setting will depend, under this model, on the natural variations in these four variables.

The importance of the four fundamental time factors for educational policy will depend on the relative ease with which they may be manipulated. It seems to us that the one variable currently most amenable to important policy modification is that of Total Allocated Exposure Time (1.). This is because there is wide variation in the amounts of exposure allocated to pupils within classes, between classes, between schools, and between districts.

Amounts of exposure may be reallocated by modifying policies that are directly under the control of states and districts. We do not need to develop a more refined technology of instruction to substantially modify this variable. The other variables may eventually be important policy foci, but action will depend on our developing a more complete understanding of the processes that determine them.

Policy Implications to Date

We have criticized the simplistic myth of no school effects and have shown that, indeed, schooling has large, important effects if we ask adequate questions such as: What is the effect of a particular amount of schooling? Our estimates of the magnitudes of the effects of schooling, in terms of quantity of schooling received, strongly require reconsideration of policy decisions resulting in less schooling. Cutbacks in the lengths of the school year and school day will result in significant drops in school achievement.

An unexpected finding of our study should alarm politicians, the education community, and concerned citizens. There are enormous differences in the amounts of education offered. State policies, manifested in compulsory education laws, have imposed a minimum amount of schooling but have failed to insure equal educational opportunity, in terms of the quantity of schooling offered. As long as budgetary district "autonomy" means nothing more than perpetuating inequality of educational opportunity, we will not fulfill basic constitutional rights.

Our results do not necessarily lead to a proposal for an equal amount of schooling for every pupil. Instead, our findings of important consequences of the quantity of schooling lead us to advocate more time for those who need it, so that more equal individual benefits of schooling will be obtained.

Our results have also stimulated us to refine the concept of quantity of schooling into more detailed components of exposure to instruction while, at the same time, maintaining the criterion that the results be usable for policy inferences. An outcome of this exploration is a proposed model for exposure to instruction and achievement. We presented it here hoping that it will be be helpful in efforts to more fully understand the educational determinants of school achievement. We also hope that the research community will join us in a redirection of efforts to implement research findings for more humane and less arbitrary education. We need to learn to ask more reasonable questions; we need to sharpen and refine our educational concepts; and we need to insure that our findings will have important consequences in educational practice.

The Treatment of
Minority Group Youngsters

Perhaps no area upon which the American public school impacts has generated more critical attention than the educational treatment accorded minority group youngsters. Many of these criticisms have been exceedingly thoughtful, grounded in solid historical and/or scientifically respectable data. Just as many have been characterized by free-flowing cliche and ideological rhetoric. There is absolutely no gainsaying the fact that, in all too many ways, the American public school has failed to extend equitable treatment to hundreds of thousands of minority-group youngsters. Even a cursory glance at our educational history will point up the fact that our record in this regard has been embarrassingly shabby.

We can, if we choose, dwell on our past transgressions. However, an unrelenting bemoaning of yesterday's sins is hardly a productive disposition to adopt. While we *must* acknowledge candidly what has been (or not been) done, we *must not* get bogged down in a morass of negativism. Rather, we must identify promising measures which we might adopt which could improve significantly the lot of those upon whom we have trampled.

The question with which this section is preoccupied is: are those who are engaged in the public school enterprise seeking to adopt political and pedagogical measures which might significantly right the wrongs of the past? If the answer is at least a qualified *yes* then our feelings of shame can be comingled with a dose of pride.

As regards the treatment of minority group youngsters, what does our current behavior portend for the future? In the initial selection, written by Robert Coles, it would appear that the razor sharp dagger of the critic might need to be somewhat blunted. While many will undoubtedly take issue with some of Coles' observations, his thoughtful essay deserves our most careful attention.

117

The next selection, by Levitan, provides us with some solid data which point up dramatically that—in terms of public school enrollment and formal educational attainment—American blacks have made very appreciable advances during the 1970s. As the discussion indicates, these gains, while impressive, are somewhat spurious in light of the low overall academic achievement level attained by all too many black youngsters. However, when interpreted within the context of potential earning power, these educational attainment trends do give us reason to be mildly optimistic about the future rate of upward social mobility among the black population. The next two readings make clear that there exists a very high correlation between educational level attained and expected earning capacity. Assuming the condition of equality of economic opportunity, the conclusion is inescapable that our public school network *is* contributing significantly to increased, upward social mobility. While increased earning power bears a questionable relationship to an increase in moral and aesthetic sensitivity, nonetheless, financial success *is* highly valued in the American society. Along this particular front, our public schools *have* contributed to the establishment of a more equitable America.

An obviously necessary step for the removal of oppressive public school conditions is an acknowledgement of their existence and a political commitment to do something about the situation. The next selection is a recently-passed statute of the state of Texas which clearly and unequivocally commits the resources of the state to a removal of language barriers which have impeded the educational performance of the state's predominantly Spanish-speaking student population.

Critics of public school efforts are fond of pointing out how dismal has been the performance of federally-funded programs designed to provide predominantly minority-group children with educational enrichment experiences. As the final reading of the section reflects, there are significant exceptions. We must be wary of rejecting cavalierly such federally-subsidized programs as Head Start and Follow Through. Whether or not these efforts will bear fruit is an open, empirical question. At this stage of inquiry, the verdict is anything but clear. Only sophisticated longitudinal studies will inform us of the effectiveness of these audacious public school experiments.

Clearly, the millenium is nowhere in sight as regards providing equality of educational opportunity for minority group students. The exceedingly deplorable condition of the nation's native-American youngsters is a damning case in point. However, it is just as clear that many of the problems with which we have saddled generations of culturally different children have been acknoweldged by political authorities. Moreover and more importantly, it is increasingly apparent that people of good will are making a sustained effort to put our public schoolhouse in order. While some who read these pages may well observe that these measures are "too little" or "too late," hopefully many will adopt a more optimistic dispostion, one which awaits the results of research studies—some of which are now in progress, some of which (presumably) are now being designed.

17
A Talk with Robert Coles

As Interviewed by
Ruth Galvin and Morton Malkovsky

I don't think any group in American society has been as severely and persistently criticized as teachers. More books have been written criticizing the American teacher, I think, than even the medical profession—which deserves it much more. And the teachers feel this. They feel that they have been the scapegoat, that they have been the subject of unwarranted, overdone, and overgeneralized assault.

A lot of this criticism is romantic in its psychological grounding, romantic in that it simply will not recognize and give justice to the honorable struggle that we all have with ourselves. What it tries to say is that we would all be lovely and idealistic and good and decent if it were not for certain institutions, particularly schools, that in some way corrupt us. So they criticize the whole school system in a blanket fashion. They say, "Let's get rid of it." Or say, "Teachers are no good. They're killers of the dream." Or, "Children are lovely and beautiful until they get into the schools. I don't think that kind of criticism addresses itself to the actuality of the lives of teachers and families.

I've seen such a range of teachers all over this nation—teachers in, say, Boston, where I've spent a lot of time, in Appalachia, or the rural South, or even in the schools for migrant children—that when I read some of the criticism of teachers I wonder which teachers they're talking about. Many are not only hard-working men and women but men and women of real sensitivity and compassion and concern and idealism and devotion and patience. And one also encounters, sometimes within the same school building, teachers of indifference and callousness, and sometimes outright meanness. But this is the problem of human beings in all professions. And

Reprinted by special permission of *Learning,* The Magazine for Creative Teaching, Nov., 1972, Copyright © by Education Today Company, Inc.

that is why I stress the importance of recognizing the particularity of people.

I work a lot with children, and many of them are poor and have had a great deal of trouble—medical difficulties and sometimes a great deal of educational difficulties—but their attitudes towards their teachers are not as critical as some of us might believe. These are not brainwashed children: they are smart, perceptive, at times belligerent children. They are very quick to speak up about a lot of things, and I have found many of them willing to emphasize the positive experiences they have had in school as well as the negative things. They're willing to talk about particular teachers who have meant a great deal to them and particular things that have happened to them in school that have been very important, as well as willing to criticize and to be saddened by or outraged by some of the experiences they've had. So I think it's important for us before we feel so sorry for the children to ask how *they* feel about their own lives.

For example, I've found migrant children, whom I described in *Children of Crisis,* for whom school has been nothing short of a redemptive experience. It's been a place where they're not only freed from the demands of backbreaking labor, but it's also a place where they have been fed well and the teachers have taken a real interest in them.

I've also seen schools in Appalachia, one-room schoolhouses that are marvelous places, where mountain children come in contact with very fine and thoughtful, beautifully idealistic school teachers of the old-fashioned schoolmarm variety, who have opened up the whole world to them. Who have used materials that many of us from the upper-middle-class suburbs might consider inadequate. But in the hands of these teachers, an old copy of a *National Geographic,* an out-of-date map, a book that many of us would consider corny, can be used to bring those children not only into the 20th century but into the whole world around us. These teachers weren't necessarily the ones who were highly accredited by schools of education, teachers who had taken all kinds of audio-visual courses. They weren't necessarily teachers who had read a lot of educational or social criticism. They were teachers who had a real capacity for firmness and toughness with their children, as well as affection.

This uncanny mixture—maybe it's God-given, though I'm not pessimistic enough to feel that it can't in some way be brought forth in people who don't seem to have it naturally—this capacity for a kind of a self-confident willingness to meet those children half way, at times more than half way, to impose standards upon them and to demand responses from them, to hope high for them, is terribly important. Oftentimes the *least* effective teachers I met were those who were too psychologically sensitive to the children. They were overanalytic. They were too passive and too "understanding." Not willing to go beyond the existential problems that the children brought in—whether psychological, economic, racial, whatever—and say: "OK, I know all this, but look, we're going to do something with this time, with this experience."

Children are not beautiful little angels who are suddenly thrust into the first grade and thereafter systematically destroyed. Teachers are up against not only the affectionate, loving, affirmative side of children but also the darker side that at times has been glossed over—the side of a child that every parent experiences years before the child ever gets to school. It's quite clear that for five years before going to school, a little boy or a little girl has been in a home, and in that home the parents and the children have had wonderful and redemptive moments, but they've also had some pretty tough times which I feel are inevitable. If you want to, use metaphors like Original Sin or fall back on psychoanalytic imagery to talk of the inevitable frustrations, anxieties, and rages children feel as they come to terms with a family. But there is no way of avoiding the fact that children have to go through periods that are very difficult for both them and those who take care of them.

Children have to be subjected to some kind of discipline and restraint. This in turn causes annoyance and frustration on the part of the child and leads to the inevitable encounter between the legitimate demands of parents who want their kids to live and the child's willfulness and assertiveness. This kind of existential confrontation between children and parents has to be taken into consideration by people who talk about what schools do to children. The child has to go to school to learn and there are restrictions there. One hopes that those restrictions are in the service of something important and valuable as the child sees it as well as the child's parents. Therefore there are satisfactions as well as pain. But pain is inevitable in life. In a functioning school system with a large number of children and with a limited number of teachers and a limited budget, there has to be some effort and mutual compromise. I don't call this killing children. I don't think children necessarily feel that they are being killed when they are asked to abide by simple rules and regulations. This isn't necessarily dampening their creativity or turning spontaneous, lovable and affectionate, outgoing, radiant children into demons or sadists or half-dead automatons. I think some of this imagery is overdone.

But beyond this, many children are severely disciplined, very fearful, and very wary children long before they ever get to school. They have to be approached with the kind of toughness and assertiveness that maybe some of us who have our own ideas about what children should be like cannot appreciate. They need control. They need authority. They've had it. They've learned to need it. And in order to reach them one has to have a certain kind of brash self-confidence and I guess what we would almost call arrogance.

Many of the children do not respect quiet, thoughtful, openly fragile and sensitive teachers. The black and white poor children that I have talked to have often been brought up in homes where there is a lot of unhesitant, somewhat authoritative discipline as the rule. And to leave that and go into a school where they're simply encouraged to generate their own kind of enthusiasms and interests is a transition that is extraordinarily difficult and at times self-defeating. So when these children come to school, it isn't simply a question of arriving at school and suddenly being brutalized by awful teachers. Many of these children have been brutalized by their life experiences long before they ever arrive at school. And for some of these children, school is a source of relief and surcease, rather than a source of new brutalization—although I do not at all deny that there are brutalizing educational experiences.

Sometimes you just can't overcome the situation outside in the ghetto. The good teacher, doing his or her work every day, is up against the child's growing appreciation that this leads to nowhere. Ghetto children really are very well behaved at a certain point in their lives, responsive to the severe discipline they get from their rather frightened parents, very obliging and quiet. And they begin to do well, or at least they try to do well. Unfortunately, about this time, when they are six and seven and eight, they are not only going to school but they're learning the facts of life in the streets. They become disenchanted and frustrated and tired because they learn from their older brothers and sisters and neighbors a cynical view of what it's going to be like for them. Believe me, anything that the most critical political scientist, sociologist, or social critic knows about Harlem or Roxbury or Chicago's South Side, these kids know and they know before they're ten.

So it's not what goes on in school but what goes on in the whole context of living in a ghetto that I think determines the kind of futility in the ghetto school system. Because, after all, if teachers know that they teach and teach and teach and yet the child is going to become another unemployed man or woman, then I think this undercuts their hopefulness.

Dr. Coles is the kind of critic who takes his convictions into the field and exposes them to the confusions and contradictions of actual experience. As he talked quietly in the musty waiting room ambience of his office, he developed a theme that armchair critics have missed: that the mass of people are not unhappy with the schools; that rather, they are disillusioned with the critics.

In the working-class suburbs of major cities, not to mention vast rural areas in the Midwest and the South and the Southwest, one finds a great degree of satisfaction among parents with what is going on in the schools. A greater degree of communion, I would almost call it, between parents and the teachers.

Teachers, you know, are working class people. Teachers are essentially white collar workers economically. They are struggling very hard to make a limited income. And a lot of the parents, too, work very hard all day. They come home quite tired and they have all they can do to have supper and go to sleep. They are only too happy to have their children just get along in school in order that they may get by, graduate, and then get on to a job. They're not thinking about a fancy university education. They don't have the money for it and often don't have the ambition for it or the sense that it is possible or maybe even desirable. They have a different attitude toward what life is all about.

Yet these families do want their children to learn well the skills, to learn well how to get a trade, and to be prepared well for the job market. They are ambitious for their children to rise in the world of blue collar workers and white collar workers. Many of these parents I have found are basically satisfied with the kind of education their children are getting.

I think the great gulf now is between on the one hand the working-class people—including teachers and including the poor who want to be working class—and on the other hand the upper-middle class intellectual people of this country. I think that gulf is much wider than that between the so-called middle American teacher and the so-called poverty stricken family. The values among the poor people I've worked with are not unlike the values of middle Americans.

After all, the American schools in the past hundred years have received millions and millions of children—children who came from families that could barely speak English, children from the whole range of social and racial and religious and ethnic backgrounds. And although they haven't turned out God's children and produced a new Jerusalem, teachers have done an astonishing job of being open, of being responsive to the poor, of assisting the rise of large numbers of people up the social and economic ladder. And this is felt by those people who are now grown up. It's particularly felt by the white collar and blue collar working people I've come in contact with in recent years. They have only cause for gratitude for what they got out of their education. They may not have gone to Harvard or Berkeley, may not have become intellectuals or college professors, but they have gotten good jobs—better jobs than their parents had—and they attribute this rise to the education they received in trade schools, in commercial schools, all through this country.

So there is a disparity between these millions of people who value certain kinds of authority and hierarchy, who value certain allegiances to the nation, to the church, to their communities, and to the various levels of authority within those communities; and on the other hand, people who criticize these values and assumptions. That criticism often has a broad scope: "Let's abolish all schools." Not: "Let families who don't want any part of these schools take their children out and find their own way." I don't think it's unreasonable for there to be a response from the people for whom these solutions are recommended. And they have responded, but we have not heard the response. It hasn't been written up; it hasn't even been documented.

I think it would be nice for some of our educational critics to talk with telephone operators, with secretaries, factory workers, construction workers, gas station owners, to find out how they felt about going to school and how they feel now as parents about the education of their children, and indeed what wheir children want from schools and teachers. I see an absence of that, I see an absence of fundamental anthropological or enthnographic data.

A lot of what we hear about bussing is not only a racial matter. They feel: people are trying to interfere in our way of life; they want to experiment with us; they want to take advantage of us; they want to push us around; they want to manipulate us. That resentment I found not only in the families but in the teachers themselves, who feel manipulated and spoken to in sermonlike fashion just too often. Bussing has become a symbol of long-suffering abuse at the hands of liberal reformers and militants. The resentment often takes the form of know-nothingism, I regret to say. People strike out in an arbitrary, irrational, and abusive form at the whole range of people and institutions they feel are insensitive to their dignity and integrity. Hence, I'm afraid that not only has the bussing issue been somewhat charged with these accumulated resentments, but I think certain politicians' careers have been enhanced by this development. The politicians sense this sad gulf between the social critics in this country, who have so much to say and offer us, and the people whose lives usually end up being the focus of this criticism. This serves only to enhance the power of reaction in this country, because when the working people of this country and the intellectuals of this country grow increasingly estranged from one another, it's the reactionaries who gain by it.

No; the families I have worked with have not lost faith in education. Quite the contrary. And I don't want to turn that off and say, "Let's not have those old-fashioned kinds of teachers with their notions of discipline and manners and forcing children into various kinds of molds." Well, I could say that, but I wonder how far I'd get. I mean I know how far I'd get because I've been up in those West Virginia hollows.

And so here we have a problem of prescribing things for people who don't want the medicine. They want what some of us feel they shouldn't have. They're brought up in a certain kind of family life with certain modes of punishment, with certain modes of getting along with children, and some of us may feel that this is unfortunate. What are we to do? Try to impose our values and ideologies on people who don't want them, for their own good? I'm not against trying to change educational practices; I'm simply concerned that the sense of community that, for example, migrants have developed—their sense of almost truculent self-support, their concreteness about life's everyday progression—be respected to the point that the schools go out to the migrants as well as the migrants go out to the schools. And that teachers who work with migrants be responsive to the strengths as well as weaknesses within migrant living.

Now, with many ghetto families there is a special situation. I should qualify the affirmative relationship I talked about between many parents and teachers and say that it is somewhat a class-bound phenomenon. As one moves into the ghetto, there is not exactly antagonism between parents and teachers—although one will find that with the militant, politically active parents and teachers, and not only black versus white teachers but also black militants versus black teachers—but the sheer weight of extreme poverty and joblessness and social disorganization makes it much harder for teachers to teach and for parents to appreciate any value in teaching. No matter how good the teachers are, if there are no jobs for the students after they leave school, then there is no reward for the teachers, good or bad.

After talking about the experiences and problems of children and parents in the different class structures, Dr. Coles turned his attention to teachers. As the scapegoats of much abusive criticism, claims Dr. Coles, teachers have good reason to feel as though they are "ineffective" and "vulnerable."

There are some structural problems that affect the way teachers think and feel both as job holders and as human beings. Namely, their political and economic weakness and vulnerability. Teachers feel abused by the entire community to which they belong, because they are paid at such a low level. And they feel vulnerable to the community authorities who can hire and fire them. They're really at the mercy of all the constricting forces within a particular community. They're not independent operators, like doctors, who somehow get off so much more easily. For one thing, doctors' incomes are higher. Their political clout, I think is more substantial. The American Medical Association is a powerful group even if it is under attack today. I don't see comparable organizational power for teachers. I don't see economic and social sanctions for teachers comparable to those given doctors and lawyers and engineers and architects and university professors.

What teachers need is more unionization, more power. Where there is real strength and power in a profession, the professional people in it are not subjected to the gratuitous whims of politicians and accrediting agencies. And I think teachers need to be encouraged to feel that they have within them the sanction and authority to be able to reach children. After all, as a psychiatrist, I know that we enter into our field fumbling, inadequate— anxious to do a good job but not sure that we can. However the status of medicine and psychiatry is such that society gives us authority and a sense of support. It says: "You can do it even if you make mistakes. We'll give you the time and the psychological sanction and general community support that will enable you to learn this art and learn the methods of communication and psychiatry and internal medicine." And a lot of it is done with patients suffering the same way schoolchildren suffer.

Teachers are not given that kind of support or sanction. If doctors had to undergo the interference that teachers have, we would not do nearly the job that we do. Every time I tried to be a little imaginative or unconventional, I would be frightened and fearful because I'd be watched and subjected to a contract renewal every year—all of those variables that teachers have to contend with. So I think there is built into teaching all kinds of constraints and restraints and inhibitions. It's much harder for a teacher to acquire the kind of civility and sense of self-confidence and self-authority that's translated into really effective teaching. They're always being watched so and they're so fearful. They can be fired so easily. I think this affects them in the classroom every minute of the day. It acts as an unfortunate retarding affect upon their generosity of spirit, their intellectual capacity, their ability to reach out or be resourceful, and their capaicty to communicate in an effective way with the children and with their parents.

Dr. Coles concluded his interview with Malkofsky and Galvin with a look at the role of school—what its obligations are, what the majority of parents expect of it—and with a hopeful note.

School is one of many institutions and it need not become subservient to the purposes of other institutions. It indeed has an obligation to assert its own goals and pursue them. I don't think a school, in other words, is a citizenship training center for the political activation of a community. I don't think a school is where children learn to understand their unconscious and learn to become more effectively mature and adult in the way psychologists or psychiatrists use those words.

The parents I talked with, poor and working-class alike, send their children to school to get what they call education. By that they mean learning to read, to write; to have the power of doing arithmetic; to learn increasingly facts, figures; to acquire the capacity to think and have ideas. Now, naturally, there is a psychological, anthropological, and sociological and political dimension to all this. But to turn away from this primary concern of education—namely the command of skills, the command of symbols, the command of the language, the command of reading, writing, arithmetic—to turn away from this is not what the vast majority of the families I've come into contact with want for their children.

This is the central issue: the nature of the profession in a particular society; the amount of respect it's granted; the amount of financial backing it's granted. One can only hope that some of this will change with the years.

One of the most hopeful things I have seen in my lifetime is that the younger college students here at Harvard, and some of the students I've met in other parts of the country in the course of my work, think that teaching is an honorable and valuable profession. In the past, these students have wanted to go into medicine, into law or architecture, and now they want to be teachers. It's lovely to see men wanting to be elementary school teachers. And to see women interested in teaching as a real professional goal for their entire lifetime. I think it does reflect some changes.

Finally, having talked so much about the gap between the social critics and the working families, I would turn that around and say that if there is a gap, there is also a kind of contact. This is a society in which all kinds of social criticism is reaching into areas where it was heretofore unheard of. And if it is creating tension, and at times a great deal of social conflict, it's also, I think, shaking things up and causing people to stop and think occasionally, too. So it's not just a negative problem. It's a problem of the difficulties that arise when various groups with conflicting ideals and assumptions run into increasingly intimate contact with one another. I think teachers get caught in the middle.

So I'm basically hopeful. Not that we're going to have an end to the problems that we've been talking about, but that these problems can be worked out. I just wish that somehow we could work a little faster, because it's the children who are caught up in this.

18
The Impact of Schooling on American Blacks

Sar A. Levitan, William B. Johnston, and Robert Taggart

The growing importance of education has challenged American ideals of equality. Education increasingly separates the economically successful from the disadvantaged and the powerful from the helpless. Despite a massive national investment in educational institutions, inequalities of educational opportunity persist. Those with better education make more money and gain more power, and the children of the successful and powerful get better education. Conversely, blacks with poor schooling have lower incomes, and children of low-income blacks tend to get poor schooling.

To break this cycle it is not enough to equalize years of school. If all are to compete on an equal footing in American society, education must produce individuals whose innate competence is as equally developed as possible. In order to obtain truly equal opportunity, education must seek to minimize environmental advantages or disadvantages and to compensate for social and economic inequalities. The vital questions concern not only gains in school attainment, but whether the education of blacks is really equivalent to that of whites, and whether it is sufficient to insure blacks equal mobility in society.

Educational Attainment

Measured by years in school, blacks are increasing their educational attainment both absolutely and relative to whites. Between 1960 and 1972 median years of black education rose from 8.2 to 10.3. Though whites were also staying in school longer, their lead narrowed from an average of 2.7 years in 1960 to 2.0 years in 1972. Proportionately, the white nonwhite differential declined from 33 percent in 1960 to 19 percent in 1972.

	Nonwhites[a]			Whites[a]		
	1950	1960	1972	1950	1960	1972
Median years of school	6.9	8.2	10.3	9.7	10.9	12.3
Male	NA	7.9	10.0	NA	10.7	12.3
Female	NA	8.5	10.5	NA	11.2	12.3

[a] Age 25 and over.

Most of the improvement in educational attainment has come from reduced high school dropout rates. Although black college graduates are increasing rapidly, they still do not contribute substantially to the average educational attainment. From 1950 to 1972 the proportion of nonwhites with fewer than five years of education fell from 33 to 13 percent; those with high school diplomas increased from 14 to 37 percent. In both categories,

Table 18-1
Comparative Levels of
Education of the Population 25 and Over

Years of education	Nonwhite			White		
	1950	1960	1972	1950	1960	1972
Percent						
Less than 5 years	32.6	23.4	12.8[a]	8.9	6.7	3.7
Less than 1 year high school	72.5	59.6	38.2[a]	45.8	39.8	23.3
4 years high school or more	13.9	21.7	39.1[a]	36.4	41.4	60.4
4 years college or more	2.3	3.5	6.9[a]	6.6	8.1	12.6
Numbers (in thousands)						
High school graduates	1,074	2,049	4,531	28,151	38,575	60,121
Some college	414	757	1,575	11,132	15,537	23,906
College graduates	176	335	797	5,108	7,253	12,567

Source: U.S. Bureau of the Census, Census of the Population, 1960, *General Social and Economic Characteristics of the Population, U.S. Summary*, PC(1)C, table 76; and *Educational Attainment: March 1972*, Series P-20, no. 243, November 1973, table 2.
[a] 1972 includes blacks only.

Table 18-2
Black 25- to 29-Year-Old High School and
College Graduates, 1940-1972 (percent of age group)

Year	Black and other races		White	
	4 years of high school or more	4 years of college or more	4 years of high school or more	4 years of college or more
1972	66.6	11.6	81.5	19.9
1970	58.4	10.0	77.8	17.3
1964	48.0	7.0	72.1	13.6
1960	38.6	5.4	63.7	11.8
1950	23.4	2.8	55.2	8.1
1940	12.1	1.6	41.2	6.4

Source: U.S. Bureau of the Census, *Characteristics of American Youth: 1972,* Series P-23, no. 44, March 1973, table 18.

Table 18-3
Median Years of School, 1972

Residence	Black	White
Total	10.3	12.3
Metropolitan	10.9	12.4
Central city	10.9	12.3
Outside central cities	11.0	12.4
Nonmetropolitan	8.3	12.1
Northwest	11.3	12.2
North central	11.3	12.3
South	9.1	12.2
West	12.2	12.5

Source: U.S. Bureau of the Census, *Population Characteristics,* "Educational Attainment, March 1972," Series P-20, no. 243, November 1972, tables 2 and 3.

the nonwhite rate of gain was faster than the white. Nonwhite college graduates increased from 2.3 to 6.9 percent while white graduates increased from 6.6 to 12.6 percent. (Table 18-1)..

These educational gains result mostly from the increased school attainment of the younger black population. Among blacks between the ages of twenty-five and twenty-nine, the proportion of high school graduates leaped from two-fifths in 1960 to two-thirds in 1972, while college graduates more than doubled from 5.4 to 11.6 percent. Whites also gained but at slower rates (Table 18-2).

Not all blacks gained equally and there are still differences in attainment between various regions and residences. In 1972 blacks in the South and those in nonmetropolitan areas lagged far behind both whites and blacks elsewhere. In suburban areas and in the West, on the other hand, blacks are much nearer equality in educational attainment (Table 18-3).

School Enrollment

The increasing educational attainment of blacks relative to whites reflects more equal enrollment ratios. At every age level (except, significantly, college years) blacks are nearly as likely—and among preschoolers, more likely—to be enrolled in school as whites (Table 18-4). Between the ages of six and sixteen when education is mandatory, almost all blacks and whites are enrolled and enrollment rates of youths through age seventeen to nineteen are nearly equal. Although blacks are still less likely to complete high school, the dropout rate is declining. In 1967, 22.8 percent of blacks between age fourteen and twenty-four had dropped out of high school without finishing, compared to 12.4 percent of whites. By 1972 the proportions were 17.5 percent for blacks and 11.3 for whites.

Through blacks are less likely than whites to be attending college, they are narrowing this gap also. Between 1960 and 1973 the number of blacks enrolled in college increased by approximately 540,000, a gain of 370 percent which raised the ratio of blacks to whites from 1 in 20 to 1 in 12. In 1973, 16 percent of blacks and 25 percent of whites in the eighteen to twenty-four age group were enrolled in college. This represented a substantial improvement over 1960, when 8 percent of blacks and 20 percent of whites were in college.

| | College enrollment (thousands) | | | |
	1960	1965	1970	1973
Black	146	274	522	684
White	2,743	5,317	6,759	7,324

Source: Derived from U.S. Bureau of the Census, *The Social and Economic Status of Negroes in the United States, 1970*, Series P-23, no. 3, table 69; *School Enrollment in the United States: October 1973* (Advance Report), Series P-20, no. 261, table 2; and *Census of the Population, 1960, U.S. Summary*, Series PC(1)-1C, table 75.

Table 18-4
School Enrollment by Race, 1973 (numbers in thousands)

Age	Black				White			
	Enrolled in school	Percent	Enrolled in college	Percent	Enrolled in school	Percent	Enrolled in college	Percent
3–4 years	292	28.9	—	—	1,364	23.2	—	—
5–6 years	835	89.9	—	—	5,270	93.0	—	—
7–9 years	1,587	99.2	—	—	9,291	99.1	—	—
10–13 years	2,210	99.0	—	—	13,812	99.3	—	—
14–15 years	1,070	96.7	—	—	6,926	97.6	6	0.1
16–17 years	967	87.7	37	3.4	6,183	88.3	247	3.5
18–19 years	377	37.8	194	19.5	2,849	43.4	2,281	34.8
20–21 years	176	20.5	164	19.2	1,924	31.3	1,865	30.3
22–24 years	156	12.4	140	11.0	1,322	14.6	1,292	14.3
25–29 years	97	6.1	89	5.6	1,174	8.7	1,152	8.5
30–34 years	67	5.0	60	4.5	502	4.5	481	4.3
18–24 years in college	—	—	498	16.0	—	—	5,384	24.7

Source: U.S. Bureau of the Census, *School Enrollment in the United States: October 1973* (Advance Report), Series P-20, no. 261, March 1974, table 2.

The universality (if not the uniformity) of the American educational system is evident from the fact that enrollment figures do not vary significantly among regions or residence areas. The variations in educational attainment between the South and North, and between central city children and suburban ones, cannot be explained by discrepancies in enrollment. Southern blacks are slightly less likely to be in school in most age groups, but the differences are very small. Among college age youth (eighteen to twenty-four years) southern blacks are more likely to be in school. The differences in school enrollment between central city and suburban and metropolitan and nonmetropolitan blacks are also insignificant. Whatever the problems of central city schools, black residents are as likely to be in school as those from other areas. In fact, between ages seven and fifteen, 98 percent or more of blacks from all types of residence areas attend school.

Educational Achievement and the Quality of Black Education

Black enrollment and attainment gains at the precollege level are paradoxical, for elementary and secondary education has become the area in which black progress is most bitterly debated. The reason for this concern is that black educational achievement on various tests and standards has not improved relative to whites. Though the extra years of education have had positive impacts, the achievement gains and the ultimate payoffs for education have been less for blacks than for whites at each level of attainment.

A number of indicators document the achievement differentials. Black children are much more likely to be enrolled at grade levels below their age groups, and this differential increases in higher grades (Figure 18-1). Whereas some white children also fall behind, this group does not seem to increase as schooling progresses. But more and more blacks fall further and further behind. By age seventeen, more than half of black males are behind their "modal" class, and 30 percent are back two grades or more. Females are less likely to fall behind, but the black-white differential is still present. Moreover, despite compensatory efforts to improve the elementary and secondary education these figures are not improving. In 1972 a slightly greater proportion of black children were behind in school than in 1968.

Tests also demonstrate lagging black achievement. The Equal Educational Opportunity survey sponsored by the Department of Health, Education, and Welfare in 1965, showed that black reading achievement was 1.5 years less than whites in the sixth grade, 2.25 years in grade nine, and 3.25 years in the senior year of high school. These data are now nine years old, and no comparably broad study has been made more recently;

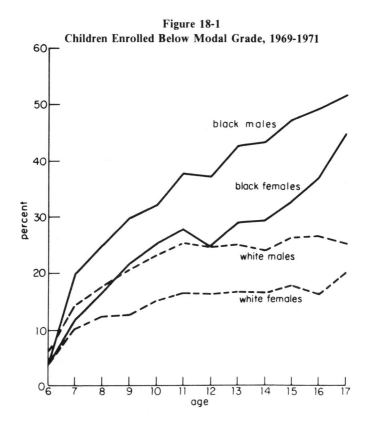

Figure 18-1
Children Enrolled Below Modal Grade, 1969-1971

Source: U.S. Bureau of the Census, *School Enrollment: October 1970,* Series P-20, no. 222, June 28, 1971, table 7; and *Social and Economic Characteristics of Students: October 1971,* Series P-20, no. 241, October 1972, table 16.

but surveys of educational needs in Title I schools and reports from heavily black central city school districts do not indicate that there has been any general improvement since 1965.

The inability of the school system to. upgrade black educational achievement is also indicated by results of mental tests of draftees (Table 18.5). Between 1950 and 1971 blacks were more than four times as likely to be rejected for military induction on the basis of mental tests as whites. Both black and white rejection rates have declined in recent years as a result of more universal education and larger draft calls which tapped better educated individuals. But the gap between blacks and whites has narrowed little.

Taken together, these figures cast a shadow on the recorded gains in black educational attainment. Not only are blacks likely to be in lower grade levels than whites, but when they are tested against the standards of those grade levels, they do more poorly. Though the census records all who have completed twelve years of school as high school graduates, it is clear that some blacks with such attainment may not have educations equivalent to those of whites.

Table 18-5
Mental Disqualification of Draftees, 1950-1971

Year	Black	White
	(percent)	
1971	33.9	4.7
1970	33.0	5.3
1969	38.2	8.1
1968	39.0	8.0
1967–1950	53.6	13.1
Average 1950–1971	49.8	11.5

Source: Department of the Army, Office of the Surgeon General, *Results of the Examination of Youths for Military Service, September 22* (Washington: Government Printing Office, 1972), table 10.

Final Examination

Given society's growing needs for educated individuals, and the controversial but real importance of credentials in determining social and economic success, the equalization of school enrollment ratios and the narrowing gap between black and white educational attainment are healthy trends. By 1973 blacks at all ages through seventeen years, and in almost all areas and residential environments, were as likely to be in school as whites. These strides in enrollment have been translated into attainment. Sixty-seven percent of blacks age twenty to twenty-four had completed high school in 1972, and the median educational attainment for blacks over twenty-one stood at 10.8 years. Black education at the college level has also improved, though blacks are still much less likely to be enrolled in college or to have attained a college degree than whites. From 1960, when blacks were 5 percent of college students, the proportion increased to nearly 9 percent in 1972, when 18 percent of blacks age eighteen to twenty-four were enrolled.

The record of black progress in education is clouded by evidence that the advancement represented by these years in school may not be equivalent to that of whites. Blacks from more impoverished backgrounds begin school at a disadvantage; they are often culturally isolated or attend schools with fewer resources than those attended by children from affluent homes. On the average, blacks are more likely to fall behind one or more grade levels and to score lower on achievement tests. Of those who do succeed in high school and go on to college, a large proportion attend black schools or integrated institutions with limited facilities and resources. One consequence is that the payoff on black educational credentials is less than for whites. Black male high school graduates may expect to earn about 24 percent more than nongraduates, while whites average 29 percent more with a diploma. A sheepskin is worth about 33 percent more to a black but it raises white earnings by 53 percent.

It would be unfair and misleading, however, to direct attention primarily toward the quality of black education as though this were evidence of overall stagnation of black educational progress. While comparisons of test scores are reminders that equality of educational opportunity is a difficult and distant goal, they do not outweigh significant black enrollment and attainment gains. The schools, whatever their shortcomings, prepare individuals for productive roles in society. Whether they still fail many blacks, few observers have suggested that those who have no schooling are better off than those who graduate. The educational advantages which blacks have gained since 1960 may be far less than optimum, and far less than what is necessary to establish true equality of opportunity, but they are crucially important steps toward that goal.

19
Educational Attainment in the U.S.

Commerce Department Figures for 1973-74

Introduction

This report contains data on years of schooling completed for persons who were 14 years old and over in March 1974. Statistical tables show data on years of schooling completed by sex, age and race; for persons of Spanish origin; and persons of metropolitan and nonmetropolitan residence. These tables follow the text of this report. Survey results for 1974 are presented in historical perspective, and the trends are analyzed in the remainder of this text.

Trends in Educational Attainment

Most indicators of educational achievement point to a steady rise over the last thirty-five years in the number of years people spend in school. Most of the males and females, both blacks and whites, are staying in school longer than their parents did. Changes over time in the educational levels of individuals 25 to 34 years old largely represent changes in the preparation of persons for entrance into the labor market. The proportion of all Americans of this age range who have four years of high school or more has risen from 37 percent in 1940 to 63 percent in 1974 (see Table 19-1). In 1940 more women than men 25 to 34 years old were high school graduates. By 1974 the situation had changed so that about the same percentage of males and females of these ages had a high school diploma, including those who had gone on to college.

The distribution of males and females by educational level differs greatly, however. Women are still more likely than men to complete high

Reprinted from "Educational Attainment in the United States: March, 1973 and 1974," *Current Population Reports—Population Characteristics,* U.S. Dept. of Commerce, Social and Economic Status Commission, U.S. Govt. Printing Office, Washington, D.C., Dec., 1974, pp. 1-4, Table D.

Table 19-1

Percent of Persons 25 to 34 Years Old Who Have Completed

Four Years of High School or More, by Race and Sex: 1940-1974

Year	White		Black		Black-white differential	
	Males	Females	Males	Females	Males	Females
1974	82.3	81.0	67.0	63.9	15.3	17.1
1973	80.2	79.7	62.3	60.5	17.9	19.2
1972	79.7	78.3	59.1	61.6	20.6	16.7
1971	78.4	76.5	52.6	58.8	23.1	17.7
1970	77.0	75.3	49.4	57.0	27.6	18.3
1969	75.2	74.7	53.9	52.8	21.3	21.9
1968	73.4	73.6	52.0	50.0	21.4	23.6
1967	72.9	72.3	49.9	54.5	23.0	17.8
1966	72.5	71.6	44.3	46.4	28.2	25.2
1965	71.0	70.5	45.2	45.8	25.8	24.7
1960	59.3	62.8	30.1	35.8	29.2	27.0
1950	51.5	55.4	18.4	22.2	33.1	32.8
1940	36.1	40.9	8.9	12.3	27.2	28.6

school but not enter college (Figure 19-1). In 1974, 47 percent of all white females 25 to 34 years old had finished high school but had completed no college, and 33 percent had completed some college. The comparable figures for white males are 38 percent with a complete high school education but no college and 44 percent with at least some college.

There is a sizeable difference, however, between blacks and whites in the percent of those 25 to 34 years old who have finished high school. In 1974, 82 percent of white males and 67 percent of black males of these ages had a high school diploma, a difference of 15 percentage points. Yet, the gap between blacks and whites in rates of high school graduation has decreased substantially, especially in the last 4 or 5 years. In 1940, a differential of 27 percentage points separated the proportions of white end black men 25 to 34 years old who were high school graduates. This differential decreased by about 6 percentage points from that point to 1974 (Figure 19-2). The latter decrease is significant at the .90 level of probability. A similar trend toward equality between the races in rates of high school graduation occurred for females.

The annual increase in the proportion of those 25 to 34 years old who have a high school diploma has been fairly constant at an average of less than 2 percentage points a year for white males since the middle 1960s. The corresponding rate of increase for black males averaged 2 percentage points a year in the late 1960s and 4 percentage points a year in the early 1970s. If the proportion of those ages 25 to 34 who have completed high school were to continue to increase at a higher rate for blacks than for whites, it would not be many years before the gap between the races in attainment of high school graduation would disappear.

Quartiles of the distribution of years of school completed, presented in Table 19-2, briefly summarize the entire distribution of educational attainment in the United States. The three quartiles divide the population into four equal amounts of educational attainment. The first quartile is the point below which the lowest 25 percent fall. The second quartile is the median, or the point at which half the people have more and half have less education. The third quartile marks the point at which three-fourths of the population has less education and one-fourth has more.

Figure 19-1
Years of School Completed for White Men and Women 25 to 34 Years Old: 1974

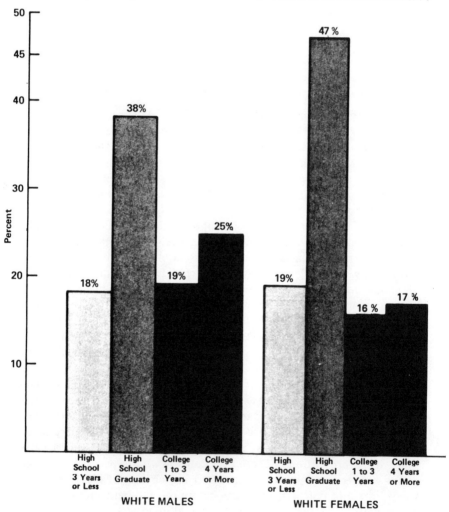

Table 19-2 shows the quartiles of the distribution of years of schooling completed by men and women 25 to 34 years old for selected years since 1940. Among males in 1940 there was about a 5-year gap between the first and third quartile, with half of the black males having between four and nine years of school and half of the white males having between eight and thirteen years of school. By 1974 one-fourth of all white males 25 to 34 years old were completing at least a four-year college education. The educational level for the highest 25 percent of black men was one year of college.

The difference between men and women in the distribution of years of school completed changed drastically from 1940 to 1974. In 1940 the top quarter of all white males and females 25 to 34 years old finished about 12.5 years of schooling. By 1974, males in the top quartile had completed four years or more of college while their female counterparts had finished only two years of college. Furthermore, there was a greater difference in educational levels of the top one-half and top one-fourth for white men

Figure 19-2
Percent of Persons 25 to 34 Years Old Who Have
Completed High School, by Race and Sex: 1940-1974

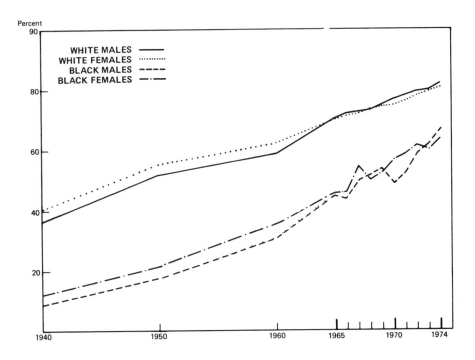

Table 19-2
Quartiles of the Distribution of Educational Attainment by Race and Sex, for Persons 25 to 34 Years Old: 1940 to 1974

Sex and year	White			Black		
	1st quartile	2nd quartile (median)	3rd quartile	1st quartile	2nd quartile (median)	3rd quartile
MALE						
1974	12.2	12.8	16.0	11.1	12.4	13.0
1973	12.1	12.8	15.3	10.5	12.3	12.9
1970	12.0	12.7	14.9	9.6	11.9	12.7
1965	11.2	12.5	14.3	8.7	11.5	12.7
1960	9.8	12.3	13.7	7.3	9.8	12.3
1950	8.9	12.0	12.9	5.3	8.0	11.0
1940	8.3	10.1	12.5	3.6	6.3	8.6
FEMALE						
1974	12.1	12.7	14.3	10.8	12.3	12.9
1973	12.1	12.6	13.9	10.5	12.3	12.9
1970	12.0	12.5	13.1	10.4	12.2	12.8
1965	11.3	12.4	12.9	9.3	11.6	12.7
1960	10.4	12.3	12.9	8.3	10.6	12.4
1950	9.3	12.1	12.8	6.1	8.6	11.6
1940	8.5	10.6	12.6	5.1	7.3	9.5

Table 19-3
Level of School Completed by Employed Persons
25 to 64 Years Old, by Major Occupation Group and Sex: March 1974

Occupation group and sex	Total	Not high school graduate	High school graduate		
			No years of college	1 to 3 years of college	4 years of college or more
Male, 25 to 64 years.........	100.0	100.0	100.0	100.0	100.0
Prof., technical, and kindred workers......	15.7	0.9	6.3	17.1	54.1
Farmers and farm managers.............	2.9	5.7	3.2	1.6	1.0
Managers, and adm., except farm........	16.2	5.5	15.5	24.2	26.3
Clerical and kindred workers..........	6.1	2.9	8.3	10.0	3.1
Sales workers.........................	5.9	1.3	5.9	10.6	8.3
Craft and kindred workers.............	22.6	25.4	29.4	18.7	3.9
Operatives, including transport workers...	17.3	29.7	19.3	8.9	1.1
Service workers.......................	6.7	10.6	7.3	6.4	1.6
Farm laborers and supervisors.........	1.2	4.7	0.6	0.4	0.2
Laborers, except farm.................	5.2	13.4	4.2	2.2	0.4
Female, 25 to 64 years.........	100.0	100.0	100.0	100.0	100.0
Prof., technical, and kindred workers......	17.1	1.0	1.6	22.5	71.4
Farmers and farm managers.............	0.3	0.5	0.2	0.3	0.3
Managers, and adm., except farm........	6.0	2.9	5.2	7.7	6.8
Clerical and kindred workers..........	32.6	6.5	19.0	46.8	13.5
Sales workers.........................	6.2	3.7	7.4	5.0	3.0
Craft and kindred workers.............	1.9	2.7	3.0	1.2	0.5
Operatives, including transport workers...	14.1	35.1	27.9	4.4	1.3
Service workers.......................	19.9	42.9	33.0	11.0	3.1
Farm laborers and supervisors.........	1.1	3.5	1.1	0.4	0.2
Laborers, except farm.................	0.8	1.4	1.5	0.7	-

- Represents zero.

than for white women which in this case illustrates the greater tendency for white men to attend college once they graduated from high school. This difference is not apparent from examination of a summary index such as median years of school completed. There was little difference in 1974 between males and females in median years of schooling completed.

Occupations and Educational Attainment

A high school diploma was a greater advantage to persons seeking work in 1940 when only one in three white men and only one in twelve black men 25 to 34 years old had finished high school than it was in 1974 when four out of five white men and two out of three black men held a high school diploma at those ages. In 1940, the high school graduate typically had more jobs in white collar occupations open to him or her than would a person with no training past high school entering the job market in 1974. A recent analysis of occupational changes, performed by the National Planning Association (1973) using the 1960 and 1970 Censuses of Population, has shown that workers with high school diplomas or some college education traditionally found employment in white collar occupations but more are now entering blue collar and service occupations.[1] The educational attainment of workers rose greatly from 1960 to 1970. The rate of growth in white collar occupations did not keep pace. A college education has become more common since 1940 and also more necessary for competition for many professional and managerial jobs in the 1970s.

Schooling acts as an important criterion for admission into most occupations. This can be seen from Table 19-3 which gives the distribution of individuals with different amounts of schooling into major occupational categories. Those occupations with the highest schooling requirements also tend to be those with the highest incomes. It can be seen from this table that men with less than four years of high school tend to be operatives or craftsmen, while their female counterparts tend to be operatives and service workers. As educational level increases so does the proportion in white collar occupations like sales or clerical workers, managers and administrators, or professional, technical, and kindred workers. Almost three out of four women and one out of two men with college degrees are in professional jobs and one out of four men with some college training is in a managerial occupation. In all educational categories females tend to be concentrated in one or two major occupational categories, whereas males tend to more evenly distributed across a wider range of occupational categories (see Table 19-3).

---

1. Harold Wool, *The Labor Supply for Lower Level Occupations,* National Planning Association, 1973, pg. 146.

20
Income and Educational Attainment

Commerce Department Figures for 1956-72

Introduction

This report presents educational attainment and income data for
selected years from 1956 to 1972 assembled from information collected in
the Current Population Survey. It updates the information previously
published for the period up to 1968 in *Current Population Reports,* Series
P-60, No. 74 and No. 56. Educational attainment estimates in this report
are limited to men with income and accordingly differ slightly from general
education statistics relating to all men. Included in the report are annual
mean income and estimates of expected lifetime income in current dollars
and in constant (1972) dollars, by educational attainment and age group,
for all males and for male year-round full-time workers. In addition,
procedures used to prepare lifetime income estimates, definitions and
explanations of terms, and sources of data are included.

Prior to 1967, mean incomes and lifetime income estimates were
computed on grouped data.[1] However, improved methodology introduced
in 1967 permits the computation of data based on the use of actual income
amounts in preparing the estimates. Therefore, for the years 1967 and 1968
lifetime income estimates and mean incomes of men are based on both
grouped and ungrouped data to illustrate the differences engendered by the
two estimation procedures. For more detailed explanation, see *Current
Population Reports,* Series P-60, No. 74, "Annual Mean Income, Lifetime
Income, and Education Attainment of Men in the United States, For

Reprinted from "Annual Mean Income, Lifetime Income, and Educational Attainment of
Men in the United States, for Selected Years, 1956-1972," *Current Population Reports:
Consumer Income,* U.S. Dept. of Commerce, Social and Economic Statistics Administration,
Bureau of Census, U.S. Govt. Printing Office, Washington, D.C., Dec., 1974m pp. 1-4.

1. Estimates based on a series of estimated mean values for specific income class intervals. The
mean income was obtained from a summation of the product of the average income and the
proportion of males for each income level.

Selected Years, 1956 to 1968," pages 20 to 22. It should be noted that since the estimates are based on a sample, they are subject to sampling variability. Moreover, as in all field surveys of income, the figures are subject to errors of response and nonreporting. Data on consumer income collected by the Bureau of the Census cover money income only (exclusive of certain money receipts such as capital gains) prior to deduction for taxes.

Mean Income and Educational Attainment

The educational attainment of the male population in the United States has increased considerably during the past 16 years. In March 1973, the median years of school completed by men 25 years old and over was 12.3 years, or about the equivalent of a high school education, whereas in March 1957 it was 10.4 years old (Table 20-1). Between March 1957 and March 1973, the proportion of males who terminated their schooling after 4 years of high school increased by about two-fifths and the proportion of males completing 4 or more years of college rose by two-thirds. As can be expected, there was a reduction in the proportion of men who terminated their schooling with elementary school, dropping from about 19 percent in March 1957 to roughly 12 percent in March 1973.

Although a large proportion of men end their formal education with a high school diploma, there has been an upward trend in the proportion of males completing their schooling beyond high school. In March 1959, about 8 percent of the 46.3 million males 25 years old and over had completed 1 to 3 years of college and in March 1973, about 12 percent of the 53.1 million males had attained this level of schooling—a gain of 48 percent. Between March 1959 and March 1973, men completing their formal education with a bachelor's degree rose from 6 percent to 9 percent. A relative gain was registered by men with post graduate studies completed. Men completing 5 or more years of college rose from 4 percent in March 1959 to 7 percent in March 1973.

In step with the rise in the educational attainment level of the male population in the United States, there has been significant changes in mean incomes received by men over the past 16 years. Thus, the mean income of all men 25 years old and over increased by 49 percent, from $6,800 in 1956 (in constant 1972 dollars) to $10,120 in 1972. An important factor in this increase is that more and more males are continuing their schooling which in turn provides the opportunity to enter into skilled occupations yielding higher income returns.

Although the mean income in terms of constant dollars for all men 25 years old and over rose from $9,600 in 1971 to $10,120 in 1972, a gain of about $520 or 5 percent, gains were recorded for men in the 35 to 44 year age group. The mean income of men 35 to 55 years old was $12,170 in 1972, $800 higher than the $11,270 mean income in 1971.

Table 20-1 shows that there is a progressive increase in income associated with each level of schooling. In 1972, men 25 years old and over who completed elementary school had a mean income of $6,700 or $1,520 more than men who started but did not finish elementary school. Male high school graduates reported a mean income of $10,430, or $1,980 higher than high school nongraduates. Males who continued their education through the college level can expect to receive considerably higher incomes than males who terminate their schooling after 1 to 3 years of college training. The mean income of men who completed 4 or more years of college was $16,200 in 1972, $4,330 higher than the mean income of men who started college but did not graduate. The income differential of graduates versus nongraduates also existed by age group.

There are monetary gains associated with successfully achieving each identifiable educational plateau. Men 25 years old and over whose education terminated after 4 years of high school received a mean income of $10,430 in 1972, or $3,680 more than men whose formal schooling ended at the eighth grade level. Men with college degrees received a mean income of $16,200, $5,770 or 55 percent higher than men whose education terminated after receiving their high school diplomas.

Of the 6.9 million males 25 years old and over in the "$1 to $2,999 or less" class interval in 1972, 19 percent completed elementary school, another 17 percent completed high school, and about 7 percent completed 4 or more years of college. In contrast, of the 9.1 million males in the $15,000 and over" class interval, about 4 percent completed their schooling with the eighth grade, another 29 percent concluded their education with a high school diploma and 42 percent received a college degree. The median years of school completed was 8.7 years for males 25 years old and over with incomes less than $3,000, and for males in the highest income interval— $15,000 and over—the median years of school completed was the equivalent of college experience—14.6 years.

Younger men (25 to 34 years old) have the highest levels of schooling completed. The median years of school completed for these men was 12.7 years in 1972, compared to about 8.7 years for men 65 years old and over. The median years of school completed for younger men in the lowest income interval was 4.3 years higher than for older men—12.4 years and 8.1 years, respectively. However, this difference in years of school completed dropped to 2.5 years for males in the $15,000 and over interval—from 15.4 years to 12.9 years.

The mean income of males completing just 4 years of college was lowest for the younger and older age groups—averaging about $11,500 in 1972—

Table 20-1
Mean Income in 1956 to 1972 of Men 25 Years Old and Over, by Years of School Completed and Age (in 1972 dollars)

Years of school completed and age	Computed from ungrouped data[1]						Computed from grouped data[2]							
	1972	1971	1970	1969	1968	1967[r]	1967[r]	1968	1966	1964	1963	1961	1958	1956
25 YEARS OLD AND OVER														
Total...........	$10,125	$9,599	$9,525	$9,623	$9,261	$8,774	$9,130	$9,482	$8,902	$8,240	$7,974	$7,653	$6,711	$6,805
Elementary: Less than 8 years.	5,235	4,903	4,778	4,842	4,785	4,436	4,571	4,919	4,536	4,451	4,205	4,193	3,661	3,960
8 years.......	6,756	6,468	6,503	6,631	6,571	6,268	6,510	6,760	6,272	6,100	6,025	5,883	5,321	5,586
High school: 1 to 3 years.....	8,449	8,252	8,221	8,309	8,136	7,842	8,115	8,393	8,111	7,629	7,306	7,218	6,443	6,718
4 years......	10,433	9,882	9,898	10,076	9,793	9,417	9,801	10,132	9,657	9,093	8,958	8,316	7,608	7,974
College: 1 to 3 years.....	11,867	11,410	11,736	11,857	11,294	10,919	11,410	11,649	11,318	10,671	10,428	10,277	9,077	9,226
4 years or more.	16,201	15,633	15,554	16,072	15,550	14,728	15,407	15,490	15,128	13,879	13,403	13,730	12,508	12,118
4 years.......	15,256	14,626	14,409	15,135	14,925	13,812	14,437	14,707	14,349	13,167	12,831	13,066	10,948	(NA)
5 years or more.	17,346	16,814	16,953	17,234	16,292	15,838	16,588	16,433	16,189	14,850	14,143	13,968	13,282	(NA)
25 TO 34 YEARS OLD														
Total...........	9,628	9,269	9,371	9,564	9,155	8,734	9,086	9,463	8,937	8,240	7,817	7,540	6,796	6,965
Elementary: Less than 8 years.	5,699	5,250	5,373	5,349	5,377	4,954	5,149	5,532	5,282	4,372	4,387	4,270	3,857	4,082
8 years.......	6,749	6,346	6,897	7,466	6,744	6,332	6,543	6,994	6,387	6,285	6,081	5,639	5,265	5,648
High school: 1 to 3 years.....	7,856	7,669	7,540	7,900	7,641	7,299	7,575	7,888	7,591	7,070	6,810	6,550	6,174	6,757
4 years......	9,451	9,002	9,027	9,284	9,054	8,658	9,011	9,389	8,866	8,333	7,944	7,492	6,900	7,345
College: 1 to 3 years.....	9,848	9,680	10,022	9,961	9,738	9,417	9,789	10,137	9,723	9,140	8,903	8,085	7,776	8,198
4 years or more.	12,165	11,768	12,255	12,591	11,799	11,511	12,020	12,061	11,735	10,916	10,068	10,463	9,722	9,052
4 years.......	11,553	11,401	11,997	12,303	11,988	11,516	12,021	12,165	11,923	10,586	9,973	10,443	9,120	(NA)
5 years or more.	12,932	12,195	12,592	12,950	11,572	11,503	12,019	11,928	11,473	11,420	10,204	10,557	10,304	(NA)
35 TO 44 YEARS OLD														
Total...........	12,172	11,369	11,314	11,463	10,956	10,388	10,882	11,345	10,640	9,794	9,458	8,999	7,855	8,098
Elementary: Less than 8 years.	7,040	6,018	6,158	6,417	6,194	5,648	5,842	6,423	5,777	5,891	5,243	5,171	4,352	4,818
8 years.......	8,508	7,789	7,713	7,740	8,073	7,421	7,773	8,310	7,678	7,124	7,061	6,702	6,140	6,498
High school: 1 to 3 years.....	9,458	9,003	9,030	9,164	8,929	8,459	8,784	9,278	8,821	8,294	8,068	7,497	7,019	7,326
4 years......	11,312	10,619	10,634	10,950	10,579	10,050	10,457	11,040	10,361	9,665	9,730	8,966	8,198	8,720
College: 1 to 3 years.....	12,858	12,842	13,156	13,151	12,722	12,187	12,788	13,202	12,711	11,537	11,126	11,302	10,407	10,305
4 years or more.	18,545	17,886	17,569	18,348	16,880	16,405	17,431	17,297	16,769	15,244	14,686	14,443	12,919	13,860
4 years.......	17,480	16,461	16,344	17,275	15,921	15,355	16,392	16,381	15,817	14,323	14,378	14,008	11,631	(NA)
5 years or more.	19,672	19,514	18,953	19,616	18,030	17,693	18,709	18,376	18,119	16,433	15,055	15,316	14,744	(NA)

45 TO 54 YEARS OLD

Total..........	12,092	11,432	11,288	11,271	10,778	10,350	10,939	10,767	10,436	9,375	9,230	8,720	7,507	7,728
Elementary: Less than 8 years.	6,834	6,363	6,121	6,027	5,977	5,647	6,155	5,865	5,688	5,556	5,344	4,980	4,272	4,672
8 years..........	8,436	8,319	7,947	8,189	7,892	7,791	8,135	8,125	7,688	6,893	7,089	7,011	6,093	6,412
High school: 1 to 3 years..........	9,586	9,424	9,360	9,220	9,136	8,876	9,409	9,197	9,240	8,452	8,056	7,822	6,757	7,274
4 years..........	11,774	11,330	11,218	11,106	10,945	10,741	11,304	11,197	10,804	10,015	9,911	9,264	8,397	8,840
College: 1 to 3 years..........	14,839	13,170	13,812	14,304	13,308	12,504	13,470	13,129	13,534	12,891	12,570	11,884	10,695	11,008
4 years or more....	20,133	19,652	19,275	19,501	18,804	17,952	18,179	18,179	18,580	16,897	16,776	16,413	16,205	16,152
4 years..........	19,414	18,847	17,308	18,207	17,166	16,518	17,056	16,956	17,335	15,862	15,098	15,323	15,339	(NA)
5 years or more.	21,096	20,617	21,801	21,292	20,701	19,520	19,417	20,271	20,343	18,405	18,792	18,273	17,661	(NA)

55 TO 64 YEARS OLD

Total..........	10,320	9,695	9,593	9,595	9,409	8,633	9,537	9,005	8,795	7,943	7,973	7,751	6,624	6,462
Elementary: Less than 8 years.	5,844	5,406	5,487	5,563	5,492	5,015	5,647	5,168	5,084	4,753	4,710	4,820	4,274	4,426
8 years..........	7,722	7,140	7,526	7,514	7,316	6,986	7,578	7,284	7,107	6,686	6,428	6,705	5,606	5,968
High school: 1 to 3 years..........	8,899	8,706	8,764	8,701	8,582	8,061	8,841	8,345	8,476	7,565	7,458	7,983	6,933	6,488
4 years..........	10,987	10,228	10,157	10,449	10,113	9,677	10,412	10,085	10,134	9,576	9,429	8,915	8,588	8,706
College: 1 to 3 years..........	13,800	13,412	12,690	12,910	11,500	11,774	12,166	12,256	11,354	10,707	11,000	10,959	9,902	9,580
4 years or more....	19,078	18,605	18,119	18,332	20,331	16,878	19,024	17,823	17,423	15,591	17,198	14,510	15,394	13,442
4 years..........	17,202	16,230	16,615	17,599	20,383	14,882	17,196	15,543	16,302	15,020	16,892	14,503	12,239	(NA)
5 years or more.	21,345	21,322	19,716	19,064	20,272	19,113	21,142	20,262	18,687	16,238	17,589	(B)	(B)	(NA)

65 YEARS OLD AND OVER

Total..........	5,384	5,176	4,847	4,916	4,793	4,469	4,839	4,528	4,298	4,544	4,172	4,130	3,307	3,526
Elementary: Less than 8 years.	3,390	3,379	3,053	3,107	2,983	2,840	3,041	2,881	2,867	3,059	2,775	2,776	2,391	2,569
8 years..........	4,503	4,381	4,234	4,137	4,219	3,893	4,250	3,985	3,714	4,162	4,004	3,660	3,366	3,429
High school: 1 to 3 years..........	5,427	5,103	5,040	5,229	4,892	5,090	5,022	5,123	4,474	4,835	4,344	4,766	3,677	3,903
4 years..........	6,761	6,311	6,207	6,046	5,952	5,556	5,921	5,642	5,584	6,362	6,105	5,224	4,152	4,972
College: 1 to 3 years..........	7,351	7,421	7,250	7,250	7,495	6,810	7,292	6,980	7,045	7,113	6,861	8,200	5,430	6,183
4 years or more....	11,933	11,167	9,595	11,378	11,137	10,323	11,303	10,315	10,290	10,441	8,766	12,098	7,860	8,298
4 years..........	11,033	10,363	9,538	9,532	10,274	9,655	9,981	9,385	8,281	10,174	8,296	(B)	(B)	(NA)
5 years or more.	13,066	12,193	11,013	14,116	12,227	11,043	12,915	11,254	12,977	(B)	(B)	(B)	(B)	(NA)

B Base less than 200,000.   NA Not available.   ʳRevised.

[1]Improved methodology introduced in 1967 permits the computation of data based on actual reported amounts.

[2]Estimates based on a series of estimated mean values for specific income class intervals.

indicating that the younger age group (25 to 34 years old) is completing their formal education before entering the labor force and that the older age group (65 years old and over) is retiring from the labor force. The income differential between the younger and older men and those in the middle age bracket was substantial, where the mean income was $17,480 for men 35 to 44 years old; $19,410 for men 45 to 54 years old; and $17,200 for men 55 to 64 years old. Even for males completing their post graduate studies, which is usually done while being gainfully employed in the labor force, the income differential was still substantial.

In addition to education, work experience is also an important variable closely associated with income. Among the 52.6 million men 25 years old and over with income in 1972, 66 percent were year-round full-time workers. In 1972, the mean income ($12,350) of men 25 years old and over working year round full time was 22 percent higher than for all men with income. This difference varied by age groupings. The difference was especially great when mean incomes of men 65 years old and over were compared against each other. Thus, in the 65 years old and over group, the mean income ($10,550) of male year round full-time workers was 96 percent higher than that ($5,380) of all men with income in this age group. In contrast, the comparable ratio was only about 9 percent higher for men in the 35 to 44 year age group.

The mean income of male high school graduates 25 years old and over working 50 to 52 weeks in 1972 was $11,570, or 27 percent higher than elementary school graduates with comparable work experience. Similarly, men completing 4 or more years of college had a mean income of $17,880, $6,310 or 55 percent higher than high school graduates. Among men working 50 to 52 weeks and who were college graduates the mean income of those men with 5 or more years of schooling was $18,980, $2,010 or 12 percent higher than those men with 4 years of schooling ($16,970).

Between 1967 and 1972, the mean income (in terms of constant dollars) of male year-round full-time workers 25 years old and over increased from $10,440 to $12,350, a rise of about one-fifth, compared with a rise of about 15 percent for all males 25 years old and over. Among male year-round full-time workers, the mean income for those completing 4 or more years of college was $17,880 in 1972 compared with $16,030 five years ago.

Lifetime Income Estimates

In this report, lifetime income estimates for different educational categories, based on data for specific years, represent a summation of the products of both mean income estimates of different age and education groups and the number of survivors in the comparable population out of 100,000 at birth from an initial stipulated age to a terminal one, divided by the comparable number out of 100,000 at birth who survived to the initial stipulated age. Thus, lifetime income estimates are a measure of the incomes that could be expected on the average by members of specific education groups in a lifetime (or for any specified span of years) if the mean income estimates by age and education, and life expectancy rates, did not change from those existing in the reference year, e.g., 1972.

The estimated lifetime income of all men from age 18 to death increased from $322,000 in 1956 (in 1972 dollars) to $471,000 in 1972, $149,000 or 46 percent.

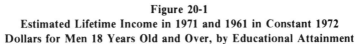

Figure 20-1
Estimated Lifetime Income in 1971 and 1961 in Constant 1972
Dollars for Men 18 Years Old and Over, by Educational Attainment

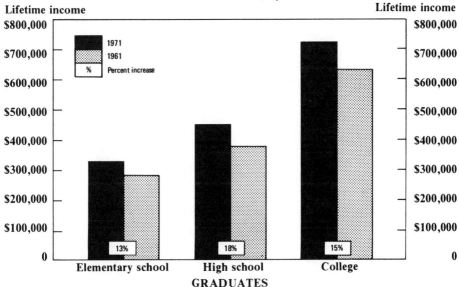

In 1972, men who completed high school could expect to receive from age 18 to death about $479,000 during their lifetime, or $135,000 more than men who completed only elementary school. The estimated lifetime income in 1972 of men completing 4 or more years of college was $279,000 higher than those who had completed only high school.

Additional schooling is associated with a substantial increase in lifetime income. As usual, the greatest income gains were at the college level. In 1972, men with 1 to 3 years of college training can expect to receive more than one-half of a million dollars in their lifetime, whereas for men with 4 or more years of college the estimated lifetime income was about three-quarters of a million dollars.

The estimated lifetime income of all men from age 25 to death was

$448,000 in 1972, a gain of about $24,000 or 6 percent over the 1971 estimated lifetime income.

Between 1967 and 1972, the estimated lifetime income in terms of constant dollars of all men from age 25 to death increased from $385,000 to $448,000, a gain of $63,000 or 16 percent. However, for male year-round full-time workers, the estimated lifetime income was $542,000 in 1972, $86,000 or 19 percent over the five-year period.

21
Texas Bilingual Education Act

Subchapter L—Public Schools

21.451. State Policy

The legislature finds that there are large numbers of children in the state who come from environments where the primary language is other than English. Experience has shown that public school classes in which instruction is given only in English are often inadequate for the education of children whose native tongue is another language. The legislature believes that a compensatory program of bilingual education can meet the needs of these children and facilitate their integration into the regular school curriculum. Therefore, pursuant to the policy of the state to insure equal educational opportunity to every child, and in recognition of the educational needs of children of limited English-speaking ability, it is the purpose of this subchapter to provide for the establishment of bilingual education programs in the public schools and to provide supplemental financial assistance to help local school districts meet the extra costs of the programs.

21.452. Definitions

In this subchapter the following words have the indicated meanings:

(1) "Agency" means the Central Education Agency.

(2) "Board" means the governing board of a school district.

(3) "Children of limited English-speaking ability" means children whose native tongue is a language other than English and who have difficulty performing ordinary classwork in English.

21.453. Establishment of Bilingual Programs

(a) The governing board of each school district shall determine not later

---

From the *Texas Bilingual Education Act—Public Schools,*1.454-Subchapter L., Bilingual Education, pp. 25-27.

than the first day of March, under regulations prescribed by the State Board of Education, the number of school-age children of limited English-speaking ability within the district and shall classify them according to the language in which they possess a primary speaking ability.

(b) Beginning with the 1974-75 scholastic year, each school district which has an enrollment of 20 or more children of limited English-speaking ability in any language classification in the same grade level during the preceeding scholastic year, and which does not have a program of bilingual instruction which accomplishes the state policy set out in Section 21.451 of this Act, shall institute a program of bilingual instruction for the children in each language classification commencing in the first grade, and shall increase the program by one grade each year until bilingual instruction is offered in each grade up to the sixth. The board may establish a program with respect to a language classification with less than 20 children.

21.454. Program Content; Method of Instruction

(a) The bilingual education program established by a school district shall be a full-time program of instruction (1) in all subjects required by law of by the school district, which shall be given in the native language of the children of limited English-speaking ability who are enrolled in the program, and in the English language; (2) in the comprehension, speaking, reading, and writing of the native language of the children of limited English-speaking ability who are enrolled in the program, and in the comprehension, speaking, reading, and writing of the English language; and (3) in the history and culture associated with the native language of the children of limited English-speaking ability who are enrolled in the program, and in the history and culture of the United States.

(b) In predominantly nonverbal subjects, such as art, music, and physical education, children of limited English-speaking ability shall participate fully with their English-speaking contemporaries in regular classes provided in the subjects.

(c) Elective courses included in the curriculum may be taught in a language other then English.

(d) Each school district shall insure to children enrolled in the program a meaningful opportunity to participate fully with other children in all extracurricular activities.

21.455. Enrollment of Children in Program

(a) Every school-age child of limited English-speaking ability residing within a school district required to provide a bilingual program for his classification shall be enrolled in the program for a period of three years or until he achieves a level of English language proficiency which will enable him to perform successfully in classes in which instruction is given only in English, whichever first occurs.

(b) A child of limited English-speaking ability enrolled in a program of bilingual education may continue in that program for a period longer than three years with the approval of the school district and the child's parents or legal guardian.

(c) No school district may transfer a child of limited English-speaking ability out of a program in bilingual education prior to his third year of enrollment in the program unless the parents of the child approve the transfer in writing, and unless the child has received a score on an examination which, in the determination of the agency, reflects a level of English language skills appropriate to his or her grade level. If later evidence suggests that a child who has been transferred is still handicapped by an inadequate command of English, he may be re-enrolled in the program for a length of time equal to that which remained at the time he was transferred.

(d) No later than 10 days after the enrollment of a child in a program in bilingual education the school district shall notify the parents or legal guardian of the child that the child has been enrolled in the program. The notice shall be in writing in English, and in the language of which the child of the parents possesses a primary speaking ability.

21.456. Facilities; Classes

(a) Programs in bilingual education, whenever possible, shall be located in the regular public schools of the district rather than in separate facilities.

(b) Children enrolled in the program, whenever possible, shall be placed in classes with other children of approximately the same age and level of educational attainment. If children of different age groups or educational levels are combined, the school district shall insure that the instruction given each child is appropriate to his or her level of educational attainment, and the district shall keep adequate records of the educational level and progress of each child enrolled in the Program.

(c) The maximum student-teacher ratio shall be set by the agency and shall reflect the special educational needs of children enrolled in programs of bilingual education.

21.457. Cooperation Among Districts

(a) A school district may join with any other district or districts to provide the programs in bilingual education required or permitted by this subchapter. The availability of the programs shall be publicized throughout the affected districts.

(b) A school district may allow a nonresident child of limited English-speaking ability to enroll in or attend its program in bilingual education, and the tuition for the child shall be paid by the district in which the child resides.

21.458. Preschool and Summer School Programs

A school district may establish on a full- or part-time basis preschool or summer school programs in bilingual education for children of limited English-speaking ability and may join with other districts in establishing the programs. The preschool or summer programs shall not be a substitute for programs required to be provided during the regular school year.

21.459. Bilingual Education Teachers

(a) The State Board of Education shall promulgate rules and regulations governing the issuance of teaching certificates with bilingual education endorsements to teachers who possess a speaking and reading ability in a language other than English in which bilingual education programs are offered and who meet the general requirements set out in Chapter 13 of this code.

(b) The minimum monthly base pay and increments for teaching experience for a bilingual education teacher are the same as for a classroom teacher with an equivalent degree under the Texas State Public Education Compensation Plan. The minimum annual salary for a bilingual education teacher is the monthly base salary, plus increments, multiplied by 10, 11, or 12, as applicable.

22
A Head Start Follow-Through Program

Juliet P. Borden, John P. Wollenberg, and Herbert M. Handley

Introduction

Data from this study indicate that disadvantaged children participating in a highly structured Head Start-Follow Through program sequence showed significant scholastic gains when compared to their counterparts who did not attend a Head Start program.

A consensus of the literature indicates that Head Start alumni generally do not compare well scholastically with their middle-class counterparts. Their performance, however, at the outset of the formal school experience is superior to their peers with comparable backgrounds who were not Head Start participants. The duration of the academic margin favoring Head Start students is questionable and apparently differs among specific programs. For this reason, the efficacy of various Head Start models is under close scrutiny and in some instances, these programs have been condemned for their failure to foster lasting cognitive gains in children.

Literature related to assessment of Head Start programs is mostly composed of reports describing the immediate effects of compensatory programs. The longitudinal impact of planned Follow Through programs designed to reinforce a comprehensive preschool experience for children has not been adequately described. In this report the results of a two-year longitudinal study of the achievement of Head Start graduates who also participated in a dynamic Follow Through program in regular school will be summarized.

The limited effect of Head Start programs as compensatory training for disadvantaged children has been documented by several investigators.

Reprinted by permission from *Journal of Negro Education,* Vol.44, No. 2, Spring, 1975, pp. 149-160. Originally titled: "Extended Positive Effects of a Comprehensive Head Start-Follow Through Program Sequence on Academic Performance of Rural Disadvantaged Students."

Jones,[1] for example, compared the language skills of Head Start and non-Head Start children and found no significant change in language skills in the Head Start group except in vocabulary use. Butts[2] studied the effects of Head Start programs on deprived children in the areas of intelligence, achievement, creativity and socialization. He concluded that no lasting effects were derived from the Head Start experience.

An analysis of the developmental status of Head Start and non-Head Start children was made by Cawley, Burrow and Goodstein.[3] Data in this study signified that no differences existed between the Head Start and non-Head Start subjects.

Other studies show that Head Start programs have a positive effect on the development of preschool children. Academic achievement, social adjustment and intellectual maturity of Head Start and non-Head Start subjects were studied by Herbert.[4] The Head Start group proved to be superior in intellectual functioning and social adaptation, but not in academic achievement. Kuzma[5] also found autonomous behavior and intelligence increased among Mexican-American and Negro children as a result of a seven-week pre-school program. Stoia and Reeling[6] investigated growth in articulatory ability among Head Start participants.Their findings indicated that articulation among culturally disadvantaged youngsters could be improved by a pre-school program.

The language ability and school readiness of disadvantaged Head Start and non-Head Start subjects were examined by Cowling.[7] As indicated by the Metropolitan Readiness Tests, the Head Starters were more prepared for school. Empirical data showed that they were significantly more advanced than the non-Head Start subjects in language ability.

---

1. K. L. Jones, *The Language Development of Head Start Children,* Unpublished Doctoral Dissertation, University of Arkansas, 1966.

2. D. S. Butts, *A Psycho-Sociological Comparison of Projected Head Start Participating and Non-participating Culturally Deprived and Non-Culturally Deprived First Graders in Durham, North Carolina,* Unpublished Doctoral Dissertation, University of North Carolina at Chapel Hill, 1970.

3. J. F. Cawley, W. H. Burrow and H. A. Goodstein, "Performance of Head Start and non-Head Start Participants at First Grade", *The Journal of Negro Education,* IX (1970), 124-131.

4. H. A. Herbert, *The Relative Effectiveness of Project Head Start to Prepare Children to Enter First Grade,* Unpublished Doctoral Dissertation, Auburn, University, 1969.

5. K. Kuzma, "Effects of Three Pre-school Intervention Programs on Development of Autonomy in Mexican-American and Negro Children", *ERIC* (ED015-006), 1965.

6. Louis Stoia and G. E. Reeling, "Better Speech for Head Start Children", *Elementary School Journal,* LXVII (1967), 213-217.

7. D. N. Cowling, *Language Ability and Readiness for School of Children Who Participated in Head Start Programs,* Unpublished Doctoral Dissertation, Lehigh University, 1967.

Turner and DeFord[8] discovered that scores on the Metropolitan Achievement Tests tended to increase proportionately in relationship to the length of the preschool experience. Additional data indicated that readiness for school and academic performance improved as a result of preschool experiences.

Love and Stallings[9] compared the achievement of first graders who had participated in a summer Head Start and a sequential Follow Through program with an equivalent group who attended Head Start and did not attend Follow Through. The children from the Follow Through program achieved significantly higher in reading than the non-Follow Through subjects.

The specific problem in this investigation was to compare the academic progress of rural disadvantaged children who attended two types of Head Start programs and also participated in a reinforcing Follow Through program for two years with that of non-Head Start students of similar backgrounds who were also enrolled in the Follow Through program. Selected measures of pupil growth included IQ scores and results from achievement tests in reading, arithmetic and spelling. Tests were given at two intervals—at the termination of the first and second grades, respectively.

Hypotheses

To structure the analysis of data, the following hypotheses were offered in the null form:

1. Students who participated in Head Start Program I will not differ significantly in IQ and achievement in selected areas from students not attending Head Start programs at the end of the first and second grade, respectively.

2. Students who participated in Head Start Program II will not differ significantly in IQ and achievement in selected areas, respectively, from students not attending Head Start programs at the end of the first and second school year.

3. Students in Head Start Program I and Head Start Program II will not differ significantly in IQ and selected achievement measures, respectively, at the end of the first and second school year.

---

8. R. Turner and E. F. DeFord, "Follow-up Study of Pupils with Differing Pre-School Experiences", *ERIC* (ED042-810), 1971.

9. H. D. Love, S. G. Stallings, "A Comparison of Children Who Attended Project Head Start Not Having a Follow Through Program and Children Who Attended Project Head Start Having a Follow Through Program," *Education*, XCI (1970), 88-91.

4. Boys from Head Start Program I, Head Start Program II and from non-Head Start programs, will not differ significantly in IQ and selected achievement measures, respectively, at the end of the first and second school year.

5. Girls from Head Start Program I, Head Start Program II and from non-Head Start programs, will not differ significantly in IQ and selected achievement measures, respectively, at the end of the first and second school year.

6. When all measures of student growth (IQ and achievement) are considered as a collective variable, students who participated in Head Start I, students who participated in Head Start II and students without Head Start programs will not differ significantly at the end of the first and second school years.

Procedures

The subjects of the study were 144 children from an elementary school in Tupelo, Mississippi. Thirty-two children attended Head Start I just previous to their enrollment in the Follow Through program as first graders for the 1969-70 school term. Forty-five children attended Head Start II and enrolled in the Follow Through program for the 1970-71 term. Sixty-seven students who had not participated in the Head Start programs served as the control sample. The control group contained 34 students who were classmates of the Head Start I alumni and 33 students who attended school with the Head Start II group.

This sample included all students who attended Head Start at the Tupelo Center during each of the respective years and who later enrolled in the experimental school and completed the longitudinal study in that school. Because of the development of new housing projects, rezoning of schools and other reasons, a portion of both Head Start-Follow Through groups and their control groups did not complete the total two-year program. The following percentages of the original subjects completed the experimental sequence and were included in this study: Head Start I, 50.0 per cent; Control Group I, 41.4 per cent; Head Start II, 81.8 per cent; Control Group II, 64.8 per cent.

To insure against an experimental mortality bias in the data which might have been effected by the dropouts, IQ scores as measured by the Otis Quick Scoring Mental Ability Test at mid-year of first grade for subjects included in the samples were compared. No significant differences in intelligence within the groups were indicated by the analysis of variance model. An F ratio of 1.21 demonstrated that all subjects completing the study were members of the same broad population in the first grade and consequently that no experimental mortality bias was introduced.

Subjects comprising the Head Start samples were selected for the programs on the basis of family income as established by guidelines from the Office of Economic Opportunity. The control group consisted of all students fitting the same criteria who did not attend Head Start and who attended Follow Through with the Head Start groups. The sample contained 127 subjects who were black and 17 subjects who were white. The white subjects were distributed among the groups.

Treatment Methods. Students enrolled in Head Start I for nine months were instructed with Distar[10] Language I materials in pre-publication form from the University of Illinois. That University provided limited consultant services. Thirty minutes daily were devoted to teaching the Distar Language format. The remainder of the school day was devoted to traditional developmental Head Start activities.

Students enrolled in Head Start II had Distar instruction outlined in published form in reading, arithmetic and language. Participants received thirty minutes instruction in each area daily in addition to other developmental activities. Regular consultant services and staff training were provided by the University of Illinois and later by the University of Oregon under a planned consultant service contract. Video-taping and continuous testing were also a part of the planned consultant service program.

The Tupelo Follow Through program selected the Englemann-Becker Model[11] for Direct Instruction as its paradym. The E-B Model is based on a behaviorist philosophy of education and is primarily academically oriented. Intense parental involvement is built into its design. In-depth teacher training and supervision for implementation of E-B teachings are also structured in the model. Instruction is administered to small groups with rapid interaction between teacher and students. A core curriculum of reading, language and mathematics is carefully programmed and sequenced. A continuous monitoring of student progress provides insight into the effectiveness of the curriculum and teaching.

Instruments. The Slosson Intelligence Test served as the instrument for collecting IQ data. Two batteries of tests, the Wide Range Achievement Test (WRAT) and the Stanford Achievement Test (Primary Level) were utilized for achievement measures at the end of the first and second grades.

Statistical Procedure. Significant differences among Head Start and

---

10. "The Engelmann Approach to Education", *DISTAR Conference Report*, Proceedings of the Conference at Boston University, March 5, 1970 (Boston, Mass.: New England Materials Instruction Center, Boston University.)

11. *Promising Approaches to Early Childhood Education, School Year 1970-71, Follow Through.* (Washington, D.C.: U.S. Government Printing Office, Catalog No. H.ES. 220: 20165, 1971).

control groups on selected measures of intelligence and achievement were determined by the use of an analysis of variance statistical model. Two independent variables, group membership and sex, plus their interaction variable, were plotted against seven dependent variables measuring pupil growth in a 3x2 matrix for each year of the Follow Through study of the children. Since the groups and subgroups whose means were being compared had unequal sample sizes, a special analysis of variance program, Veldman's[12] AVAR23 model, was employed for data analysis. Whenever the model showed a significant difference predicted by a variable, t tests were computed to determine where significant differences lay between means of the different groups.

To compare the overall achievements of students who attended Head Start I, students who attended Head Start II and students who attended no Head Start at all, a discriminant analysis program, BMDO5M, from the Biomedical Computer Program series[13] was used. In the manner outlined by Cooley and Lohnes[14] the individual test scores on all measures of intelligence and achievement were transformed into a single discriminant score. That score indicated the individual's spatial relationship to the mean of all three groups. Another statistic, D2 or V, which is equivalent to a chi square, was also derived in the discriminant studies and used to test the null hypothesis that collective group means for the subjects of all characteristics were the same at the end of each year; i.e., that no significant differences existed among the groups of students when all dependent variables were considered simultaneously.

Results

Results derived from the analysis of variance studies in testing the first three null hypotheses are given in Tables 22-1 and 22-2. In Table 22-1, group means and F ratios predicted for all measures made at the end of the first school year are indicated. Data for group comparisons on the same measures at the end of the second school year are given in Table 22-2.

No significant differences in intelligence and achievement among the groups were shown for the first grade by the analysis. At the end of the second grade, however, significant differences in reading, arithmetic and spelling achievement were noted. In further analysis to compare each pair of group means, no significant differences between pupils who participated

---

12. D. J. Veldman, *Fortran Programming for the Behavioral Sciences*, (New York: Holt, Rinehart and Winston, 1967).

13. W. J. Dixon (Editor), *BMD Biomedical Computer Programs* (Berkeley, Calif,: University of California Press, 1970).

14. W. W. Cooley and W. R. Lohnes, *Multivariate Measures for the Behavioral Sciences,* (New York: Wiley, 1962).

in Head Start I and students who attended no Head Start program were calculated. Students from Head Start II, however, outscored those from both the control and Head Start I programs in the areas of reading, arithmetic and spelling on the Stanford Achievement Tests.

Significant differences favoring the Head Start II alumni were predicted at the .01 level for all measures in the Stanford battery except for reading. The Head Start II group showed more growth in reading than did the group at the .05 level of significance and scored significantly (.01 level) higher than did Head Start I group on the same measure.

To determine differences in achievement for boys among the Head Start and control groups, the interaction portion of the group, a sex variance model was studied. F ratios indicating significant differences found on the seven measures in intelligence and achievement for the end of the first and second years of school, respectively, are given in Table 22-3.

Table 22-1
Achievement of Students in Post Head Start and
Control Groups at the End of the First School Year

| MEASURE | MEANS | | | |
	HEAD START I (N=32)	HEAD START II (N=45)	CONTROL (N=67)	F RATIO
IQ, Slossom	95.31	99.51	95.07	1.37
Reading, WRAT	20.69	19.13	17.37	2.18
Stanford	13.69	11.51	11.34	1.38
Arithmetic				
WRAT	16.97	16.78	15.98	.59
Stanford	13.88	14.71	13.87	.97
Spelling				
WRAT	15.97	15.64	16.26	.10
Stanford	13.69	11.51	11.34	1.38

No differences were observed when the means of boys' scores in each of the three groups were compared at the end of first grade. After the second year, significant differences were discovered for boys' groups in reading (.01 level), arithmetic (.05 level) and spelling (.01 level) as measured by the Stanford tests. Here, significant differences were found between boys from Head Start II and their counterparts from the control group. At the .01 level of confidence the boys from Head Start II scored higher on arithmetic, spelling and reading.

No significant difference in arithmetic achievement was indicated for the boys in Head Start II when their progress was compared to the Head Start I boys at the end of the second year. Significant differences, however,

Table 22-2
**Achievement of Students in Post Head Start and
Control Groups at the End of the Second School Year**

| | GROUP MEANS | | | |
MEASURE	HEAD START I (N=32)	HEAD START II (N=45)	CONTROL (N=67)	F RATIO
IQ Slossom	97.25	97.38	95.52	.18
Reading				
Wide Range	20.69	19.13	16.63	2.68
Stanford	18.31	22.71	18.94	10.63**
Arithmetic				
Wide Range	24.53	24.13	23.06	.68
Stanford	20.16	26.56	20.57	9.01**
Spelling				
Wide Range	22.12	25.76	21.54	2.98
Stanford	19.62	32.13	20.52	20.73**

*Significant at .05 level (F ≥ 3.06)
**Significant at .01 level (F ≥ 4.75)

favoring the Head Start II group existed in the areas of reading (.05 level) and spelling (.01 level) when the comparison was made.

When the achievement of girls was compared within the three groups, one significant difference in the area of reading was discovered at the end of the first year. Achievement of girls as measured by means of each of the tests are summarized in Table 22-4. At the .01 level of confidence girls who had attended Head Start I learned more in reading as measured by the Wide Range test than did their control group. Girls from the Head Start II group also scored significantly higher (.05 level) in reading than did their control group. At the end of the first year no difference in reading was predicted on the same instrument between the Head Start I and Head Start II girls' groups.

At the end of second grade, four measures—two of reading achievement and one in arithmetic and spelling, respectively—indicated significant differences in achievement of girls among groups. As determined by the WRAT instrument, the Head Start II girls still scored significantly higher in reading (.01 level) than did their control group. Again, no significant differences were indicated in the achievement of the Head Start I and Head Start II girls on this measure. Also, the achievement gain shown for the Head Start I group over its control group at the end of the first year had apparently disappeared. No significant difference in the reading achievement of girls in Head Start I and control groups were indicated by the Wide Range Test at the end of the second year of study.

Similar to the comparison in the boys' subgroups, significant differences

Table 22-3
Comparison of Means for Head Start Boys' Achievement with Mean
Scores of Control Group at the End of the First and Second School Years

CRITERION	HEAD START I (N=18)	HEAD START II (N=30)	CONTROL (N=37)	F RATIO
IQ, Slosson				
First Year	99.94	100.33	95.38	1.40
Second Year	101.11	100.87	95.35	1.15
Reading, Wide Range				
First Year	17.50	17.47	16.03	.33
Second Year	30.56	35.10	28.35	1.53
Reading, Stanford				
First Year	8.43	6.67	6.83	.32
Second Year	17.67	21.87	18.95	5.33**
Arithmetic, Wide Range				
First Year	16.61	16.30	14.50	1.15
Second Year	25.00	23.27	21.54	1.69
Arithmetic, Stanford				
First Year	12.94	14.13	12.32	2.45
Second Year	19.89	26.17	19.73	4.79*
Spelling, Wide Range				
First Year	13.67	14.57	14.43	.19
Second Year	10.00	13.73	12.86	.55
Spelling, Stanford				
First Year	12.06	9.97	8.65	1.66
Second Year	17.00	29.03	19.22	13.31**

**Significant at the .01 level (F = 4.87)
*Significant at the .05 level (F = 3.10)

in achievement among girls in reading, arithmetic, and spelling were indicated on the Stanford tests at the end of the second year. No differences were indicated when the girls' means from Head Start I and control groups were compared in all three areas. In all cases on the Stanford tests, girls from Head Start I showed more academic gain (significant at the .01 level) than did girls from the control group. At the .01 level of confidence girls from Head Start II also scored better in reading, arithmetic, and spelling than did girls from Head Start I on the tests.

No differences in IQ scores on the Slosson test were discovered statistically significant among any of the group means during either phase of the data analysis. Apparently the intelligence measures as indicated by this instrument remained relatively constant for all groups throughout the experiment.

In testing Hypothesis 6 by use of the discriminant analysis model, accurate group membership was predicted for 68.8 per cent of the subjects

Table 22-4
Comparison of Means for Head Start Girls' Achievement with Mean
Scores of Control Group at the End of the First and Second School Years

CRITERION	HEAD START I (N=14)	HEAD START II (N=15)	CONTROL (N=30)	F RATIO
IQ, Slossom				
First Year	89.36	97.87	91.80	.90
Second Year	92.29	98.92	95.10	1.75
Reading, WRAT				
First Year	24.79	22.47	17.07	4.17*
Second Year	37.86	51.47	32.43	3.61*
Reading, Stanford				
First Year	8.43	8.47	8.10	.01
Second Year	19.14	24.40	18.97	6.36**
Arithmetic				
First Year	17.43	17.73	15.47	1.32
Second Year	23.93	25.87	24.77	.37
Arithmetic, Stanford				
First Year	15.07	15.87	13.67	2.34
Second Year	20.50	27.33	21.70	5.08**
Spelling, WRAT				
First Year	18.93	17.80	15.63	1.98
Second Year	21.06	24.73	20.41	2.42
Spelling, Stanford				
First Year	15.79	14.60	11.30	2.55
Second Year	23.00	38.33	22.17	11.34**

*Significant at .05 level (F ≥ 3.15)
**Significant at .01 level (F ≥ 4.98)

at the end of their first year in school. At the end of the second school year, when each subject's scores were plotted against the mean discriminant score for each of the three groups—Head Start I, Head Start II, Control (control combined Control Group I and Control Group II)—the computer accurately assigned group membership to 76.5 per cent of the students. The analysis from the D^2 given in Table 22-4 when the profiles of the three groups, as determined by the seven measures of achievement and IQ collectively, are compared at the end of each of the two years gives an overall summary of group differences. Differences in Head Start II and control summary of group differences in Head Start II and Head Start I groups on the collective measure approached significance ($X^2 = 14.07$, df = 7) at the end of the first school year. Within the accepted error limits, no significant differences among the profiles of the three groups were discovered at the end of the first school year.

At the end of the second year, significant differences in the overall profiles of the students from the Head Start II and Control groups were established at the .01 level. Students from the Head Start II group on the collective profile also achieved significantly higher than did the Head Start I group alumni at the end of two years, as indicated by the D^2 or equivalent chi square statistic.

Discussion

Students who attended the Head Start II program offering comprehensive instruction in reading, language, and arithmetic and also participated in the two-year Follow Through exhibited significantly more academic gain than did the members of the control group. In most cases, also, they were achieving at significantly higher levels than were the students who had attended the Head Start featuring language only instruction and who had enrolled in the same Follow Through.

Significant gains in achievement were not indicated for the Head Start II group until the end of the second year of Follow Through and these comparative gains were generally noted on the Stanford Achievement Test data. A possible explanation for this phenomena may be that the Head Start II instructional program gave time and emphasis to teaching basic concepts which support the structure of subsequent teaching. All students, both Head Start and controls, participated in a behaviorally structured Distar program in the two years of Follow Through. This Follow Through Model is specifically designed to nurture pupil participation and to encourage total pupil involvement in highly structured learning activities. In this program the Follow Through activities apparently reinforced the experiences offered for disadvantaged students in the Head Start II program particularly well.

When an overall comparison was made among the profiles of the groups by the D^2 statistic in the discriminant analysis at the end of the first school year, differences in Head Start II and control group subjects on the collective measures approached significance ($X^2 = 14$, df = 7). Similar difference was observed in the overall profiles of the Head Start I and Head Start II groups at that time. Apparently, achievement gains by Head Start II participants were cumulative in the two years of public school to the extent that a significantly higher achievement for this group was recognized at that time. The discriminant analysis at the end of second grade demonstrated that the Head Start II alumni were distinctly superior to either the control or the Head Start I group when all growth measures taken were considered collectively as one operant variable.

With the exception of one comparison among groups, all significant gains in achievement in the Head Start groups were indicated by scores on the Stanford Achievement Tests. Head Start II girls scored significantly higher on reading as measured by WRAT at the end of both the first and second years than did their control group. Generally, though, the basic skills in students in the comprehensive Head Start program and fostered by the Distar Follow Through are discriminated better by the Stanford, rather than the WRAT battery of tests.

Since the data reported in this investigation involves outcomes from only one Head Start Center and one Follow Through program, similar studies in other locations must be done to evaluate the external validity of the generalizations observed.

It is felt, however, that these data offer substantiation for the observation that structured, long term Head Start experiences, coupled with a Follow Through program which continuously builds on these experiences, can make a significant difference in the achievement of disadvantaged rural children in their later school work.

SECTION FIVE

Are the Schools Inflexible?

Another frequently mouthed complaint is that our public schools are notorious for their stylized, stilted ways. They are—so the indictment runs—inevitably caught up in some variety of "cultural lag."

Some of these accusations are clearly valid. That many policies and practices of our public schools have not kept pace with an increasingly interdependent "future shock" world is not to be denied. Shortcomings in the area of sex education, for instance, come readily to mind.

It is sheer folly to try to *justify* some of the absence of imaginative, innovative public school measures, but the situation can, in part, be *explained*. The point can and should be argued most vigorously from a philosophic perspective, but it is an historical fact that our schools—and I dare say almost all public schools anywhere and at all times—have been established deliberately to help preserve and conserve the culture which we have evolved. (Hopefully, this evolutionary process is not narrowly ethnocentric.) Except for revolutionary conditions and/or select totalitarian regimes, public schools have always been perceived as vehicles of cultural transmission. Whether or not this conserving function is logically and morally defensible is not the issue in the present context. What is at issue is the recognition that almost all political cultures have regarded the public school as a traditional bastion of mores and folkways.

Let's grant the point that our public schools—along certain selected dimensions—have been "behind the times," indeed, in some cases quite well ossified. In this area, as in all others examined in this book, sweeping negative generalizations reflect more rhetoric than reality. The most cursory look at public higher education will illustrate the point. While some of the "student power" criticisms of the sixties and seventies were justified, the record indicates that in many significant ways, our publicly supported state colleges and universities have not been lacking in imaginative innovation. The development of agricultural research and the explosive expansion of the community colleges are but two examples among many which can be cited to refute, in part, many of the categorical condemnations which have been (and continue to be) in vogue.

On the elementary and secondary levels, too, charges of gross inflexibility are at best half truths. The selection on alternative schools reflects an increasing willingness on the part of public school policy makers and practitioners to engage in bold, innovative schooling experiments. What appears to be a burgeoning national trend is hardly indicative of a rigid, unresponsive public school system.

The other reading in this chapter suggests that innovative schooling approaches, which affect small localized groups of students, *are* being attempted. How representative this Harlem school is of teaching dedication and sensitivity it is impossible to say. Hopefully, it is (or soon will become) part of a national pattern.

23
Optional Alternative Public Schools

Vernon H. Smith

In recent years the concept of educational choice (optional schools, alternative schools—call them what you will) has penetrated deeply into the American system of education. It seems likely that in the foreseeable future many different types of schools will exist side by side within the total educational structure, each designed to meet a different set of specified learning and living needs of young people. These schools will not be competitive with nor antagonistic to one another, but rather will be complementary in effort and thrust, helping American education redeem its long-term commitment to the fullest education of every child.

While the standard school certainly will continue to be the major institution in American education, it will not be the exclusive one. Other types of schools will develop, seeking to provide more fully for the total educational needs of the community. Widespread educational options— the coexistence of many types of alternative schools and programs— should strengthen American education as a whole.[1]

The development of optional alternative public schools is based upon four simple concepts:

1. In a democratic society people should have choices about all important aspects of their lives. Our present monolithic structure for public education, in which children and youth are assigned without choice to a public school, evolved more by accident than by intent. Students, parents, teachers, and administrators should all have options among a plurality of schools.

2. Different people learn in different ways. This is all too obvious, but

Vernon H. Smith, "Optional Alternative Public Schools: New Partners in Education,"*The North Central Association Quarterly* 49, No. 3 (Winter 1975). Reprinted by permission.

1. North Central Association Task Force on Non-Standard Schools, *Proposed Policies and Standards for the Accreditation of Optional Schools and Special Function Schools,* revised first draft (December 1973), p. 1.

remember the psychology of learning is much newer than the organizational structure of the public schools. If we know that different people learn in different ways and at different times, what sense does it make to assign all the eight-year-olds in the neighborhood to one school and one classroom within that school?

3. Learning in schools should not be isolated from the world outside the school. Four national reports on secondary education published within the last year are unanimous in their criticism of the schools for isolating youth from society and for segregating youth from adults and from other age groups in the schools.

4. Those closest to the action, the individual school, should have the biggest share in the decision making. The local community, the families involved, and the teachers and administrators should all have a share in decisions that affect their lives.

Today it is no longer necessary to justify the need for alternative public schools. Since 1970, at least a dozen national reports on education have recommended the development of optional alternative public schools. Recently the *Report of the National Commission on the Reform of Secondary Education* urged that, "Each district should provide a broad range of alternative schools and programs so that every student will have a meaningful educational option available to him."

The North Central Association has already recognized the development of optional alternative public schools with the publication of *Policies and Standards for the Approval of Optional Schools and Special Function Schools,* which were approved in March 1974.

Over two thousand optional alternative public schools are in operation today, and at least several thousand more are being planned and developed throughout the country. These alternative public schools provide options for students, parents, and teachers within their communities. When I describe some of the types of alternative public schools in existence, many of you will nod to yourselves, "Oh yes, we have that." You do not have the kinds of options that we are considering here unless every family in your school district has choices among different schools in the community at no extra cost.

When a community has several optional alternative public schools available, the conventional school itself becomes one of the options. And as you might expect, it is usually the most popular option. Obviously, the advantage that the optional schools have over the earlier reforms is that they do not require consensus. The families who are satisfied with the conventional school still have that option. For those families who opt for something other than the conventional, the risk is low. If the alternative proves to be unsatisfactory for some students, they can return to the conventional school. The alternative schools will not replace the conventional or standard school. They will be complementary to it so that coupled together, the alternatives and the conventional will be able to provide educational programs that are more responsive to the needs of more students.

Types of Optional Alternative Public Schools

Because alternative public schools usually develop as responses to particular educational needs within their communities, there is no single model or group of models that would encompass their diversity. We can identify at least a dozen different models today, but the great majority would fit into the following types or into combinations of these types:

Open schools with learning activities individualized and organized around interest centers scattered throughout the building.

Schools without walls with learning activities throughout the community and with considerable interaction between school and community.

Learning centers with a concentration of learning resources in one location available to all of the students in the community. These would include such facilities as magnet schools, educational parks, and career education centers.

Continuation schools with provisions for students whose education in the conventional schools has been (or might be) interrupted. These would include dropout centers, re-entry programs, pregnancy-maternity centers, evening and adult high schools, and street academies.

Multicultural schools with emphasis on cultural pluralism and ethnic and racial awareness, and usually serving a multicultural student body.

Free schools with emphasis on greater freedom for students to determine their own educational goals and to plan appropriate learning experiences. Although this term is more frequently applied to nonpublic schools, a few are available by choice within public school systems.

Schools within schools with a small number of students and teachers involved by choice in a different educational program. This would include the *mini school* within the conventional school building and the *satellite school* at another location but with administrative ties to the conventional school. The school-within-a-school would usually belong in one of the six categories above.

A recent development has been the school that is a complex of mini-schools. Haaren High School in New York City, Quincy II in Quincy, Illinois, the New School in Cleveland Heights, Ohio and Ravenswood High School in East Palo Alto, California, are all large high schools that consist of a number of mini-schools. As far as the educational program is concerned, there is no longer an identifiable conventional school or program.

Not all alternative public schools would fall into these types. There is at least one school in which all learning activities are based on behavioral modification (Grand Rapids, Michigan) and another that is a nongraded continuous progress school (Minneapolis, Minnesota).

Many alternative schools operate as voluntary integration models within their communities—in Louisville, Kentucky; St. Paul, Minnesota; Philadelphia; and Chicago, for example.

Special function schools that serve students who are assigned or referred without choice would not be included. A school for disruptive students may be highly desirable in some communities, but it should not be confused with optional alternative public schools.

What Do These Schools Have in Common?

Whereas each alternative public school has been developed in response to needs within its community, most of them share some or all of the following characteristics:

1. As previously stated, the school provides an option for students, parents, and teachers. Usually the choice is open to all within the community, but there must always be choice for some so that the alternative school has a voluntary clientele. The school population should reflect the socioeconomic and racial makeup of the entire community. There is no need for public alternative schools that are elite or racist.

2. The alternative school has as its reason for existence a commitment to be more responsive to some educational need within its community than the conventional schools have been.

3. The alternative school usually has a more comprehensive set of goals and objectives than its conventional counter-part. Although most alternative secondary schools are concerned with basic skill development and with college and vocational preparation, they are also concerned with the improvement of self-concept, the development of individual talent and uniqueness, the understanding and encouragement of cultural plurality and diversity, and the preparation of students for various roles in society—consumer, voter, critic, parent, spouse....

4. The alternative school is more flexible, and therefore more responsive to planned evolution and change. Since the alternatives are being developed in today's age of accountability, they rely more on feedback

and formative evaluation in the development and modification of their curricula.

5. The alternative schools tend to be considerably smaller than our comprehensive high schools. The median enrollment in alternative public schools would be around two hundred. Because they are smaller, the alternatives tend to have fewer rules and bureaucratic constraints on students and teachers.

The size of both elementary and secondary schools has been increasing for the past twenty years. Critics are now suggesting that schools cannot be large and humane too. Proponents of alternative schools suggest that when students choose their school, there is a stronger loyalty to that which is chosen over that which is compulsory. Alternative schools report less vandalism and violence, less truancy, and fewer absences on the part of students (and teachers) when compared with other schools at the same level in the same school district. This may be partly because the students in the smaller school have a bigger share in determining the rules and regulations. Shared decision making is another characteristic of many of the alternative public schools.

Developing More Responsive School Systems

The development of optional alternative public schools is probably too minor a move to be called major reform. I prefer to think of it as a strategy for self-renewal. The development of optional public schools within the system is a simple and effective way to provide a total educational program that is more responsive to the needs of more families within any community.

Within every community and every public school system, the development of optional alternative schools should be considered. Many communities will find that alternatives are needed immediately; many will not. Dialogue within the community is critical so that parents, teachers, and students will understand the availability of options. After such dialogue, a decision that the community has no need for alternatives at this time is just as healthy as a decision that the alternatives are needed.

Earlier I stated that the alternative shcools would not replace, but would be complementary to, the conventional schools. Let us look at some of the ways in which these options will complement the standard program within a community.

Of course, the first and most obvious way is that these alternative schools will be responsive to the needs of some students that are not currently being met by the existing programs. Some kids need schools that provide for their different styles of learning. Some kids need small schools. Some kids need schools in which they have more opportunities for self-determinism and decision making; some kids benefit from more learning experiences in the community, including work experiences.

The alternative schools can provide an exploratory or pioneering function. We can try out innovations in the smaller school that might be resisted in the larger school, particularly if they were to involve all students and all teachers.

The alternative schools will encourage the conventional schools to look at themselves more carefully. In many communities, there are long waiting lists for admission to the alternative schools. This creates a healthy self-examination on the part of the faculties in the conventional schools.

The alternative schools provide for more community involvement in the educational process—first, through exploratory dialogue on the need for optional alternatives; second, by offering families choices and thus compelling them to make decisions; and third, by involving community members in the regular function of the alternative school.

The alternative structure provides a simple mechanism for continuous change and improvement. Already in some communities we are seeing the development of alternatives to the alternatives. The alternatives provide a structure that is more responsive without additional layers of bureaucracy.

The alternative schools can provide an exploratory or pioneering function. We can try out innovations in the smaller school that might be resisted in the larger school, particularly if they were to involve all students and all teachers.

The alternative schools will encourage the conventional schools to look at themselves more carefully. In many communities, there are long waiting lists for admission to the alternative schools. This creates a healthy self-examination on the part of the faculties in the conventional schools.

The alternative schools provide for more community involvement in the educational process—first, through exploratory dialogue on the need for optional alternatives; second, by offering families choices and thus compelling them to make decisions; and third, by involving community members in the regular function of the alternative school.

The alternative structure provides a simple mechanism for continuous change and improvement. Already in some communities we are seeing the development of alternatives to the alternatives. The alternatives provide a structure that is more responsive without additional layers of bureaucracy.

The alternative schools provide opportunities for exploring and trying a wide variety of learning facilities. They are already making use of the different kinds of space available within their communities. However, the smaller, more flexible school could become a proving ground for new concepts in school design, new combinations of hard and soft facilities, and new approaches to matching learning environments with learners and teachers.

The alternatives provide new opportunities for the cooperative development of better teacher education programs. They provide a field base for new cooperative ventures between the public schools and the teacher education institutions.

However, most important of all, the alternatives will provide educational choice within the community. Attitudes of the community toward the schools will become more positive when they see real options available. Students and parents will feel a stronger loyalty to that which is chosen. Teachers and administrators will benefit from a clientele that comes by choice, rather than compulsion.

The alternative schools provide an additional level of accountability to the school system. When alternatives are available by choice, you have a consumer market in education. When thousands of families place their children on the waiting list for a few hundred openings in the alternative schools, as is the case in several communities today, those alternatives must be meeting a perceived educational need. Community control of the schools is a highly controversial topic. Here we are talking about consumer choice, with or without community control.

I have intentionally omitted cost because there is little to say. Some alternative schools cost more; many cost less. In general, however, they operate on the same per pupil budget cost as the other secondary or elementary schools within their communities. Sometimes modest funds are necessary for planning and development; sometimes they are not. Anyone planning an alternative school should plan to operate on the regular per pupil cost of education within the community, and should avoid the use of external funds in the basic operation of the school. As a district moves to alternative schools, there may be transitional expenses just as there are minor added expenses each time a new conventional school is opened.

An Idea for which the Time Has Come

As for me, I see unity through diversity. A diversity in educational design that will permit parents moving from Houston, New York, or Los Angeles to find a curriculum program and an organizational pattern amenable to their thinking. I see absolutely no need for uniformity of organization or standardization of design. There is room in this sprawling system for alternatives and there is a place for the varied educational philosophies of both educator and patron.

To pretend that administration or supervision of these alternatives is an easy task is to display managerial ignorance. Flexibility and diversity are difficult to manage but, to me, the alternative to diversity is educationally untenable. The alternative is standardization and comformity. It is untenable because now in education we speak of uniqueness, of individuality. This mandates alternatives.[2]

Five years ago, I doubt if we could have found a single reference on the optional alternative public school. Today we can find hundreds if not thousands. To my knowledge no one was really pushing them, but here they are. To me, the most powerful and most impressive aspect of the current development of alternative public schools is the unbelievably widespread support that they have gained in such an incredibly short time, as educational changes go. I am forced to conclude that the alternative public school is "an idea for which the time has come."

---

2. Bruce Howell, *Superintendent's Bulletin*, 44, No. 2 (Tulsa Public Schools, September 4, 1973):1.

24
Innovation is Tradition in West Harlem

Henry S. Resnik

Nine eighth-graders waited nervously outside the principal's office at
Junior High School 43, in Manhattan's West Harlem. The girls, six of
them, were seated on a wooden bench and almost visibly trembling. The
three boys paced up and down or wandered occasionally into the hall, then
back. It was near 10 o'clock, the principal was late, and the small group
clearly wanted very much to conclude this visit.

The principal, George Manley, a warm and patient black man who took
charge of 43 in the middle of the 1970/71 school year, was delayed because
he was busy dealing with the week's prize crisis: The nineteen-year-old
sister of one of his students had died of a drug overdose a couple of days
earlier. Right now the principal was meeting with representatives of the
school's parents' association to discuss the matter. It was the sort of thing
that could seriously depress the morale of a school where, in the words of
one teacher, "the usual problems" had begun to make the faculty
increasingly uptight, increasingly insistent on order and discipline.

But the nine eighth-graders, all either black or Spanish-American,
happened not to be discipline problems, even though that is usually the
only reason kids in this sort of school get to see the principal. They were
waiting instead to talk with Manley and a group of parents and teachers
about redressing certain fundamental wrongs. They were fighting back, but
they were nervous. They'd never tried this kind of thing before.

Their fight had started with two eighth-grade teachers, Charles and
Gioia Shebar, who have been married for sixteen years and who have
taught for most of that time. With the principal's support, the Shebars'
classes comprised a quasi minischool with fifty-nine students in which they
had virtual carte blanche to make of the school day whatever they wanted.
What they particularly wanted was what they found the parents of their

Henry S. Resnik, "Innovation is Tradition in West Harlem," from *Saturday Review*, Aug. 19,
1972. Reprinted by permission.

students wanted: the kind of solid background in basic skills without which no student ever has a chance at academic success.

The Shebars' style blends their nuts-and-bolts, system-beating determination with casual, easy warmth and a genuine respect for their students. Last year, in addition to studying basic skills, their kids built a huge gerbil farm in an old bookshelf. Art was a daily activity. And the relationship of teachers and students in their small community—literally off in a corner of the school—was intimate enough to resemble an encounter group.

It was this atmosphere that encouraged fourteen-year-old Renee Jones to approach the Shebars last October with the proposal that if she worked hard enough she might be allowed to make up for the year she'd been left back. Renee is an unusually tall, striking-looking black girl with a keen interest in fashion and enough drive for any two people. But she had failed first grade. Now, finally, she had found a place where she could express her wish to make up for her failure.

Her failure. It doesn't do to dwell on the phrase. When Renee and the Shebars finally recruited eight others from the class for their little program, the kids all realized that their reasons for being left back fell into two general categories: either they couldn't remember, or they had only recently arrived in the country and spoke no English. Most had failed very early grades. And now they were getting a chance to make up.

The mechanism they decided on was deceptively simple. First they discussed their idea with the principal and got his approval. Then they consulted the assistant principal in charge of the ninth grade and learned exactly what they would have to do to meet criteria commensurate with the ninth-grade curriculum. And finally they set up an independent program aimed at completing both the eighth and ninth grades in one year. This involved several hours of extra work each week after school, work sessions on Saturdays at the Shebars' home (the two teachers volunteered their time), special assignments, drill work, and the compiling of a portfolio of tests, essays, and other papers. Most of the kids also read books on Africa and studied map-making skills. No fancy "innovations," no special technical wizardry, no untried miracle cures. In fact, this rather daring and unusual educational experiment really meant more of the same kinds of work—but in more intensive doses.

Belkis Suero, for example, wrote a report on Latin America, a subject that would ordinarily have been studied in ninth grade. Jose Rivera did pages of drawings and diagrams in connection with his study of the human body. Gwen James wrote a series of poems. Most of the actual work was done at home, leaving the afternoon and Saturday sessions free for planning and review.

The Shebars believe that "teaching and judgment" should be distinct from each other, and at their suggestion the eighth-graders invited a special panel to review their work and to decide whether they had earned the right to proceed to work on the ninth-grade level and thence to the tenth grade.

The panel consisted of Erwin Rosenfeld, the ninth-grade assistant principal, Maude Katz, the president of the parents' association; Luz Caban, whose daughter, Juana, was one of the group; and Principal Manley.

And so after several months of work the nine eighth-graders had arrived at the day when they would make their first presentation to the panel. The girls were dressed in their best—Renee, the leader, resplendent in a luminous orange blouse and black pants. The boys looked as if they were ready for church. And all of them carried large manila portfolios containing the papers they'd brought for the panel to examine. It seemed a little like taking orals in graduate school.

At last the principal was ready to see them. The group filed into the office and took seats at a large rectangular table. Dittoed sheets for each student listing the contents of each portfolio and the hours of extra work done were distributed to the panel members. (The sheets also included space for the panel members to record their decisions.) After much nervous giggling, everyone was finally ready.

"First of all, welcome," Mr. Manley began. His voice had the mellifluous tones of a minister—but a friendly minister, the sort one might want to chat with after the service. "Mrs. Katz, Mr. Rosenthal, and I are very pleased to greet you this morning and to say how pleased we are with the whole procedure. We in the older generation have been telling you, 'If at first you don't succeed, try, try again.' We hope you'll always continue pushing ahead."

Gioia Shebar proceeded to explain, casually mixing in fluent Spanish for the benefit of the one parent who spoke little English, that the group had asked her to say a few words before they began—that they had all been held back once, that they had written when and why on their individual dittoed sheets, and that if they were judged able to do ninth-grade work they would remain with the Shebars and be allowed to take ninth-grade tests "and other atrocities" and then take tests for entrance to high school. "Charles and I will not give an opinion," Gioia said. "And the judgment is not whether they will go to the tenth grade but whether they will be allowed to do ninth-grade work."

"Last fall I went to Mr. Shebar and asked if I could go to the ninth grade," Renee told the panel. "We have all done work at home, and we've done work on Saturdays, too. We feel that some of our group is better than the ninth-graders now." Then Renee proceeded to introduce Sondra Collier, the first of the eighth-graders to make her formal presentation.

Throughout the next hour the tone of the meeting was somewhat less formal than that of an inquisition. What had they done for extra work? The panelists asked. What books had they read recently? Why did they choose the particular high schools they'd listed on their dittoed sheets? "I read a book that Mrs. Shebar gave me," one of the boys answered at one point. "I got to page eighty, but it was a hard book."

And when one girl with an excellent record said she wanted to be a nurse, the principal countered with, "Why be satisfied with just being the assistant? Why not be the doctor?"

Finally the session was over, but the tension of that meeting lingered for almost two weeks as the principal of 43 became increasingly preoccupied with "the usual problems" and found that he had little time to make a thorough examination of the bulging folders. When he did get around to looking at them, however, he found that some bulged more than others. The Shebars had deliberately refrained from pushing their students. A few had done very little; others had submitted pounds of paper. "They had been very severely turned off to what had been happening to them in schools," Charles Shebar observed after the first meeting with the panel. "Some of them weren't achieving at all. Originally, we saw the program as a motivational device to see whether they could handle the whole thing themselves. One boy in particular did almost no work. I reminded him of it fairly often; he thought I was going to say something at the meeting of the panel. But I told him that we weren't going to say a thing, that it was up to him. Toward the end he started to understand. He suddenly began to do good work. Some worked very steadily throughout—especially the girls."

Finally, about two weeks after the first session with the panel, the eighth-grade group reassembled once again in the principal's office to hear the verdict. This time the kids were dressed in ordinary school clothes, but they seemed more nervous than before. "The panel and I have considered everything that you did," Mr. Manley told them. "We considered the work in the folders and the manner in which you responded during the interview. We want to say how much we appreciate the effort put forth by the majority of you. However, as you can see, not everybody put forth the same amount of effort." And then briefly the principal returned each student's dittoed sheet and folder with a brief comment on how he or she had done. Seven of the nine were passed to the ninth grade without qualification. The remaining two were still expected to complete more work. "But," Mr. Manley said, "clearly there's still hope. There has been no out-and-out disapproval."

As the kids filed out of the office, even the ones who weren't smiling seemed satisfied. Their expressions seemed to say that justice had indeed been done.

SECTION SIX

Public School Teachers

Critics seem to revel in characterizing the American public school teacher as a mindless, bungling sub-professional. More often than not this stereotyped creature is represented as oppressive and dogmatic, or wishy-washy, or... *you* choose the unflattering adjective! Undoubtedly, this image does correspond to some who style themselves professional educators. However, this portrait does not reflect the characteristics of most teachers. Many, if not most, are diligent, dedicated professionals who labor under frequently inadequate working conditions for a less than handsome salary.

The first reading calls attention to the remarkable dedication and compassion of an inner city public school teacher. The second reading points up, as its title indicates, that "what teachers do does make a difference."

These two selections could be supplemented by many more. Certainly, the often vilified, frequently libelled public school teacher is deserving of a better "press" than that established by many an unsympathetic contemporary critic. Our teachers are not angelic, far from it. But, neither are they diabolic. Like any and all professions, American public education has its share of "dead wood." But like these other professions, it boasts a large number .of fine practitioners who are rendering the public an outstanding service.

25
A Teacher from Detroit

An Interview with Cheryl Greene

In her mid-twenties, white, unmarried, Cheryl Greene has been teaching English at Cooley High School since September 1966. She grew up in a small, very white town near Rochester, N.Y., went to a Catholic girls' high school and to Marygrove, a Catholic women's college "which is in Detroit; that's how I got to Detroit." She had considered other occupations. "I throught teaching was what a woman did if she couldn't do anything else. But I was more interested in English than in most other things, so..." She entered the school system on trial, calmly resolved that if she found it distasteful or inwardly unrewarding she would not remain.

I like it very much. There are times when I get very excited about being here, when things look very, very hopeful. Then, sometimes I get downright discouraged. At the beginning of this semester I saw some positive things coming across, especially like individual discussions with students. They were coming to ask me if there was something they could do for a particular project, or how they could get certain courses (mostly, black studies) incorporated into the curriculum. They were showing that they wanted to do something very positive.

And of course, when we had the disturbances—everybody for a couple of days afterward just is hurt. I think that's the inward reaction, although we go to objective things to discuss, like security in the building, student committees and things like that. But we're all dealing with it at such a time from a very subjective basis, just a personal kind of discouragement. It hurts. It's disappointing.

"The disturbances" at Cooley erupted, as they did in many schools throughout the country, immediately following the assassination of Martin Luther King on April 4, 1968. At Cooley, the black students were obliged to

Reprinted by permission from *The Real Teacher*, Philip Sterling, ed., (New York: Random House, 1972), pp. 190-203. Originally titled: "Cheryl Greene, Detroit"

*confront an aggressive white youth group, Breakthrough, from outside
school. In the course of the year, black students reacted by organizational
effort to deal with issues directly affecting their lives within Cooley.*

I have thought of returning to do some more graduate work but the fact
is that, no, I don't want to go to a suburban school. I really don't. I like this
school. I think this is very exciting. I don't mean because of demonstrations
and fights; I mean exciting when good things happen, and there are many
good things. Name some? Yes. Being able to take something like Othello in
a very contemporary situation, even though maybe Shakespeare didn't
mean it to be; taking it from two points of view and having them vocalized
in the classroom.

Or coming in from a false alarm (an aspect of "the disturbances") and
having a black student come up to you and say, "That upset you, didn't it?"
And I say yes and that student says, "Let's go for a walk around the halls
and talk about it."

There are learning experiences here for me, too. Like being able to say to
a black person when something (a conflict of some kind) happens: " I feel
very prejudiced," and having that black student say,"Yeah. I know what
you mean. I do too." To me that means we could both recognize we weren't
being objective and we trust each other enough to say so.

Or today. I just came back from the post office with two students, one
black, one white. We were driving along, looking for the place, and I saw a
mailman. So I pulled up and I called out, "Sir . . ." and that didn't register.
Oliver, he's sitting alongside me, says, "Hey, brother." I was embarrassed . . . Later I said, "That man must have thought I was yelling
'Hey, brother' and he was probably wondering 'Who's she trying to kid?' "
but Oliver said, "Well, what were you calling him 'sir' for?" That Oliver,
he's really something—and it was just an awfully good moment, an awfully
positive thing. Something like that out there, that workshop, that gets me
excited.

*"Out there," is the spacious sunlit library beyond the door of the small
conference room where we are talking. A constitutional convention of
student delegates is deciding the forms, functions and powers which it will
propose to vest in the Student Union which is undergoing a long,
controversy-laden reorganization.*

I've listened all morning to what's going on . . . Many students out there
will be graduating in four weeks. They could say, "I don't care. I'm not
going to be here." Yet they're in there, talking about things that will
concern other students next year. They're dealing with issues, and very
logically. Many times we do them an injustice when we simply say, "Give us
your ideas," instead of "How would you put your ideas to work?" Because
then they're involved in the real practical aspects of it. The idea of a student

council sounds great but how are you going to make it work? When they start talking to each other about this, they realize it isn't easy and yet they're trying to be really fair about it.

This problem of student representation within the school is really difficult. A student council should be fully representative and yet it is so easy to charge them with not being so. How should it be? Students who are elected may not necessarily be involved themselves in extreme movements or extreme ideas. They can be, but they should be knowledgeable of every element within the school. They should be able to go through the halls and talk to somebody they wouldn't normally talk to and find out how he would vote on this issue and what he thinks of that question. If he is a person who is from the extreme, in one corner or another, he should be able to approach the person in the middle and find out what that person thinks, and vice versa.

What's extreme around Cooley and what's conservative?

I guess I judge it by the means which are used to achieve what you're asking for. I think some of the people who form demonstrations out in front, who are very much concerned about it being orderly but effective, are not extreme. They are taking a direct, perhaps very dramatic way of showing something, but they do not necessarily, to me, form the extreme elements, those who seem to have lack of consideration for any of the other elements involved.

What is there here to demonstrate about?

The Student Council, if they didn't think it was representative ...We have a group formed by some of the very concerned black students, Black United Front, which has proposed several lists of demands to the office: incorporation of black literature in the English courses, various workshop projects, including sensitivity workshops for the faculty. Some faculty members favor it, some feel it's a complete waste of time, some are reticent but willing to try it.

Then there are proposals for changing the cultural orientation within the building, that the names of some of the study halls should be changed to represent black figures in history. The art work in the halls could be changed because it's antiquated anyway but also because it isn't representative of their own culture; many black students feel it should be. And many of them aren't simply saying "black-oriented" but more of an international flavor (with Third World implications). And they want more of the students' own work represented on the walls. One student who graduated from here is doing murals at the request of black students in another school. This kind of thing is, you know, an excellent idea for their own relationship to the building...

One of the main issues is student representation: What is the role of the student in determining the direction of a high school...I think the demand is voiced more strongly at Cooley than in predominantly white schools. They are asking for a more immediate proof of these things coming into action, in a reality...You also might find that financially there is a greater need here for an immediate answer than in a school where the money is there and the parents want it and know they can get it right away, whereas these students feel they're really going to have to speak up to get the sort of thing they need.

We had one Saturday workshop, on a voluntary basis. About thirty-five teachers were involved in that, which is about one-fourth of the faculty, plus a few parents and students. I thought that was a very good kind of workshop. I enjoyed it very much. Another one was for the entire faculty and more students, on a much larger scale. I think everybody found it unsatisfactory. That could be because you got people who didn't want to attend. I don't know, maybe faculty people and students who were not as cooperative as they should be. Also, we had people in large groups. I'd rather see three teachers and five students go out had have a hamburger together, you know, and sit around and talk...There should be more of that than there is.

Okay, you get along well with the black students. But would you say that expressions of hostility, suspicion, by black kids toward white teachers is not uncommon?

Yes, that does happen. It's happened to me. It's a very difficult thing to deal with. If someone says you're prejudiced, what do you say—"No, I'm not!"? You can't prove it any other way than the way you act and believe. I was also accused once, by a white student, that I was "prejudiced in reverse." Prejudice—it's a charge that once made cannot be really properly refuted. How? Not by giving a better grade if it's undeserved. A person who leans over backward to prove that he isn't prejudiced is obviously probably more prejudiced...It's a really delicate issue, especially for a teacher who has worked to relieve that kind of issue...It's a very delicate thing...

Are there any prejudiced white teachers here? I would guess that that is true. But I wouldn't say it exists any more in this building than in any other. I would think that for a person who is prejudiced this situation would be extremely uncomfortable. Because certainly students are well enough aware of that kind of tendency. They have been schooled well enough in the reactions of a prejudiced person to identify it and react to it.

Teaching language and literature, what are your general goals? What are you trying to accomplish with your students?

First, clarity of thought: absolutely the most important thing, in the students' interpretation of literature and in the presentation of their own ideas. If they're going to be involved in things that are at all controversial, and they are—that's what almost every part of life is concerned with now—they've got to be able to look at something and ask, What is the basic thing

that is being said here?...If it's an idea, then I've got to look at the proof
and see what is proof. And, am I saying something when I explain my point
of view? Or am I so subjective about the fact that it's my idea that I'm going
to assume that everybody already understands it? Am I really trying to
communicate and prove it?...

In our college preparatory English course, twelfth grade, this semester
the students have done research papers on subjects of their own choosing.
We've read Thomas Hardy's *Return of the Native.* Then we took *Black
Voices,*[1] principally the short stories and poetry. Now we're doing *Othello,*
for two reasons. One, because of the idea of a supposedly tragic black
figure, and secondly, I like Shakespeare. I try to get them to like it...It's
too bad we can't do more with the crossing of time barriers in literature. I
read them a passage from *Les Miserables* about the French Revolution:
"This revolution is based on two mounds, one of suffering and one of
ideals..." and I said, "Date this. Where would it be?" They had no idea.
They were very much surprised at the date of it because it sounded so
contemporary. They were surprised how phrase after phrase in the whole
passage seems to be reflective of things they hear today. I said, "Relevance
does not necessarily mean that it has to be written in the last five years.
Relevance does not necessarily have to do with the date of the work"...

I'm concerned with form to the extent that your work should reflect what
you value in yourself, how you value yourself; that it has some kind of
dignity about it, that it shows what *you* think of what you think. Content
should be varied; it's a kind of intellectual diet. If I concentrate too much on
one area I'm doing students an injustice, even though a teacher's got to
realize that not everybody is going to like everything...

Sometimes I wish we had a setup where a teacher would teach a certain
specialized area, somewhat like the college setup, partly for the students'
sake but mainly for myself, selfishly, because there are areas— I teach
Shakespeare better than anything else; and the essay, maybe because the
concentration in thought and presentation interest me. Also American
literature, but poetry is a difficult thing for me to teach just simply as
poetry, from an anthology. I'm sure every teacher has his or her preferences
about this kind of thing. I like Sandburg and Whitman, for example,
because they are so people-oriented...

*You've got a big population of black students here who are hollering for
relevant—*

Black literature? Yes... I think Richard Wright is really fantastic in his
understanding of the psychological reactions in a man. I've read Wright
more than I have any of the other black writers. I think this is something

---

1. *Black Voices: An Anthology of Afro-American Literature,* by Abraham Chapman, with an
Introduction and Biographical Notes (New York: New American Library, 1968).

that is absolutely going to have to be incorporated into college curriculums. When I was going to college there were no courses in black literature. It would have been very pertinent for me . . . People don't seem to study things like that independently when they're busy accumulating credits toward a degree. And there simply wasn't an accredited course. I feel handicapped in my own background. You can bone up on something because you know it's important but that's not quite the same as having it taught to you in a classroom two or three years before you need to use it. I need a period of assimilation so that I can *bring something* to the material, to make it relevant.

There is some form of black literature incorporated into each semester here. This has taken place in the past year, maybe a year and a half . . . There were no real examples of black-literature study before that time (the period in which black students learned to press for curriculum changes). Part of the problem was that the teachers were not prepared, were not that knowledgeable themselves in some areas of black literature, and I'm not saying that we are now. It's a slow process[2] . . . I feel there is a great deal I'm not familiar with in respect to black literature. I think there are other teachers who know much more than I do. Two or three of them are white and a couple are black.

As far as black writers are concerned, most of the students tend to be interested in the novelists rather than the poets. The poems in the anthology we used were, I thought, a little outdated. Quite often the poets' tendency was to portray a situation and their own reactions to society, their feelings about the situation, but then counter with the idea that "this is something I must accept or that I will suffer through." I'm not saying this about the whole body of work by any poet but only of the selections in the anthology. I found in the prose writers a little more bitterness, a little more of the sense of struggle than I found in the poetry. Of course, you're dealing with the difference in approach between two types of literature. I guess the prose is just a little more effective, maybe because you become attached to a figure more closely. And maybe this is simply so for me, as a white person; I can see it better because I've been given more time to associate. A black person may be able to respond immediately to something a black poet says because he may not need this kind of building up of an empathy; it's already there.

I'm not saying that poems we took were not relevant but prose selections like Richard Wright's "The Man Who Lived Underground" or excerpts from *The Invisible Man* made a much greater impression.

I found the first time that I taught *Black Boy* there was much more response from the white students than the black—discussion,

---

2. Beginning in September 1971, Cooley planned to offer an elective course in black literature.

interpretation, questions. I was surprised. But this semester I'm getting equal response from the black students.

I gave them reading assignments in the book, and study questions to be discussed in class the next day: What was Richard Wright's first reaction to the sight of the prisoners as they came from a distance? What were the motives that went into his burning the curtains? This type of thing. Then the discussions grew from that, so we could follow the theme from the beginning of the book to where it narrowed down toward the end.

They were very honest and direct about their answers and I don't think that any of the questions skirted issues. What was Wright's own first experience or racial prejudice? He stood in line with his mother... You know. Why was his grandmother considered black when she looked as white as any of the other people he saw on the train?

Of course you have some students who are very vocal anyway and they are going to be quick to raise their hands. Yet, I think the (white) student who found black literature the most revealing might be the one I never got to know about. Many of those students who are sitting there very quietly are seeing things they never saw before. They wouldn't be comfortable enough to discuss it...

Do your students show any independent curiosity about literature?

I know I've had students who looked through my bookshelves when they stopped over at my house and who became interested in a book just because it was there. And they'd say, "Hey, can I take this?" I think this is the best way to instill an interest in literature, this casual kind of thing: "Hey, did you ever read such-and-such? Because it's a little like, or very different, from something else, with which both of us are already familiar."

Are these visits from your students casual, too?

I had one class for two semesters at Cooley. After they graduated I said I want to have you all over for dinner, so they came over one night... We sat around and talked for four hours and I'm sure I had a better time than they did. I thoroughly enjoyed it. I have had on occasion somebody call up and say, "Would it be all right if we stop over to see you?" Well, "All right. Fine." I'm not married, which makes my schedule more flexible, of course. I don't think that the hours I spend here can be spent with total informality, but I've always felt that my free hours are their hours and that's a time to talk, to fool around and they can just come in here; that's fine. The paperwork I can always do at home. It depends on a teacher's personal life. If she's married, with four or five kids, that's something else, and it doesn't mean she isn't a good teacher. But much of the contact, like going to the post office with those two students today, that was more a part of the whole thing of being a teacher than any formal class. I have found that personal feeling is—so much.

Usually the kids call me because they're involved in Student Council work which takes place after school hours. Sometimes it's kind of like being a parent. You drop 'em off at a meeting and then they call you up when they're ready to come home and you pick 'em up and take 'em home. There was a time at the beginning of the semester when it was not unusual to be in the building from seven A.M. until ten thirty at night. Maybe go home and get something to eat and come back. But a person can't do that every day.

Personal feeling counts for so much in what respects? How?

We've had a Community Council here, comprising representatives of the teaching staff, the Student Council, the student newspaper, the parents, the community. It's not functioning now. One of the meetings . . . it —it was re-e-ally involved. There was so much conflict. It was just very disturbing and I thought, Oh, I want to leave; but I had to take some of the kids home afterward. I got in the car feeling almost hopeless about the general situation at Cooley High School: I just don't care. It's so sticky. Why get involved? Then the kids got in and we started talking about the value of the faculty workshop, about the suspension of a student, about the representation of students before the administration and the school board—many points. We talked. Any my attitude changed entirely, toward teaching, toward the issues. At that big meeting, where you'd think there would be the most objectivity, people were just making their own point. But when we got together in a small group where we knew everybody liked everybody else, we just dealt with the issues objectively. We (Cheryl Greene and the students in the car) had opposite views. Both sides, if you want to call them sides, stayed with their own opinion, but the thing was that each side could see there were other points of view that had to be dealt with.

Is the division of opinion on the issues in and around Cooley mostly a racial division?

There is obviously an element of race involved. But I don't say, and I've really talked to lots of students about this, that the division was that clear among the students. The issue can be racial but the people who are taking sides don't necessarily take sides along the racial division. We (the Student Council) were talking about the (established) school paper and the (new) Student Council newsletter. Is the newsletter going to conflict with the paper, compete with it? Some people made the charge that the paper was white-oriented, therefore the newsletter should be black-oriented. Now, this is a racial issue. But at the meeting a white student came to talk for the Black United Front, and a black student who was on the paper talked for the paper . . . These situations are never *simply* racial. They aren't simply one issue. There's so much division within a person about what he thinks is right, or what he believes or how he would react to a certain situation. The fact that you've got a friend, you take gym with her or something. And then you're thrown into a demonstration where the black students are outside and the white students are inside . . . The kinds of decisions that these students have to make place a great deal of pressure on them to know themselves, and what they believe in and how they're going to react in a certain situation, and dealing with things that I never had to deal with. I mean, it's just unbelievable, the kind of issues and the kinds of contradictions they face every day.

What is the essential contradiction at Cooley, and at similar schools?

I'd only be guessing. I would say (a twenty-second pause) maybe (another pause, eight seconds) present situation versus past situations — uh—for everybody.

26
What Teachers Do Does Make a Difference

Jane A. Stallings

Do classroom practices make a difference in how children grow and develop? In order to answer this kind of question, the government over the past seven years has funded a group of planned educational experiments. A variety of educational theories have been put into practice in a program called Follow Through Planned Variations.

The program began when the government invited educators to submit plans for establishing their various teaching models in public schools in order to test whether their individual approaches could improve the educational achievement of economically disadvantaged children. From the group who came forward, twenty-two were eventually selected to implement their programs in the Follow Through study. These educators are called "sponsors" because they each sponsored a particular model of education. Although the project varied somewhat from year to year, ultimately Follow Through models were implemented in 154 Follow Through projects within 136 urban and rural communities in all regions of the country.

The theory and practices proposed by the various educational sponsors were quite diverse, and from the program's inception in 1969, government agencies and educators asked: "Does planned variation exist, and, if so, how do the various educational programs effect children?"

The purpose of a recent report by Stallings and Kaskowitz was to study the classroom implementation[1] of seven Follow Through sponsors' models to evaluate whether or not the planned variations were in existence. Three

Jane A. Stallings, "What Teachers Do Does Make a Difference—A Study of Seven Follow Through Educational Models," (original title), reprinted by permission from *Perspectives on Education,* Allen B. Calvin, ed., (Reading, Mass.: Addison-Wesley Publishing Co., 1977), pp. 49-66.

1. Implementation means the ability of the sponsor to teach inservice teachers to use the materials and methods the sponsor has specified. The sponsor's staffs trained inservice teachers through the use of video tapes, workshops, demonstrations, discussions, observation sessions in model schools, and self-reports.

previous studies of Follow Through implementations were limited to one or two locations per sponsor. With such small samples, few generalizations could be made regarding the sponsors' performances at other locations. Realizing that a study of greater scope was needed in order to make generalizations regarding the sponsors' ability to implement their models in many locations, the Office of Education commissioned the Stallings/Kaskowitz study, which is summarized here. (The study assessed the impact of the various classroom instructional processes used by sponsors on the growth and development of children, as well as the implementation of the Follow Through sponsors' programs in the classrooms.)

(The data presented in this report were collected in the spring of 1973 in thirty-six project locations.) The sample represents approximately twenty first-grade and twenty third-grade classrooms for each of seven Follow Through sponsors, at five or more sites per sponsor. Program implementation in the classroom was judged on the basis of two criteria: (1) the extent to which a sponsor's classrooms were found to be uniform on selected implementation variables, and (2) the extent to which a sponsor's classrooms differed from the traditional Non-Follow Through classrooms on the same set of variables.

Classroom Implementation

Methodology Used in the Study of Implementation

The first step in the assessment of classroom implementation was to describe each educational model in detail. The model descriptions were prepared by The Standard Research Institute and reviewed by the sponsors and then revised according to the sponsor's specifications. With assistance from Follow Through sponsors, an observation instrument was developed to collect data that would describe each sponsor's educational program. The observation instrument recorded information regarding the materials used in the classroom, the activities that occurred, the grouping of adults and children, and the interactions that occurred between the adults and children.

After the observation instrument was developed, training materials were prepared and observers from each location were trained to at least a 70-percent reliability on all sections of the observation instrument.

Data were collected at each location using the observation instrument. From these data, variables were created to see whether or not critical components of each sponsor's model could be observed in the classrooms. For example, were children in models that tried to teach inservice teachers to provide individualized instruction receiving more such instruction than children in traditional classrooms? A list of variables was prepared by the staff that described representative elements of each model. Each sponsor was sent the list of variables and asked to rate each variable according to (1) its critical importance to her or his model, and (2) the frequency with which the variable was expected to occur in a conventional classroom. Thus, a list of variables was selected for each of the seven models. Admittedly, the critical list of variables describes a sponsor's model only in part and there is considerable overlap among the critical variables (see Table 26-1). Some of the important subtle processes of the programs, such as developing self-motivation in students or concepts of time and space, have not been assessed. Reducing a model of a list of variables can provide only a partial picture of implementation.

Since the Follow Through Programs are intended to be innovative and to represent alternatives to the conventional classroom, a pool of Non-Follow Through classrooms was used as the standard from which Follow Through classrooms were expected to differ in specified ways. The standards were established separately for first and third grades.

For each sponsor's classroom, an implementation score was computed for each variable of each sponsor. Table 26-2 illustrates the computations for one variable, "Wide Variety of Activities," for one sponsor (Far West Laboratory). A total implementation score for each classroom was also computed.

To measure how well each Follow Through sponsor's model was implemented in the classrooms, a total score was computed for each Non-Follow Through classroom using each sponsor's set of implementation variables. The average score of all Non-Follow Through classrooms was reported for each sponsor's set of variables. Comparisons were made separately for first and third grades to show the differences between the Follow Through sponsors' classrooms and the Non-Follow Through classrooms.

Implementation Findings

Implementation was judged on two criteria: (1) Were the sponsors' classrooms different from the comparison Non-Follow Through classrooms? (2) Were the sponsors' classrooms similar to each other in the frequency of specified processes used? In other words, do all four first grades in Salt Lake City have similar scores on the variables and do the four first grades in Berkeley have scores similar to first grades in Salt Lake? (See Table 26-2.)

On the first criterion, all seven of the sponsors' implementation mean scores for both grade levels differed significantly from the Non-Follow Through classroom means. For the most part, on the second criterion the twenty first grades and twenty third grades of each sponsor appeared remarkably similar regardless of the site. There were some instances for

Table 26-1

List of Critical Variables Selected by Sponsors

No.	Description	Far West Labs	University of Arizona	Bank Street	University of Oregon	University of Kansas	High Scope	EDC
24	Child selection of seating and work groups	X	X	X			X	X
25	Games, toys, play equipment present	X	X	X			X	X
39	General equipment, materials present	X				X		X
65	Guessing games, table games, puzzles		X			X	X	
66	Numbers, math, arithmetic	X	X	X	X	X	X	X*
67	Reading, alphabet, language development	X	X	X	X	X	X	X*
70	Sewing, cooking, pounding		X				X	
71	Blocks, trucks						X	
74	Practical skills acquisition	X†						
83	Wide variety of activites, over one day	X	X	X			X	X
86	Teacher with one child	X	X	X			X	
87	Teacher with two children			X				
88	Teacher with small group		X	X	X	X	X	
92	Aide with one child	X		X				
94	Aide with small group		X	X	X	X	X	
114	One child independent	X	X	X	X	X		X
115	Two children independent							X
116	Small group of children independent	X		X				X
239	Math or science equipment / Academic Activities	X		X			X	X
240	Texts, workbooks / Academic Activities				X	X	X	

*Third grade only.

†First grade only.

(cont'd)

Variables No.	Description	Far West Labs	University of Arizona	Bank Street	University of Oregon	University of Kansas	High Scope	EDC
343	Child to adult, all verbal except response	X	X	X	X		X	X
344	Individual child verbal interactions with adult	X	X	X	X	X	X	X
350	Child questions to adults			X				
363	Child group response to adult academic commands/requests or direct questions				X			
372	Child presenting information to a group			X			X	
375	Adult instructs an individual child	X						X
376	Adult instructs a group				X			
390	Adult task-related comments to children	X		X				X
394	All adult acknowledgment to children				X	X	X	
398	All adult praise to children		X		X	X	X	
412	Adult feedback to child response to adult academic commands/requests, questions				X	X		
420	Adults attentive to a small group	X			X		X	
421	Adults attentive to individual children	X	X	X	X	X	X	
423	Positive behavior, adults to children	X	X	X				
435	Total academic verbal interactions				X			
438	Adult communication or attention focus, one child	X		X		X	X	X
440	Adult communication or attention focus, small group				X		X	
444	Adult movement	X						
450	All child open-ended questions							X

(cont'd)

Table 26-1 (cont'd)

No.	Description	Far West Labs	University of Arizona	Bank Street	University of Oregon	University of Kansas	High Scope	EDC
451	Adult academic commands/requests and direct questions to children	X			X	X		
452	Adult open-ended questions to children		X	X			X	X
453	Adult response to child's question with a question						X	X
454	Child's extended response to questions			X			X	
456	All child task-related comments	X	X				X	
457	All adult positive corrective feedback	X	X		X	X		
460	All child positive affect	X	X					X
469	All adult reinforcement with tokens					X		
509	Child self-instruction, academic				X*			
510	Child self-instruction, objects			X			X	X
513	Child task persistence			X		X	X	
514	Two children working together, using concrete objects						X	
515	Small group working together, using concrete objects						X	
516	Social interaction among children	X		X				X
574	Child movement	X		X				X
599	Child self-instruction, nonacademic	X	X				X	
	Total number of Critical Variables	28† 27*	21	27	16† 17*	17	29	20† 22*

*Third grade only.
†First grade only.

some sponsors where one site or one or two classrooms had implementation scores as low as, or, in one case, lower than Non-Follow Through. However, considering the diverse locations and the enormous task of making educational theory come alive consistently in the classrooms, we conclude that the seven models have been implemented to a remarkable degree.

Classroom Processes and Child Outcomes

The study of implementation would be of little importance if we did not believe that differing educational theory and practices affect children differently.

Like educators in general, Follow Through sponsors feel that the development of basic skills in reading and computing is important, but that it is also desirable for children to develop such attributes as task persistence, attending ability, cooperation, inquiry behavior, and independence. While these attributes appear to be elusive, we have been able to operationally define and systematically observe some of these behaviors.

Child Behavior

In a study based on 105 first-grade classrooms observed and tested in the spring of 1973, we are finding some interesting relationships between classroom processes used by the teacher and observable behaviors on the part of the children. These relationships have been adjusted to take account of entering ability. The classroom process data were collected on different days from the observed child behavior data. We do not know whether the findings are causal relations, but they do suggest hypotheses to test. The desirable child behaviors that will be discussed in this paper are independence, task persistence, cooperation, and question asking. Twenty-eight classroom process variables were correlated with these child behaviors.

In our study, independence is defined as a child or children engaged in a task without an adult. This type of independent behavior is more likely to be found in classrooms where teachers allow children to select their own seating and groups part of the time, where a wide variety of activities are available, and where an assortment of audiovisual and exploratory materials are available (see Table 26-3). The adults provide individual attention and make friendly comments to the children.

Fewer independent children are found in classrooms where textbooks and workbooks are used relatively more frequently. Fewer independent children are found in classrooms where adults ask relatively more direct questions regarding the subject matter. Fewer independent children are

Table 26-2
Wide Variety of Activities, Over One Day (Variable 83)

Sites	First-grade classrooms with implementation scores of					Third-grade classrooms with implementation scores of				
	Poor	Fair	Good	Very good	Excellent	Poor	Fair	Good	Very good	Excellent
Berkeley, Calif.				4					1	3
Duluth, Minn.			3	1					1	3
Lebanon, N.H.				4						4
Salt Lake City, Utah				4				1	1	2
Tacoma, Wash.				4				2	1	1
Total Classrooms			3	17				3	4	13
Percentage of classrooms				15%	85%			15%	20%	65%

found in classrooms where adults praise children a lot (the variable describes praise in general, not for specific tasks or achievement).

The negative relationship between praise and independence is very high. This finding appears to support John Holt's description in *How Children Fail* of the child who is dependent upon teacher's praise. Holt says such children are "teacher watchers"— they pitch their ears to what the teacher wants rather than behaving independently in relation to their own thoughts or tasks. This suggests that if teachers want to help children become independent in working on tasks, they should use praise sparingly and specifically.

However, praise does not affect all outcome measures in the same way. There is a positive correlation between praise for academic achievement and reading and math scores. A more thorough study of the relationship of praise to achievement in math showed that first-grade children in classrooms where the average entering ability was low had achievement scores in math that were more positively related to praise than did first-grade children in classrooms where the entering ability was higher. Third-grade children were less affected by praise.

The next dimension we will consider is task persistence. For this study, task persistence is defined as a child engaged in self-instruction over a designated period of time (a matter of a few minutes or more). If the child becomes engaged in a conversation with someone else during the task, task persistence is no longer present, and the observer no longer codes task persistence. The highest positive relationships indicate that task persistence occurs most often when textbooks and workbooks are used in the classroom. Where adults instruct one child at a time, the children are also likely to be more task persistent. This may be because young children often have difficulty understanding group instructions. However, in settings where adults work on a one-to-one basis, children can have a question answered or directions clarified and then persist in the task at hand.

For this study, cooperation is defined as two or more children working together on a joint task. This kind of cooperation is more likely to be found in classrooms where a wide variety of activities occur throughout the day, where exploratory materials are available, and where children can choose their own groupings. If the adults interact with two children, asking questions and making comments about the task, the children seem to be encouraged to join each other in cooperative tasks. In classrooms where textbooks and workbooks (which a child uses by himself or herself) are used a great deal, fewer children are coded as cooperating. (The negative correlation is strong.)

Educators have long recognized the value of a child's asking questions as a primary means to gain information. Previous research indicates that question-asking is positively related to test scores. In our study, we found that first-grade children asked more questions where there was a one-to-one relationship between an adult and a child in the classroom, where adults responded to children's questions, and where adults made general conversational comments to children. Children asked fewer questions in classrooms where adults focused their communication toward a small group.

Our observations indicate that the Educational Development Center's Open Education Program, Far West Laboratory's Responsive Educational Program, the University of Arizona's Tucson Early Education Model, and High/Scope's Cognitively Oriented Curriculum Model, all of which try to help children become independent and cooperative, have succeeded in their efforts. These Follow Through children are independent and do cooperate with each other more often than do the children in comparison Non-Follow Through classrooms. The children in the Bank Street College of Education Approach and EDC's Open Education Program were observed to show more pleasure through laughter and smiles than do comparison children in Non-Follow Through classrooms. Children in classrooms using Far West's Responsive Educational Program and University of Arizona's Tucson Early Education Model ask questions more often than do comparison children in Non-Follow Through classrooms.

Test Scores

In a study of 105 first-grade and 58 third-grade classrooms in the fall of 1973, we found that several classroom processes are related to achievement

Table 26-3
Partial Correlations of Instructional Variables and Child Behaviors (Fall 1971 WRAT Partialed Out)

Instructional Variables	Independence		Task persistence		Cooperation		Child questions	
	Corre-lation	Signifi-cance level	Corre-lation	Signifi-cance level	Corre-lation	Signifi-cance level	Corre-lation	Signifi-cance level
Child/Adult ratio	.23	.02	.09		.02		-.15	
Children select groups and seats part of the time	.36	.001*	-.22	.03	.19	.05	.03	
Instructional materials used	-.01		.11		.09		-.07	
Audiovisual equipment used	.13		-.25	.01	.15		-.12	
General equipment and materials	.22	.02	-.08		.09		.005	
Total resource materials used	.13		-.23	.02	.18		.03	
Wide variety of activities occur concurrently	.22	.03	-.12		.15		.09	
Wide variety of activities occur during the day	.43	.001	-.36	.001	.32	.002	.14	
An adult with one child	.57	.001	-.16		.08		.14	
Use of TV	-.03		-.10		-.11		-.03	
Audiovisual equipment used in academic subjects	.24	.01	-.25	.01	-.01		-.04	
Exploratory materials used in academic subjects	.34	.001†	-.22	.03	.27	.006	-.11	
Math or science equipment used in academic subjects	-.18		.17		-.18		.11	

Instructional Variables	Independence		Task persistence		Cooperation		Child questions	
	Correlation	Significance level	Correlation	Significance level	Correlation	Significance level	Correlation	Significance level
Textbook and workbooks used in academic subjects	−.33	.001	.31	.002	−.49	.001	−.04	
Puzzles and games used in academic subjects	.16		−.07		.09		−.07	
Adults asking children questions	−.17		.03		−.17		−.04	
Adult instructs an individual child	−.09		.23	.02	−.17		.22	.05
Adult comments to children	.22	.03	−.12		−.13		.36	.001
Adult task-related comments to children	.12		−.24	.02	.39	.001	−.16	
Adult acknowledges children	−.16		.15		−.11		.04	
Adult praises children	−.60	.001	.20	.05‡	−.21	.03	.02	
Adult speaks to one child	−.01	NS§	.13		−.06		.38	.001
Adult speaks to two children	.29	.003	−.13		.28	.004	−.03	
Adult speaks to a small group	−.15		.19	.05	.01		−.32	.001
Adult asks direct question about subject matter	−.41	.001	.07		−.28	.005	.03	
Adults ask open-ended thought-provoking questions	.16		−.12		.13		−.07	

*.001 = 1 chance in 1000 that the relationship would occur by chance.
†.01 = chance in 100 that the relationship would occur by chance.
‡.05 = 5 chances in 100 that the relationship would occur by chance
NS = Not Significant
Note: Number of Classroom units used in the correlation computations = 102.

test scores as tested on the Metropolitan Achievement Test in reading and math (MAT). Test scores were adjusted to account for differences in scores children received on the Wide Range Achievement Test when they first entered school.[2] Statistical tests were computed to see whether children in classrooms with high test scores were taught in similar ways; that is, did their teachers use similar instructional processes.

In first-grade classrooms, we found that children with higher test scores were most often taught in small groups of three to eight children. In third-grade classrooms, children with higher test scores were taught in larger groups of nine or more children.

Another finding indicated that children had higher test scores in classrooms where teachers more often used a stimulus-response-feedback interaction. In this kind of instructional process, the teacher provides a bit of information and asks a question about the information; the child responds, and the teacher immediately lets the child know whether the response is right or wrong. If the child is wrong, the child is guided to the correct answer (positive corrective feedback). If the child is correct, praise, a token, or some form of acknowledgment is given by the teacher to the child. This type of interaction is related to higher test scores in reading and math in both first and third grades.

Child self-instruction and task persistence are correlated with reading and math achievement. Also, in classes where social studies are taught, there is a positive relationship with reading scores. Obviously, reading skills are used in social studies projects, but it is interesting to note that just the occurrence of social studies activities improves reading scores. In addition, the use of instructional aids such as programed materials, Cuisenaire rods, or Montessori materials is positively correlated with math scores.

Variables describing the average amount of time children spent in reading or math (either formal or informal) were highly correlated with math and reading achievement. A study of third-grade children's ability when they entered school indicated that the amount of time a child spent in math was more closely related to achievement in classrooms where the children's entering school ability was lower than in classrooms where the children's entering school ability was higher. This finding suggests that third-grade teachers should allocate more time to children who had lower scores when they entered school than to those who had higher scores. The relationship of praise to achievement in math was similar. This type of interaction treatment study could be useful in planning educational programs to enhance the learning of children with differing abilities.

University of Oregon and University of Kansas, both structured models

---

2. These are called adjusted gain scores.

that instructed teachers to use the processes described above, have the highest scores of all sponsors in first-grade reading, and University of Kansas has the highest score in first-grade math. In third grade, the University of Oregon has the highest scores in both reading and math.

In general, a low absence rate, high independence, and high scores on Raven's Coloured Progressive Matrices (a test of nonverbal perceptual problem solving) tend to be associated with the more flexible classroom where a wide variety of materials are used, many different activities occur, and children are allowed to select their own groups and seating part of the time. In these more flexible classrooms, adults interact with children on a one-to-one basis, questions are more open ended, and children show more verbal initiative. Far West, University of Arizona, Bank Street, High/Scope, and Educational Development Committee use these processes. For the most part, children in these model classrooms have higher scores on the Raven's, lower absence rates, and show more independence than do children in either University of Kansas or University of Oregon, which are classified as structured models.

The Intellectual Achievement Responsibility Success Scale shows a positive correlation with variables describing the more open classrooms. Our results indicate that children from the more flexible classrooms take responsibility for their own success but not for their failure. Children from the more highly structured classrooms take responsibility for their own failure, but attribute their success to their teacher's compentence or other forces outside themselves.

Outcomes Explained by Entering Ability and Classroom Processes

Whether or not classroom procedures affect the growth and development of children has been seriously questioned by other researchers such as Coleman, Jencks, Herrnstein, Moynihan, and Mosteller. Their research has indicated that a child's entering aptitude is of primary importance and, in fact, governs what the child will achieve in school. The study reported here, however, found that observed classroom procedures contributed as much to the explanation of test score differences as did the initial ability of children. Table 26-4 presents findings from a stepwise regression where the Wide Range Achievement Test score was entered into the regression first. The third and seventh columns report that part of the differences in test scores is explained by what the teacher does in the classroom; these are called the classroom process variables.

In both first and third grades, child behavioral outcomes were only slightly explained by entering aptitude. As might be expected, these behaviors were much more related to classroom processes.

Very little of the absence rate was explained by entering ability, in either first or third grade. Approximately 60 percent of the variance was

Table 26-4
Summary Statistics for the Stepwise Regression Analyses

Outcome Variable	First grade (N = 105)				Third grade (N = 58)			
	R² WRAT	R² WRAT, Process variables	Process variables (unique)	Number of process variables (included in regression)*	R² WRAT	R² WRAT process variables	Process variables (unique)	Number of process variables (included in regression)*
Behavioral Outcome Variables								
Child questions	.00	.28	.28	2	.00	.29	.29	3
Self-esteem	.00	.48	.48	5	.01	.42	.41	6
Child independence	.00	.67	.67	5	.01	.41	.40	3
Task persistence	.00	.44	.44	9	.06	.61	.55	6
Cooperation	.00	.32	.32	2	.10	.61	.51	5
Verbal initiative	.00	.22	.22	3	.00	.38	.38	2
Days Absent	.01	.67	.66	14	.07	.69	.62	6
Test Outcome Variables								
MAT math	.32	.74	.42	10	.17	.81	.64	8
MAT reading	.50	.73	.23	8	.42	.79	.37	7
Raven's	—	—	—	—	.41	.86	.45	9
IAR—success	—	—	—	—	.18	.57	.39	4
IAR—failure	—	—	—	—	.04	.83	.79	11

* These columns contain the number of process variables that entered the stepwise regression with an "F-to-enter" that was significant at .05.

explained by the instructional procedures used in the classroom, suggesting that what occurs in classrooms is related to whether or not the child stays away from school.

The achievement of children in math at the end of first grade can be attributed in part to their ability as it was measured when they entered school, but even more so by the instructional practices used by their teachers. In first grade, entering ability accounts for approximately 40 percent of the achievement (Table 26-4). By the third grade, less of the achievement can be attributed to entering school ability and more to classroom practices.

One of the most important findings centers around the Raven's test of nonverbal reasoning or preceptive problem solving (considered to be a culture-fair test of fluid intelligence). The abilities required to function well on this test have not been considered to be influenced by environment. This study found that ability to perform well on the Raven's test was related to the classroom environment and strongly suggests that children who, for a period of three years, have been in classrooms that use a wide variety of activities and provide a wide variety of manipulative materials have learned to see the relationship between parts and wholes. At any rate, they learn to see spatial relationships similar to those tested on the Raven's.

Summary and Conclusions

Our evaluation suggests that it is possible to find out what a teacher can do to bring about desired child behaviors. In the more academically oriented classrooms, where there is a high rate of drill, practice, and praise and where the children are more frequently engaged in reading or math activities, the gain scores on reading and math are higher. These children also take more responsibility for their failure as tested on the Intellectual Achievement Responsibility Scale. These findings are supported by the fact that the sponsors that use these processes in their classrooms (University of Oregon and University of Kansas) also have higher scores on these tests.

In the more open, interdisciplinary classrooms, where a wide variety of activities are occurring, where a wide variety of materials are available, and where children can select their own groupings part of the time and engage in activities without adults, children have higher scores on the Raven's perceptual problem-solving test. They are also absent less often, and take more responsibility for their success as measured on the Intellectual Responsibility Scale. They are more independent, cooperate more often, and ask more questions.

Classroom instructional processes (what teachers did) predicted as much or more of the outcome score variances as did the entering school test scores of children. On the basis of these findings, we conclude that what occurs within a classroom does contribute to achievement in basic skills, good attendance, and desired child behaviors.

SECTION SEVEN

Public Schools and Social Ills

An area where the public school is presumably vulnerable is its record of inducing, or not inducing, desirable changes in the culture at large. In this regard, critics have accused the schools of having failed to help rid us of everything from juvenile delinquency to banal taste in art. Whether or not some of these allegations are partially valid, one thing is crystal clear: they are frequently simplistic. In too many cases, it is assumed naively that there exists a clear cause-and-effect relationship between what the school does (or does not do) and a particular social condition. It takes little imaginative reflection to realize that social problems are infinitely complex and that what the school does or does not do is but one variable which impinges upon these conditions. Many critics conveniently seem to forget that the school is but one part of a rich, organic whole. Whatever might be the schools' potential role in helping rid us of social ills— hopefully it *is* significant—there are some, such as our first writer here, who insist that the school will contribute to this alleviation only when other institutions are 'ready' for the desired change.

Whether Levin's analysis is essentially sound is a matter of a great deal of scholarly dispute. As the companion reading demonstrates, there have been other prominent educational spokespersons who insist that yes, the school *can* rather singlehandedly induce social change through cultivating the process of reflective inquiry.

Is Levin right? Is Counts right? Obviously, we cannot know with any degree of precision. Our response depends in large measure on our particular historical and philosophic disposition. Hopefully, one thing is clear from this brief excursion: our public schools must be examined within the total social and cultural fabric. To refrain from so doing—as has been the wont of many critics who feel the schools need but wave a magic wand and social problems will vanish—is to articulate a naive, destructive position.

27
Educational Reform and Social Change

Henry Levin

In virtually every modern society, educational reform is expected to generate social reform—a view which implies that the educational system can be shaped and used as a tool of social engineering to transform society. In this paper I shall argue, however, that significant changes in education occur only as a consequence of changes in the overall social, economic, and political relations that characterize a polity; no set of educational reforms will succeed if they violate the major tenets of our social, economic, and political system. In any stable (nonrevolutionary) society the educational system will always be a major vehicle for transmitting the culture and preserving the status quo, academic debates and utopian visions notwithstanding.

Does Society Dominate the Schools?

Much of the literature and debate on educational reform (e.g., Silberman)[1] is grounded upon the rarely explicit assumption that the limits of the schools' ability to change society are conditioned only by the limits of our imagination and the difficulties of obtaining consensus. In contrast, I shall argue that schools exist as an agent of the larger social, economic, and political context which fosters them. Accordingly, they correspond to the institutions of the larger society and serve the functions which are assigned to them for reproducing the social, economic, and political relationships

Reproduced by special permission from *The Journal of Applied Behaviorial Science.* "Educational Reform and Social Change,": by Henry M. Levin, Vol. 10, No. 3, pp. 304-320, Copyright by NTL Institute for Applied Behaviorial Science, 1974. An earlier version of this paper was prepared for the Conference on "The Public Interest in Education: Toward a Policy for the United States." sponsored by the Center for the Study of Democratic Institutions, Santa Barbara, California, March 19-20, 1973.

1. Charles B. Silberman, *Crisis in the Classroom,* New York: Random House, 1970.

reflected in the prevailing institutions and ideologies.[2] As such, schools serve society, and meaningful educational reform is not possible. In brief, the former view suggests that schools dominate society; the latter, that society dominates its schools.

Which view is more correct? The attractiveness of the former is considerable. Schools have been such a salient factor in the lives of all educated people that we tend to assume that they are a principal, independent force for determining the shape of society. It is little wonder that students who opposed the war tried to destroy universities rather than munitions plants. The frustration caused by a nonresponsive government was visited upon the father figure of the school.

In addition to the psychological underpinnings of movements for educational reform, there is also the compulsion of logic, which argues that if we change the modes of schooling we change the modes of socialization, and if we alter socialization patterns we alter social institutions. Although the argument seems sound, it assumes that schools can be modified independently of the demands placed on them by the dominant political, economic, and social institutions—an argument which lacks empirical support.

Finally, a romantic image of schools, promulgated by the early works of such philosophers as Horace Mann and Henry Barnard, persists. Thus Silberman views the 'crisis in the classroom' as only a lack of good ideas and commitment—and so does his revisionist adversary, Colin Greer.[3] After attempting to demonstrate that schools have historically served to reproduce the class structure, Greer concludes that if only they would pay more attention to their lofty rhetoric of equality they would succeed. Underlying both points of view is the romantic notion that the schools can remake society.

Our psychological dependency on schools and the apparent logic and romantic tradition of school reform lend strong support to the view of schools as a mechanism of social change. Accordingly, the remainder of this paper argues that, though schools adapt to changes in the polity, the traditional view that school reform can effect change in the sponsoring society is an improbable and unsupported one.

The Correspondence Principle

The most important tenet underlying my approach is the

---

2. S. Bowles, "Unequal Education and the Reproduction of the Social Division of Labor." In Martin Carnoy (Ed.), *Schooling in a Corporate Society*. (New York: David McKay, 1972, pp. 36-64).

3. C. Greer, *The Great School Legend* (New York: Basic Books, 1972).

correspondence principle, which suggests that the activities and outcomes of education serve and therefore mirror those of society at large. Indeed, this correspondence should be evident across societies, in that differences in their social relationships should be discernible in their schools.[4] Specifically, if a society supports inequities in political, economic, and social status, those inequities will be expressed in unequal educational outcomes, e.g., schooling attainment for various student populations and differences in the quality of education provided. Moreover, we would expect to find that the financing, governance, and operations of schools reinforce those inequalities rather than mindlessly reproducing them.[5]

Stated more strongly, we would expect to find that if a society emphasizes competition and authoritarian relationships, then its schools will reflect those attributes.[6] If the work force requires workers to labor for extrinsic rewards and to accept alienation from and boredom with their work, then schools will prepare their children by socializing them to and legitimating those conditions. It takes little imagination to see the correspondence between grades for school performance and wages for work performance; between the alienation and boredom of the assembly line and the classroom; between the competition among students for grades and among workers for advancement; and between the teacher's imposition of his values in the classroom and the boss's on the job (neither has the legitimacy of authority that results from a democratic election).

The validity of the correspondence principle is only apparently contravened by the publicly declared intentions most countries assign their schools. Thus, if schools invest far more in the children of the rich than in the children of the poor, this is a better indicator of intent than the liturgy of equal opportunity.[7] If tracking and curriculum sort and select children in such a way that the children of low-income or welfare parents and the children of the elite are socialized for positions consonant with their class or origin, then we need not torture our senses by suggesting that these are inconsistent with intent. In a mature and long-standing institution, its actual operations and outcomes can be considered the best reflection of the true intent of that institution.

---

4. U. Bronfenbrenner, *Two Worlds of Childhood: U.S. and U.S.S.R.* (New York: Russell Sage Foundation, 1970).

5. Silberman, *Crisis in the Classroom,* states unequivocally: "What makes change possible, moreover, is that what is mostly wrong with the public schools is due not to venality or indifference or stupidity, but to mindlessness" (p. 10).

6. For an analysis of some of these attributes see R. Dreeben, *On What Is Learned in School* (Reading, Mass.: Addison-Wesley, 1968); for similar implications see W. Jackson, *Life in Classrooms* (New York: Holt, Rinehart and Winston, 1968); and for empirical data see H. Gintis, "Education, Technology and the Characteristics of Worker Productivity," *American Economic Review,* May 1971, LXI (2), 260-279.

7. J. E. Coons, W. H. Clune, and S. D. Sugarman, *Private Wealth and Public Education* (Cambridge, Mass.,: Harvard University Press (Belknap Press), 1970).

Figure 27-1
The Educational Sector

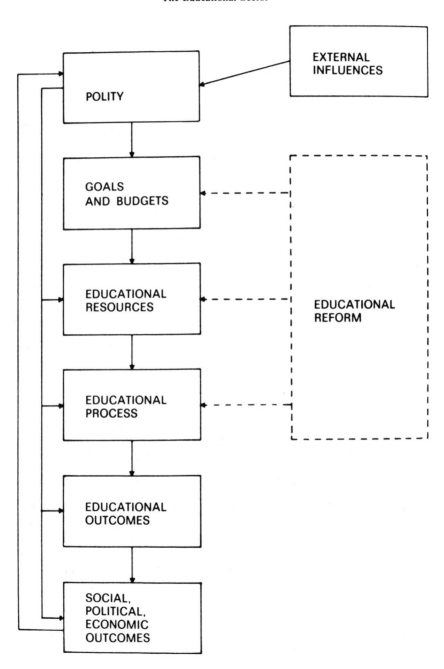

In short, according to the correspondence principle, the school, along with other agencies of socialization such as the family, the church, and the community, prepares children for adult roles in society; thus its modes or organization and activities are congruent for the most part with the society which sponsors it.

The Educational Sector— Mirror of Society

In order to analyze the applicability of the correspondence principle to schools more systematically, this section reviews briefly the various activities which constitute the educational sector, particularly their relationships with one another and with the sponsoring society.[8]

Figure 27-1 shows a flow diagram of the educational sector. The activities of the sector are described by a set of six boxes connected by a series of arrows describing a closed loop and a seventh box representing external influences on the system. The arrows represent flows of decision outcomes, resources, and socialization outcomes from one state to another. Throughout this description we shall be referring to the formal educational sector or schooling sector as if the two were identical. Although discussion of other educational influences is omitted, I do not believe that their inclusion would modify the pattern of interpretation.

1. Polity. 'Polity' refers to an organized society with a specific ideology and form of government. Thus, the polity has various properties which create demands on its educational sector. These properties include such characteristics as the nature of the economic and political system; social, religious, and cultural factors; the level of industrial development; and relationships with other societies. Emanating from the polity is a set of demands or socialization objectives for transmitting the culture and maintaining the economic, political, and social order. These demands take the form of laws that define and affect the schools; governing relationships that will inevitably weigh the demands of some constituencies more heavily than others; and a resource or budget that will be allocated to educational activities.

In addition, the polity will affect educational activities by creating values and expectations with regard to the roles of its citizens and the educational requirements for fulfilling them. To this degree, the educational values and expectations of any individual will themselves emanate from the role that he perceives for himself (or that his parents perceive and transmit to him). A large portion of the differential

---

8. A parallel description is presented, and somewhat more detail is provided with regard to describing the political dimensions for the process in H. Levin, "Accountability in Education," *Saturday Review,* May 1974, 82 (3).

socialization effects of schools and families are apparently related to the roles assigned by the polity to different classes of individuals. For example, Melvin Kohn has found the values of children to be consistently related to the social class of their father.

> The higher their class position, the more highly they value self-direction and the less highly they value conformity to externally imposed standards (p. 171).[9]

Other researchers (Olin, Hess, & Shipman)[10] have drawn similar conclusions regarding family position in the class structure and the values transmitted to children by the mother that affect learning, attitudes, and attainments. That is, the reality that individuals experience in their daily lives leads to educational and social expectations as well as to perceptions of the 'rules for success.' Persons occupying different vantage points in highly stratified societies will emerge with different values and expectations. These studies suggest that the children of working-class families will be more adept at taking, and those of ruling-class families more adept at giving, orders. These attributes will not be treated neutrally by schools that select children by testing and curriculum assignment in order to fill out the class structure for the next generation.[11]

Thus, in explaining educational outcomes we should be cognizant not only of the formal government policies but also of the values and attitudes and expectations inculcated by the polity with regard to itself and others. It is the subtle interaction among the governmental outcomes of the polity, the direct demands of government and private agencies, and the effect of the polity on the formation of individual and class values that will determine the operations and results of its educational sector. Accordingly, Figure 27-1 shows that the influence of the polity extends not only to the determination of budget and goals; it also determines the selection of educational resources, educational processes, and educational outcomes, and how educational outcomes are translated into social, political, and economic outcomes.

2. Goals and Budgets. One of the most direct ways in which the polity dominates the educational sector is its determination of goals and budgets. The goals reflect the formal and informal demands that the society visits upon its schools; budgets represent the resources that are allocated to fill those demands.

---

9. Melvin Kohn, *Class and Conformity* (Homewood, Ill.: Dorsey Press, 1968).

10. E. G. Olin, R. D. Hess, and V. Shipman, "The Role of Mothers' Language in Mediating their Pre-School Children's Cognitive Development," *School Review*, Winter 1967, 75.

11. L. Althusser, *Lenin and Philosophy and Other Essays* (New York: Monthly Review Press, 1971, pp. 127-186).

In most cases the goals will not be transmitted directly, but implicitly in the laws, operating procedures, licensing requirements, curriculum, and personnel requirements that are mandated upon the educational system. It is difficult to find any list of objectives communicated to the schools by the polity other than the ambiguous and rhetorical ones, which have little operating value, e.g., 'equality of opportunity' and 'training for literacy.' In fact, these objectives are often discharged through the mere expansion of school enrollments or through the assumption that any person completing a particular level of schooling (e.g., the fifth grade) is literate, while the actual goals of the polity are found in its policies on personnel selection, school organization, compulsory attendance, and budgetary allocations.

The budget represents the monetary value of the resources that the polity wishes to allocate to schools, e.g., teachers, administrators, buildings, books, and other instructional material. In most cases budget allocations are determined by forces far removed from the schools where the money is spent. That is, budgets are not lump-sum amounts allocated to individual schools according to the professional views of their educators or the priorities of local communities; they often specify, in remarkable detail, the number of teachers, nature of facilities, and other inputs to be used in the educational process.[12]

3. Educational resources. In large measure the impact of the budget on educational outcomes will be contingent upon the types of resources brought into the schooling process. As noted above, most of those decisions are made by the polity, so that in many respects the determination of the budget and the resources it will purchase are made concurrently.

The choice of personnel is one area of resource selection that deserves special scrutiny. To a large extent, educators seem to be hired less for their skills than for their values. The licensing and selection requirements rarely focus on intellectual proficiencies or success in attaining educational objectives. Rather, high-level administrators are chosen according to their "philosophies" of education, and they are expected to hire other educators according to such values. In addition, the control of certification of educators permits the polity to assure itself that teachers will be socialized in a manner consistent with the interests of the state. In fact, the training programs themselves act as self-selection devices in filtering out individuals who do not subscribe to the values and content that underlie teacher-training programs and licensing requirements.

---

12. There is a close parallel between the conditions that await workers and those that await pupils. In both cases the tacit assumption that underlies "production" is that they are interchangeable and that the fine details of their circumstances can be set without specific knowledge of their attributes other than their class origins.

4. Educational process. Educational resources are organized to produce certain educational outcomes. For example, schools are arranged in hierarchical fashion with respect to administrators, teachers, and students. Curriculum requirements are set with regard to how personnel and students will interact in any particular setting. Various types of competitive activities, academic and athletic, are sanctioned. A particular amount of time is normally spent in each activity and grade level, and so on. In addition, success according to the norms of the school is sanctioned with strong social approval and such extrinsic rewards as high grades and high class rankings, while poor performance is punished with detention, other coercive sanctions, and low grades.

Children are tested and on the basis of such results are allocated to the various curricula. Counselors attempt to shunt students toward schooling paths and careers with which their academic grades, test scores, and "interests" are consistent, and students who represent "problems to the school are stigmatized by visits to school psychologists, low grades, dismissal, or other devices which punish a failure to fulfill school norms. Educational settings are usually dominated by the educators themselves, in that few choices are made by the students; most of the decisions that will affect the school experiences of each child are made by teachers, administrators, and governing agencies in the form of inflexible personnel configurations, curriculum, lesson plans, and so on.

5. Educational Outcomes. Contrary to those who suggest that the above processes are mindless, I maintain that they are functional in producing outcomes which the policy desires. What are some of these outcomes? Because the popular appeal of the school is based upon its contribution to increasing literacy and knowledge, we often tend to think of schools as producing only cognitive outcomes. That is, it is common to identify effective schools as those which produce students with high proficiencies on standardized tests of reading, mathematics, and general knowledge.

But the demands of modern industrial societies on their citizens are far more complex than the requirements suggested by cognitive goals. All kinds of values and personality attributes are also necessary for effectively functioning social units. Accordingly, much of the energy and organization of the schools is devoted to the transmission of attitudes and values. As we noted above, in this context the hierarchical structure of the school, the boredom, the alienation from one's activities, the emphasis on conformity in some settings and intense competition in others are functionally related to the demands of the hierarchical work organizations that characterize modern societies.[13]

---

13. For a more extensive discussion of the correspondence between educational outcomes and

6. Social, political, and economic outcomes. The end product of schooling is the social, political, and economic results desired by society. The economic system depends on an adequate supply of persons who are properly trained and inculcated with the attributes that sustain both production and consumption. Adults must be politically acculturated in order to contribute to an effectively functioning political system. Social and cultural traditions must be accepted in order to maintain a stable social order from one generation to the next. In this respect, schooling has an important role in preparing people to assume their ultimate responsibilities as adults.

The results of schooling are usually stated more positively. Thus, it is widely asserted that schools contribute to economic and political development and increase the amount of social mobility within the polity.[14] Schooling is considered to be a nationally unifying force because it promotes a common set of values among the diverse populations that it touches. Moreover, schooling is supposed to generate a more interesting and diverse cultural milieu by increasing the level of literacy, artistic activity, and cultural appreciation. Whether schooling does all of these things has been much less explored than the popularity of these claims suggests.

Finally, whatever the effects of schools, their impact on the polity occurs in a dynamic setting. Their relationship is thus a reciprocal one, which is reflected in the arrows in Figure 27-1 that feed back the social, economic, and political outcomes to the polity as well as stem from the polity through its influence upon educational outcomes. Thus, the values and goals of the larger society and those of the educational sector operate in a continuous and reinforcing flow.[15]

---

the social relations of production, see Gintis, *Education, Technology and Worker Productivity;* Gintis, "Towards a Political Economy of Education," *Harvard Educational Review* (Feb. 1972, 42 (1), 70-96); Bowles, *Unequal Education;* and Althusser, *Lenin and Philosophy.* A general view of socialization for competence is found in A. Inkeles, "The Socialization of Competence," *Harvard Educational Review,* Summer 1966, 36 (3), 265-283. The Inkeles view does not deal with the requirements for differential socialization in hierarchical societies; rather, it addresses itself to a general set of competencies that all citizens are "expected" to possess. In contrast, the literature that links schooling to the social relations of production tends to focus on differential socialization for differential competencies of a hierarchical nature.

14. Greer, *The Great School Legend*

15. Since the translation of educational results into social, economic, and political results is itself influenced by government policy, market factors such as discrimination, and other characteristics of the polity, even changes in educational outputs will not necessarily be converted into expected social, economic, and political changes. That is, not only does the polity control the educational process, but it also controls the reward or value structure for converting educational results into social results.

Contradiction and Change

The assertion that the educational sector reinforces the existing social order should not be construed to mean that change does not occur. On the contrary, a dynamic process of social change is constantly evident, but it is not attributable to deliberate educational policy.

There are three ways in which the polity can change with regard to its structure, organization, and values. First, *natural disasters* such as earthquakes can have an enormous impact on the shape of all social, economic, and political institutions. Second, societies which are highly dependent on external factors can be affected deeply by them: for example, immigration or emigration, wars, and substantial changes in export and import prices for key commodities. Finally, a society can change because of internal contradictions that arise. Since the first two sets of forces are largely self-explanatory with regard to their change-inducing properties, I shall concentrate on change through contradiction.

Although the forces that dominate society attempt to reproduce and maintain their relationships from generation to generation, contradictions emerge through unforseen consequences. To sustain the existing social, political, and economic order it is necessary to eliminate those contradictions by adapting to them while attempting to preserve the traditional order. For example, the invention of simple and inexpensive methods of birth control affected the size and therefore the nature of families, the life style of individuals, the growth of economic markets; and, as the composition of the population changes, so does the pattern of its political behavior. Those consequences were largely ignored by the developers of the new technology but they represent new conditions and potential contradictions in the existing social, political, and economic order, to which legal, economic, political, educational, and other institutions must adapt.

Thus, if a society alters its traditional economic, political, and social relationships, its schooling must likewise change or remain incongruent with such changes. Accordingly, I would predict that planned changes in the educational sector would parallel the transition in the society at large in order to remain functional—a prediction born out in the cases of Cuba,[16] Tanzania, and China; and congruent with the Marxian dialectic of thesis-antithesis-synthesis.[17]

---

16. S. S. Bowles, "Cuban Education and the Revolution Ideology," in Martin Carnoy (Ed.), *Schooling in a Corporate Society* (New York: David McKay, 1972, pp. 272-303), and R. Fagen, *The Transformation of Political Culture in Cuba* (Standord, Calif.: Stanford University Press, 1969).

17. Mao Tse-tung, "On Contradiction," in *Selected Works of Mao Tse-tung,* Vol. I (Peking: Foreign Languages Press, 1967, pp. 311-347).

Contradictions can also emerge within the educational sector. Assume that for some unforeseen reason the schools produce citizens whose attributes do not correspond to those which are functional in the polity. For example, the legitimacy of schooling as a selection device and an agent of social mobility requires a constant expansion of enrollments at successive levels in order to absorb the social demand for increases in educational opportunity and access. But job opportunities for educated persons have not expanded commensurately with increases in educational attainments. Expectations of higher-level jobs have not been met, and the overall social system has therefore contradicted itself. In response, many persons with higher educational attainments have begun to reject the normal world of work and choose instead to exist marginally on welfare payments and food stamps under communal or semicommunal arrangements. In many cases they have chosen to pursue arts and crafts and other countercultural endeavors as well as to partake of drugs and seek new religious experiences. It is clear that in order to preserve the relationship between schools and work, some radical changes will have to take place. We will describe one such possibility in the concluding section. What is important to note is that schools can only serve as an agent of change when their activities and outcomes are contravened by changes in the larger social order.

The School Cannot Remake Society

In contrast, the educational reformer assumes that changes can take place in education without reference to the polity, and that the results of such planned change will be social change. This view is symbolized by the dotted box to the right of the flow diagram in Figure 27-1. The three dotted arrows suggest that educational reforms are directed at altering the budgetary support and goals of the educational sector, the types of educational resources used, and the organization of these resources in the educational process. Presumably, the reforms would create different educational outputs as well as social, economic, and political outcomes and would result in a change in the polity. But to the degree that such reforms do not correspond to the social, economic, and political order, our previous analysis suggests that they must fail.

Indeed, I believe that a review of major school reform movements that violated the precepts of the polity would show that they either failed to be adopted or failed to show expected results. One need only compare the criticisms of the major turn-of-the-century reformers with recent critiques. John Dewey's trenchant indictment of school practices written in his 1899 essay on "The School and Society" is strikingly similar to that of Charles Silberman in his 1970 work, *Crisis in the Classroom*: yet the two works were separated by seven decades of school reform spearheaded by Dewey's own progeny, the "progressive education movement."[18]

There have been several more recent attempts to change substantially the ways in which the schools function, but in each case the reforms were inconsistent with the values and premises of our larger social system, and thus failed: e.g., attempts to individualize instruction, which obviously violated the need for conformity and class-related interchangeability among individuals in the hierarchical organizations that characterize both industry and government in our society.

Attempts to provide "compensatory education" for youngsters from low-income backgrounds have also failed.[19] Again, the correspondence principle suggests that the schools are not going to succeed in reducing the competitive edge of the advantaged over the disadvantaged in the race for income and status. The failure of the Supreme Court's 1954 Brown decision to put an end to racial segregation in the schools is but another example of the failure of school reform; and there is every indication that the attempts to equalize financial support of the schools will also fail since society regards the ability to provide a better educational background a privilege of the rich rather than a right of every citizen.[20] In short, only when there is a demand for educational reform by the polity will educational reform succeed. The historical record bears out the view that the "turning points" in the functions of the schools coincided with major movements that changed the social order.[21]

---

18. See L. A. Cremin, *The Transformation of the School* (New York: Vintage Books, 1964), and J. Dewey, *Democracy and Education* (New York: MacMillan Co., 1916).

19. See the evidence on this in H. M. Levin, "Serrano-type Expenditure Increases and Their Effects on Educational Resource Allocation and Effectiveness," Occasional paper in the *Economics and Politics of Education,* No. 72-12, School of Education, Standord University, December 1972. This does not mean that there were not a few individual successes. Rather, the assertion is that such policies will not succeed in a systematic sense. That is, the real question is whether so-called compensatory education policies have shown success on the average rather than in isolated instances.

20. See Levin, "Accountability in Education," for a political model that would predict this result. This view is also supported by the recent (March 21, 1973) decision of the U.S. Supreme Court to overturn the decision of the Federal District Court in the case of *Rodriguez vs. San Antonio.* The lower court had ruled that the present system of financing education in Texas— and by implication in all other states except Hawaii—violated the equal protection clause of the Fourteenth Amendment because it provided greater educational support to children in wealthier school districts than in poorer ones. In Levin (1972), I have argued that even if similar decisions are upheld in individual states, the educational outcomes among children drawn from different class origins are not likely to change.

21. R. Callahan, *Education and the Cult of Efficiency* (Chicago: University of Chicago Press, 1962); M. Katz, *The Irony of Early School Reform* (Boston: Beacon Press, 1968).

Contradiction and Educational Reform

In order to apply the concepts that have been presented, I shall attempt to demonstrate that certain educational reforms that would not be adopted on their own merits might be acceptable as reforms insofar as they correspond to modifications in the larger social order.

As we noted above, the swift upgrading in educational attainments has recently generated extensive contradictions between work and schooling. Each of those contradictions has led to a rising dissatisfaction with the conditions of work that await educated persons. What are some of these inconsistencies? First, despite the enormous increase in the number of young persons with college credentials, traditional job opportunities for college graduates have not expanded as rapidly as the number of graduates. The result is that individuals with college training are being increasingly employed in jobs which formerly required only high school credentials. Thus, one of the normally expected relationships between more education and higher productivity is violated as more and more highly educated persons assume relatively low productivity and low-status occupations.

Second, increasing job expectations that cannot be met by the occupational structure has led to rising dissatisfaction with work itself. That is, most college enrollees expect their additional educational accomplishments to be reflected in occupations with higher prestige, earnings, and greater entrepreneurial options, or at least greater control over activities on the job. As it becomes obvious that their expectations exceed the actual opportunities and jobs available, dissatisfaction with work itself ensues.

Third, the constant tendency for technological change and specialization to reduce the number of functions of workers means that workers increasingly feel redundant. At virtually all levels of employment, from professional positions such as physicians, lawyers, and professors to production workers, the tendency toward greater specialization of function is evident. The fact that more schooling has increased exposure to a wider variety of cognitive experiences while job requirements have become more highly specialized has certainly contributed to worker dissatisfaction.

Symptoms of these contradictions between education and jobs are increasingly found. For example, the quality of workmanship has been deteriorating in recent years, and quality control is one of the most serious problems faced by industry. Moreover, industry and government are plagued by rising incidences of diminished productivity due to alcoholism and drug usage; employee absenteeism and turnover appear to be rising, and production is increasingly disrupted by wildcat strikes and employee sabotage.[22] The specter of increasing sabotage is especially frightening to

---

22. See *Work in America* (1973) especially Chapters 2 and 3.

employers because relatively simple acts can do vast amounts of damage to sophisticated machinery, and the interdependence of particular manufacturing and service activities means that a single act of sabotage can disrupt production even for those plants and equipment that are intact.

These problems have been recognized at the national level by a recent report of the U.S. Department of Health, Education, and Welfare, "Work in America" (1973), which suggests that if the nature of work does not increase the participation of workers in decision making and reduce worker alienation, major disruptions of normal production activities and reduced productivity can be foreseen. Such an adaptation would preserve the underlying ownership of capital while reducing the threat of costly distruction and disruption. These attempts to increase productivity by changing the nature of workers' relationships to the firm and its decision making mechanisms can all be thought of as attempts to increase the degree of "industrial democracy."[23] Recent experiments in the United States and abroad with industrial democracy suggest that this phenomenon will become increasingly important as a strategy for improving worker satisfaction and output.

Given major changes in the organization of work, important changes in the function of schools are implied. Industrial democracy will require that workers possess characteristics that enable them to participate more fully in decisions regarding the production process. A glimpse of those processes suggests that workers will need abilities and interpersonal traits that are not required at present or developed by existing educational institutions. For example, industrial democracy will lead generally to somewhat less specialization in production tasks, and individual initiative will be encouraged through cooperative or team production and decision making. The rewards of work will become substantially more internally oriented than under the present system.

Corresponding changes in schooling are likely to emerge. Cooperation in learning, mastery of particular skills, the ability to handle new situations and learning opportunities, and other worker traits that follow from increased control of the work process would be emphasized. It would not be surprising to see schools accept such reforms as Bloom's mastery learning approach, which would assure that all workers have mastered the minimum competencies required for their participation;[24] the open classroom advocated by Charles Silberman, (Section III), which would provide students with experience in taking responsibility for particular

---

23. G. Hunnius, D. Garson,and J. Case (Eds.), *Workers' Control: A Reader on Labor and Social Change* (New York: Vintage, 1973); C. Pateman, *Participation and Democratic Theory* (New York: Cambridge University Press, 1970); and *Work in America.*

24. J. H. Block, *Mastery Learning* (New York: Holt, Rinehart and Winston, 1971) contains several essays and a description of the literature on the mastery learning paradigm developed by Benjamin Bloom.

school (and thereby production) decisions; and the tutorial communities where students assist other students in learning new proficiencies.[25] Even the deschooling proposed by Illich would be likely to be partially accepted as it became more useful for students to acquire some of the necessary competencies for worker democracy through on-the-job training programs rather than through formal schooling.[26]

Paradoxically, if the scenario that I have sketched takes place, the advocates of school reform will celebrate the victory of having changed society through educational "progress." Indeed, the coincidence of the work reforms with the educational ones will reinforce their view of the world. But such a conclusion will derive from a misinterpretation of the data, in conjunction with their own educational reform ideology, for an active commitment to social change on the part of the polity will have preceded these educational changes.[27]

25. This was advocated by J. Dewey (1899) and is reflected in a number of educational projects. In particular, the New York City-based National Commission on Resources for Youth headed by Judge Mary C. Kohler has been promoting and implementing the "kids tutoring kids" approach on a national basis.

26. Ivan Illich, *Deschooling Society* (Garden City, L.I. New York: Doubleday, 1971).

27. It is important to recognize that the speed of adaptation will depend on the availability of implementable ideas. In this sense the educational reformers will tend to increase the rate of change in the educational sector in response to contradiction if they can provide models for change that can be readily diffused.

28

Dare the School Build a New Social Order?

George S. Counts

Like all simple and unsophisticated peoples we Americans have a sublime faith in education. Faced with any difficult problem of life we set our minds at rest sooner or later by the appeal to the school. We are convinced that education is the one unfailing remedy for every ill to which man is subject, whether it be vice, crime, war, poverty, riches, injustice, racketeering, political corruption, race hatred, class conflict, or just plain original sin. We even speak glibly and often about the general reconstruction of society through the school. We cling to this faith in spite of the fact that the very period in which our troubles have multiplied so rapidly has witnessed an unprecedented expansion of organized education. This would seem to suggest that our schools, instead of directing the course of change, are themselves driven by the very forces that are transforming the rest of the social order.

The bare fact, however, that simple and unsophisticated peoples have unbounded faith in education does not mean that the faith is untenable. History shows that the intuitions of such folk may be nearer the truth than the weighty and carefully reasoned judgments of the learned and the wise. Under certain conditions education may be as beneficent and as powerful as we are wont to think. But if it is to be so, teachers must abandon much of their easy optimism, subject the concept of education to the most rigorous scrutiny, and be prepared to deal much more fundamentally, realistically, and positively with the American social situation than has been their habit in the past. Any individual or group that would aspire to lead society must be ready to pay the costs of leadership: to accept responsibility, to suffer calumny, to surrender security, to risk both reputation and fortune. If this price, or some important part of it, is not being paid, then the chances are that the claim to leadership is fraudulent. Society is never redeemed

George S. Counts, "Dare the School Build a New Social Order?" reprinted with alterations from the book of the same title, John Day Co., Inc., 1932.

without effort, struggle, and sacrifice. Authentic leaders are never found breathing that rarefied atmosphere lying above the dust and smoke of battle. With regard to the past we always recognize the truth of this principle, but when we think of our own times we profess the belief that the ancient roles have been reversed and that now prophets of a new age receive their rewards among the living.

That the existing school is leading the way to a better social order is a thesis which few informed persons would care to defend. Except as it is forced to fight for its own life during times of depression, its course is too serene and untroubled. Only in the rarest of instances does it wage war on behalf of principle or ideal. Almost everywhere it is in the grip of conservative forces and is serving the cause of perpetuating ideas and institutions suited to an age that is gone. But there is one movement above the educational horizon which would seem to show promise of genuine and creative leadership. I refer to the Progressive Education movement. Surely in this union of two of the great faiths of the American people, the faith in progress and the faith in education, we have reason to hope for light and guidance. Here is a movement which would seem to be completely devoted to the promotion of social welfare through education.

Even a casual examination of the program and philosophy of the Progressive schools, however, raises many doubts in the mind. To be sure, these schools have a number of large achievements to their credit. They have focused attention squarely upon the child; they have recognized the fundamental importance of the interest of the learner; they have defended the thesis that activity lies at the root of all true education; they have conceived learning in terms of life situations and growth of character; they have championed the rights of the child as a free personality. Most of this is excellent, but in my judgment it is not enough. It constitutes too narrow a conception of the meaning of education; it brings into the picture but one-half of the landscape.

. . . .

That the teachers should deliberately reach for power and then make the most of their conquest is my firm conviction. To the extent that they are permitted to fashion the curriculum and the procedures of the school they will definitely and positively influence the social attitudes, ideals, and behavior of the coming generation. In doing this they should resort to no subterfuge or false modesty. They should say neither that they are merely teaching the truth nor that they are unwilling to wield power in their own right. The first position is false and the second is a confession of incompetence. It is my observation that the men and women who have affected the course of human events are those who have not hesitated to use the power that has come to them. Representing as they do, not the interests of the moment or of any special class, but rather the common and abiding interests of the people, teachers are under heavy social obligation to protect and further those interests. In this they occupy a relatively unique position in society. Also since the profession should embrace scientists and scholars of the highest rank, as well as teachers working at all levels of the educational system, it has at its disposal, as no other group, the knowledge and wisdom of the ages. It is scarcely thinkable that these men and women would ever act as selfishly or bungle as badly as have the so-called "practical" men of our generation—the politicians, the financiers, the industrialists. If all of these facts are taken into account, instead of shunning power, the profession should rather seek power and then strive to use that power fully and wisely and in the interests of the great masses of the people.

That the teachers should deliberately reach for power and then make the most of their conquest is my firm conviction. To the extent that they are permitted to fashion the curriculum and the procedures of the school they will definitely and positively influence the social attitudes, ideals, and behavior of the coming generation. In doing this they should resort to no subterfuge or false modesty. They should say neither that they are merely teaching the truth nor that they are unwilling to wield power in their own right. The first position is false and the second is a confession of incompetence. It is my observation that the men and women who have affected the course of human events are those who have not hesitated to use the power that has come to them. Representing as they do, not the interests of the moment or of any special class, but rather the common and abiding interests of the people, teachers are under heavy social obligation to protect and further those interests. In this they occupy a relatively unique position in society. Also since the profession should embrace scientists and scholars of the highest rank, as well as teachers working at all levels of the educational system, it has at its disposal, as no other group, the knowledge and wisdom of the ages. It is scarcely thinkable that these men and women would ever act as selfishly or bungle as badly as have the so-called "practical" men of our generation—the politicians, the financiers, the industrialists. If all of these facts are taken into account, instead of shunning power, the profession should rather seek power and then strive to use that power fully and wisely and in the interests of the great masses of the people.

. . . .

Our generation has the good or the ill fortune to live in an age when great decisions must be made. The American people, like most of the other peoples of the earth, have come to the parting of the ways; they can no longer trust entirely the inspiration which came to them when the Republic was young; they must decide afresh what they are to do with their talents. Favored above all other nations with the resources of nature and the material instrumentalities of civilization, they stand confused and irresolute before the future. They seem to lack the moral quality necessary to quicken, discipline, and give direction to their matchless energies. In a recent paper Professor Dewey has, in my judgment, correctly diagnosed our troubles: "the schools, like the nation," he says, "are in need of a central purpose which will create new enthusiasm and devotion, and which will unify and guide all intellectual plans."

This suggests, as we have already observed, that the educational problem is not wholly intellectual in nature. Our Progressive schools therefore cannot rest content with giving children an opportunity to study contemporary society in all of its aspects. This of course must be done, but I am convinced that they should go much farther. If the schools are to be really effective, they must become centers for the building, and not merely for the contemplation, of our civilization. This does not mean that we should endeavor to promote particular reforms through the educational system. We should, however, give to our children a vision of the possibilities which lie ahead and endeavor to enlist their loyalties and enthusiasms in the realization of the vision. Also our social institutions and practices, all of them, should be critically examined in the light of such a vision.

. . . .

As the possibilities in our society begin to dawn upon us, we are all, I think, growing increasingly weary of the brutalities, the stupidities, the hypocrisies, and the gross inanities of contemporary life. We have a haunting feeling that we were born for better things and that the nation itself is falling far short of its powers. The fact that other groups refuse to deal boldly and realistically with the present situation does not justify the teachers of the country in their customary policy of hesitation and equivocation. The times are literally crying for a new vision of American destiny. The teaching profession, or at least its progressive elements, should eagerly grasp the opportunity which the fates have placed in their hands.

Such a vision of what America might become in the industrial age I would introduce into our schools as the supreme imposition, but one to which our children are entitled—a priceless legacy which it should be the first concern of our profession to fashion and bequeath. The objection will of course be raised that this is asking teachers to assume unprecedented social responsibilities. But we live in difficult and dangerous times—times when precedents lose their significance. If we are content to remain where all is safe and quiet and serene, we shall dedicate ourselves, as teachers have commonly done in the past, to a role of futility, if not of positive social reaction. Neutrality with respect to the great issues that agitate society, while perhaps theoretically possible, is practically tantamount to giving support to the forces of conservatism. As Justice Holmes has candidly said in his essay on Natural Law, "we all, whether we know it or not, are fighting to make the kind of world that we should like." If neutrality is impossible even in the dispensation of justice, whose emblem is the blindfolded goddess, how is it to be achieved in education? To ask the question is to answer it.

To refuse to face the task of creating a vision of a future America immeasurably more just and noble and beautiful than the America of today is to evade the most crucial, difficult, and important educational task. Until we have assumed this responsibility we are scarcely justified in opposing and mocking the efforts of so-called patriotic societies to introduce into the schools a tradition which, though narrow and unenlightened, nevertheless represents an honest attempt to meet a profound social and educational need. Only when we have fashioned a finer and more authentic vision than they will we be fully justified in our opposition to their efforts. Only then will we have discharged the age-long obligation which the older generation owes to the younger and which no amount of sophistry can obscure. Only through such a legacy of spiritual values will our children be enabled to find their place in the world, be lifted out of the present morass of moral indifference, be liberated from the senseless struggle for material success, and be challenged to high endeavor and achievement. And only thus will we as a people put ourselves on the road to the expression of our peculiar genius and to the making of our special contribution to the cultural heritage of the race.

A Critique of the Critics

This final section of the book contains several essays which challenge the validity of the positions advanced by many of the more prominent public schools critics. In the considered judgment of the writers cited in this section many aspects of the more popular public school criticisms suffer from one or more of the following weaknesses: 1. A weak or distorted sense of history; 2. an insensitivity to the social context; 3. inadequate research designs and statistical procedures; 4. a refusal to acknowledge materially important facts; 5. "leaps" in logic; 6. ideological distortion; 7. simplistic reasoning; 8. morally questionable inferences and implications. These are weighty charges, indeed. Whether or not they are convincing and compelling is a judgmental conclusion which the careful student of American education is in a position to make only after a thoughtful consideration of the evidence. For many years we have been exposed to the testimony of the prosecution. This section and sections three through seven constitute part of the brief for the defense. Is the public school guilty as charged? Only an informed, responsible jury can render a just verdict.

The initial reading selected for this section draws together rather succinctly much of the evidence presented in sections three through seven. In addition, the author suggests several other considerations which bear upon our public schools' performance. He strikes out at the critics for having conveniently ignored many of the indisputable achievements of the American public schools.

The second reading takes pains to acknowledge the invaluable service rendered by many of the more thoughtful critics. The essay insists that a professional educator should not only welcome constructive criticism; he or she should actively encourage it. The author takes pains to insist that public school fault finding should be done in an intelligent, responsible way, not in a carping, acrimonious way as has been the wont of all too many contemporary critics.

The next writer frontally attacks some of the procedures and conclusions reflected in the writings of the critics Silberman and Freidenberg. Moreover, insists this respondent, these critics— and others of their persuasion—glaringly ignore the palpable fact that the quality of our public schools reflects the commitment which the public at large invests in them. A great deal of the burden of guilt for some of our schools' admitted shortcomings must be borne by a sometimes anti-intellectual, sometimes apathetic public.

Our next essay is essentially a highlighting of the attacks propounded by six of the more vocal, more visible contemporary school critics. After pointing up some of the inadequacies of these positions, the author concludes his discussion by insisting that the professionals which staff our teacher preparation programs are blameworthy for not having vigorously responded to the critics' accusations.

The next writer looks at contemporary public school critics from a refreshingly unique perspective. According to his interpretation, it is supremely ironic that many liberal academicians who have heretofore been among the staunchest proponents of public schooling are now counted among the ranks of the critics who insist that schooling experience has little relationship to fruitful student gains. He suggests that many of these upper middle class, politically liberal writers—especially some of our more prominent social scientists—are propounding an essentially elitist position.

The next writer responds to the deschooling position articulated by the most radical critics. He suggests that for a variety of reasons the notion of abolishing our public schools is totally untenable. It is sheer folly, suggests this writer, to assume that youngsters, left to their own devices, will manifest the motivation needed to engage in the ongoing process of becoming educated.

Our last selection, by Fred and Grace Hechinger, summarizes eloquently the thesis advanced in this book. A balanced, judicious appraisal of our public schools' performance ought to be one of pride tempered by an acknowledgment of our shortcomings. Rather than despair, those committed to American public education ought to make a firm commitment to engage in the ongoing perfecting of the process of educating our nation's youth.

29
Does Education Make a Difference?

Bernard C. Watson

For the past decade a debate has been raging in this country. Ignored by and unknown to most Americans, it finally penetrated the consciousness of the man in the street when daily newspapers began to report and serialize a book written by Christopher Jencks, *Inequality*. Simply stated, the major thesis of the book was that education made little difference in reducing inequality, educational or otherwise. And further, adding more money to public school budgets would do little to equalize opportunity and life chances between the affluent and poor, black and white. And thus the issue was joined in public debate.

But Jencks' book was only the latest of a series of social science documents and theories. Daniel Moynihan's *Maximum Feasible Misunderstanding*, Edward Banfield's *The Unheavenly City*, and Nathan Glazer's "The Limits of Social Policy," to name a few, had all contributed individually and collectively to the effort by some to roll back governmental attempts to improve the lot of minorities and the poor. Simultaneously, from another vantage point, there was a resurgence of the old/new theories of racial superiority/inferiority stated most openly by Arthur Jensen, William Shockley, Richard Herrenstein, and H.J. Eysenck. And gilding the lily were the counsels of Herbert Kohl, who advised that one good year was not enough, and Jonathan Kozol, who informed us that schools were racist, brutal, joyless killers of intelligence, youthful creativity, and institutions of stultifying conformity. And as if these were not sufficient to destroy all hope for the average citizen, advice from the wings told us that deschooling was the answer; decentralization and community control, alternative education, free schools and eliminating the mindlessness of educators would lead us to the promised land. Lower the age for compulsory attendance some advised, create a new breed of teacher

Bernard C. Watson, "Does Education Make a Difference," reprinted by permission from *In Spite of the System,* Copyright 1974, Ballinger Publishing Company.

and administrator, reduce the size of classes and/or schools. Go to the market place: create a voucher system so parents can purchase the education they desire for their children. Desegregate. Integrate. Separate the boys from girls. Create open classrooms. But remember, counsel the modern day sophists, education doesn't really make that much difference.

This whole dialogue is mind boggling to many Americans who have always believed that education made a difference. It was more than a belief, it was an article of faith. At almost any other time in our history, serious discussion of whether education makes a difference would have been unthinkable. It would have been met with suspicion, incredulity or mystification. Does education make a difference? One might as well ask whether food, sleep or oxygen make a difference.

Of course, we are not really talking about education, which is not limited to what takes place in schools, but about schooling. That is what is under discussion (one might almost say under attack) today. The whole complex process whereby children and young people are sent to certain buildings and required to spend eight or twelve or sixteen years acquiring certain skills and understandings under the direction of certain people labeled teachers, administrators, and supervisors.

One may argue, with considerable justification, about whether some schools are better than others, or one might even discuss the proposition that formal schooling as we know it is antithetical to good education. The response to this seems obvious. Certainly some schools are better than others. Why else would families who have the option to decide where and how their children are to be educated automatically gravitate to neighborhoods where schools have a reputation for high teaching standards, good administration, or fine facilities? Or why would well-to-do families send their youngsters, who have the benefit of every imaginable "cultural advantage" at home, to private schools nearby or to the great boarding schools such as Groton, St. Paul's, and Miss Porter's? There seems to be no question in the minds of these families about whether education makes a difference: they willingly pay exorbitant sums—in high suburban tax rates or in tuition bills or both—to obtain the best kind of education available. And they certainly do not rely on their children's ability to simply absorb, by a kind of osmosis, the intellectual and cultural skills which they will later need to run family corporations or become successful professional men.

If we look back through history, we find no evidence to indicate that anyone has ever seriously raised the question with which American citizens are asked to deal today. Quite the contrary. Political philosophers, beginning with Plato and Aristotle, have usually devoted much of their teaching to education, on the assumption that the state's health and welfare depend on the proper training of the young in the duties of citizenship.

Indeed, education has been seen as the key to enabling men to become fully human, to exercise their peculiarly human attribute of rationality. Similarly, religious teachers have always urged on parents their duty to train their children in the traditions and precepts of their religion. Without education, it seemed obvious that neither the church nor the state could long survive.

Think of how education has been viewed by the aspiring poor of every age and nation. Think of the stories we have all heard—some may be part of one's own family history—of parents who struggled and saved and even scrimped on necessities in order to see that their youngsters made it to school, or to college, or to the university. It never occurred to them that education made "no difference"—they *knew* that it was the key to security and status that they had never known but which their educated children could enjoy. Education has, of course, been feared by members of some ruling elites: they knew all too well that education was a liberating force which, if put in the hands of slaves and peasants, might well turn the world upside down. Rightly perceiving that education was threatening to their own designs, they burned books, closed schools and universities, and generally reserved educational opportunity to the chosen few who could be counted on to be loyal to the goals of the existing regime. Other rulers have turned education to their own ends by insisting that the young be indoctrinated with political propaganda, along with reading and arithmetic. (To an extent, all societies do this. After all, schooling is one of the primary means of socialization in every society.)

It is incredible that something that "makes no difference" should have been viewed for so long as both threat and promise; should have absorbed so much of the time and energy of so many. Whatever we are, whatever we have accomplished, is a tribute to the power of education, broadly conceived. One generation after another has absorbed the learning of the past, moved beyond it or added to it, and passed on to their children not only their own knowledge, but the thirst for more. Why, then, is the question being asked: Does education make a difference? Partly, no doubt, it is a symptom of the temper of our times—when most traditions, conventions, and commonly accepted values are subject to doubt and questioning, or are even being abandoned. But even more significant, the question is evidence of the social and political reaction which is rampant in this country at present. It is raised—scornfully by some, hesitantly or sadly by others—as a challenge to the most basic of American beliefs: the belief that through education a society of free men might have equal opportunity to succeed in life and, even more important, to maintain control over their chosen government.

But before we explore the reasons why this question is being posed at this particular time and in this context, it seems appropriate to attempt to respond to it directly. Does education make a difference? Or, in other words, what evidence is available on the success of education in achieving its objectives? One way to approach this is to take the question apart and look at each of its key components in turn. First, what kind of "evidence" is being requested? What will satisfy the judge and jurors? It has previously been indicated that history is replete with examples of how education did, in fact, make all the difference. Let us remember the persistence with which the former slaves (and their abolitionist allies) struggled to get schools and teachers—although they were confronted at every turn by scorn, contempt, patronizing words, and outright refusals to have tax monies used for the education of former slaves. As early as 1866, the various freedmen's associations had established nearly 1,000 schools attended by some 90,000 pupils—a number which increased to almost 112,000 the following year. James McPherson, the Princeton historian, noting that "the children came from a cultural environment almost entirely devoid of intellectual stimulation," says that progress was slow but he adds:

> The freedmen had an almost passionate desire to learn to read and write, and children laboriously taught their parents the alphabet and multiplication tables during their spare time. Teachers invariably testified that despite their disadvantages in background, training and environment, Negro children learned to read almost as well and as rapidly as white children.

Despite the collapse of Reconstruction and the ensuing establishment of strict segregation and dual facilities, the proportion of the black population attending school climbed steadily. Black people knew that education made a difference—and so did their oppressors. Gunnar Myrdal, in his classic book *An American Dilemma,* describes the abysmal conditions in black schools in the South during the 1930s. He writes:

> ...Negro education still does not have a fixed legitimate acknowledged place. It is realized that something must be done in order to keep the Negro satisfied and in order to uphold the American slogan of free schools for every child, but it is rare that a community has any real interest in planning or building a wise system of education for the race. Politically, it is not admitted that a Negro has a right to schools...

Those who carefully engineered an inferior school system for blacks (a program whose nature and extent has been well documented not only by Myrdal, but by such other scholars as Ambrose Caliver, Horace Mann Bond, and Henry Allen Bullock)—whether in the rural South or urban North knew very well the power and liberating force inherent in education. Had schooling been made available to the black child on the same terms as to the white, the myth of his inferiority would very quickly have been shattered.

Yet many of the youngsters did manage to complete this inadequate schooling and went on to the black colleges, which for the last century have provided almost the sole opportunity for higher or professional education available to blacks. Indeed, as late as 1969, Meharry and Howard were educating all but a tiny number of black medical and dental students, and 27 percent of all black law students were enrolled in four black schools. Without these institutions, the black community would have been almost completely without medical and legal services—which are still much scarcer for minorities than for the white population of this country. One must ask again: how is it possible to entertain the possibility that education makes no difference? The oppressed and ignorant slaves knew better, and generations of their descendants, whether themselves graduates of universities or simply beneficiaries of the specialized training of fellow blacks, know better.

Similarly, the thousands upon thousands of immigrants who came to these shores, fleeing from famine and oppression elsewhere, counted on education to break down language barriers, to help them adapt to the customs and culture of their newly adopted land. And, whether in formal or informal settings, these people and even more their children, quickly (though not always without pain and stress) adopted American ways. What evidence do we have that education succeeds? They would point to their sons and grandsons who, within a generation, began to take their places as respected citizens, landowners, and professional men in the new country.

If one prefers another kind of evidence, why not recall the critical role education has played in meeting various national goals? In wartime, for instance, workers were trained without previous factory experience (many of them housewives and adolescents) to operate complex machinery; youthful officers were taught to become fluent in another language, in only months; jets and rockets and the atom bomb were developed, crass youth were taught to build, operate, and maintain the most complicated equipment in the history of man. Our feelings about war may be more ambiguous now than in the 1940s when we were in a desperate race with time and the most efficient and educated war machine ever established. Without the determination and ability to educate our people to meet the crisis, history might have run a very different course.

More specific evidence can be found, however, in the history of agriculture: Five percent of the population of this country feeds the other 95 percent. The unusually high standard of living enjoyed in this country could not have been achieved had we not discovered how to provide for this most basic of human needs—food. It was not done by accident, but through education: think of the role played by the land-grant colleges, the agricultural extension stations and labs, the field agents, who trained farmers in new methods and machinery by which they could increase their land's yield. In other parts of the world today, one hears of the "green revolution"—discoveries from scientists which are helping to ameliorate the ancient spectre of famine. Agricultural education has already accomplished much in some of the Third World countries—and now that indigenous farmers have learned to operate modern equipment, they require further education in order to be able to maintain it.

One hardly needs to mention the space program—so clear is the relationship to education. A single space shot, the Russian Sputnik, was responsible for widespread curriculum changes in this country. And in turn, the graduates of our science programs—engineering, biology, chemistry, and a host of other specialities whose names one has difficulty pronouncing, let alone understanding—succeeded within ten short years in breaking the barrier between man and the moon. What evidence do we have about the difference made by education? What more evidence do we need?

If statistical evidence is more convincing, that, too, can be provided. Henry Levin, Stanford economist, and his colleagues put together a study not long ago for the Mondale Committee—and calculated that inadequate education (which they defined as less than high school completion) for working-age males in this country would cost, over their lifetimes, some $237 billion in lost income, $71 billion in lost tax monies, and some $6 billion in costs for welfare and prison. And very recently, the Census Bureau published a survey establishing the relationships between level of education completed and earning power. The mean annual incomes for each group ranged from $5,950 for those with less than eight years of schooling to $16,698 for those with four or more years of college.[15] These aren't theories, or models, or somebody's projections: these are facts, culled out from the ever growing masses of data collected by the government to let us know what is actually happening to people.

Let us move on to the second key word in the question: "success." How is "success" to be defined? One really can't talk about success in the abstract, because it has to be connected with something else—namely, the objectives one deems appropriate for education. In an admirable move toward defining educational objectives more precisely, teachers are sometimes required to specify their goals in behavioral terms, so that one can measure the extent to which they have succeeded or not. But educators often lose sight of the broader role played by the educational system in our society. We take it for granted (although again one must remind himself that perhaps it is no longer taken for granted) that education is the chief, if not the only, means whereby people, especially the poor and minorities prepare for some jobs, increase their income, move upward socially, participate in democratic affairs. Yet there are also the "latent functions" of the vast educational system: to provide a place and activities for those too young to enter on a career; to keep them out of mischief and off the streets; to look after them while parents (and increasingly both parents) are at work outside the home, either from necessity or from choice. Some of the more romantic educational philosophers, of course, see and condemn these "latent functions" of education—but they seem ill prepared, despite the flow of rhetoric about schools as prisons, to present workable alternatives for the care and supervision of millions of children.

And let us not forget the schools as employers. They provide jobs and income and status for millions of people and, for the poor and minorities, in particular, a major opportunity for upward mobility. If one were to consider education's success only in performing these latent functions, then our task would be relatively simple. At present, the vast majority of youngsters under sixteen are in school, off the streets, and out of the factories. And the few exceptions—children of migrant workers or urban dropouts—are cause for particular concern just because they are exceptions. The school systems, as caretakers of the young and as key employers, are certainly making a difference.

But what about the specifically educational functions? We have all been in conversations where someone launched into a tirade about what the schools should be doing, or what would happen if they would just start doing something else. What do people have in mind when they think of educational "success," even in a vague and general way? Sometimes they seem to mean that one would have total employment: everyone would be working, no one would be on welfare—if the schools were successful. Others seem to have visions, similar to those of the old utilitarians, of universal happiness: no riots, no unrest, no apathy, no alienation— everybody happy. Is that what is meant by success when education is being evaluated? Or is one interested in the relationship between schooling and citizenship, and does one judge successful education, therefore, on the basis of statistics about participation in the last election? Of course, one might feel that education should produce cultured people. One would then measure success by sales of books, or attendance at cultural events, or amount of amateur activity in the arts, crafts, music, and dance.

Obviously, it is not possible to make sense of "success" without specifying education's objectives. But first one must consider the third key word in the question, namely "education." Well, here again one has to ask, what is meant by "education"? Obviously there is a distinction between formal and informal education, and few would deny the critical importance of what is learned informally; in families, over the air waves, on the streets, in movie houses. Some people, in fact, regard this type of learning as so important, so "meaningful" or "relevant" that they would have us abandon the schools so that everyone might devote himself to such informal learning. But we are here concerned with formal education: that which takes place, for the most part, in special buildings under the guidance of specially trained personnel. Still, one needs to ask again specifically, what is meant when one uses the word "education." Are we referring to public or private or parochial education? To elementary, secondary or higher education? To liberal arts or vocational education? And when these questions have been answered, one must still know what kinds of schools one is talking about: rich or poor, in what part of the country, rural or urban? And what kind of atmosphere is in them: mindless or purposeful; permissive or rigidly structured; loving or tension-ridden?

Sloppy writing or speech, old-fashioned English teachers would say, is a sign of sloppy thinking, and I heartily concur, when I hear people ask questions about "education" as though that conveyed to me in and of itself a crystal clear concept which I could then discuss. "Define your terms" has been the first rule for debate since men began to argue, but we still avoid doing so all too often, not least of the reasons being that it is so much easier to talk in generalities, to talk about "Society" or "The Economy" or, as here, "Education."

As noted earlier, "success" in education, as in any other enterprise, is inextricably tied up with "objectives." It is not possible to discuss educational success without reference to educational objectives, goals, and purposes. And although others have developed this point more fully in scholarly discourses, let me mention just two of the most important objectives of the educational process: socializing the individual, and making him, at the same time, self sufficient.

Societies have used their formal educational system to socialize the young, that is, to indoctrinate them with the values and standards of the group, to teach them to distinguish between acceptable and unacceptable behavior, to give them a sense of pride in the history and traditions of their country. In other words, the young have to learn, and do, to a greater or lesser degree, that they are and will always be dependent on one another. But simultaneously they must also learn to be independent: to develop an identity, a feeling of self-worth, and skills and abilities which will allow them to reach their personal goals. So the broadest objectives of education—socialization and individual self-sufficiency—are frequently in contradiction. But the tension between them can be a creative tension. As the student learns about his group, his society and his country, he also learns to reflect on them, and as he reflects, he criticizes. It is significant that reform, rebellion, and revolution have so often been sponsored and led by students.

Does education make a difference? Most people I know would be surprised to know that this question is being asked, let alone seriously considered. Certainly the minority group members of this society would be astonished. So would the poor, in Appalachia or in the heart of any one of our cities. So would the immigrants to these shores. And farmers and space scientists and oceanographers.

Restating the question doesn't help very much, either. We have looked at another version—What evidence is available of the success of education in meeting its objectives?—and we have seen that each of the key terms is so imprecise that the question as a whole is almost meaningless.

30
Challenging the Critics

Paul J. Schafer

Alice, the heroine of the great Victorian fantasy, *Alice's Adventures in Wonderland,* follows a rabbit down a rabbit hole and is immediately immersed in a strange and wonderful world. At one point she stops to examine the events taking place around her and makes an immortal comment on life: "Life is becoming curiouser and curiouser." Modern educators find themselves in a similar position. One needs only to look at recent criticism of education to justify the assertion that, indeed, life is becoming "curiouser and curiouser."

Schools Have Become Scapegoat

In the modern world, especially in the United States, the schools have become a modern scapegoat. On October 4, 1957, the Soviet Union launched Sputnik I, thereby seizing, temporarily, the space lead. When many people traced the "blame" for this United States failure, they found that the responsibility and blame came to rest at the neighborhood schoolhouse. Curiously, a few years later when the space endeavors of the United States surpassed those of the Soviet Union, no one traced the credit for this feat to the local schoolhouse.

Recent critics have not only been harsh and incredulous, but they have verged on ridiculousness. A responsible person needs only to look at the titles of some recent books highly critical of our American educational system to realize the extremes to which the critics have gone: *Death at an Early Age, They Die So Young, Murder in the Classroom, Our Children Are Dying, Children Under Pressure, and Crisis in the Classroom* —to name but a few of the more obvious titles. Unfortunately, titles such as these seem to go on interminably. One is reminded immediately of Mark

Paul J. Schafer, "Challenging the Critics," reprinted by permission from *National Association of Secondary School Principals Bulletin,* Feb., 1974, pp.1-6.

Twain's comment when he heard reports concerning his death: "Reports concerning my death are greatly exaggerated." Likewise, reports concerning the mutilation and murder of children in the classroom are also "greatly exaggerated." If the American people were to take such unorthodox criticism seriously, they would be extremely reluctant to wave good-bye to their children at the front door. Fortunately, the American people are accustomed to gross exaggerations and faulty generalizations. They have learned through television advertising, political campaigns, and other types of propaganda to be wary of gross exaggerations. Indeed, the American people have learned to give little consideration to unfounded and quixotic criticisms.

Criticism Is Contradictory

Much of the criticism concerning American education is not only grossly unjust but downright contradictory. Consider, if you will, James Conant who, during the early fifties, scurried around the country sounding the alarm that a tough and rigorous high school curriculum was essential if the American schools were to be saved. A decade later Conant and his supporters were mysteriously and suprisingly quiet when the "romantic" critics ushered in the humane and flexible curriculum. Then, it was their turn to scurry about the country calling for school to be fun and joyful.

Likewise, many critics of our modern educational system are calling for a more relaxed and humane school. They are demanding more flexibility, more freedom, and more open classrooms. They decry the tyranny that, they insist, dominates our public schools. Holt, Kozol, Dennison, Goodman, and Silberman, to mention the more vocal of this group, are making strident demands for a type of school which is more humane and free.

Parents and taxpayers, on the other hand, do not see lack of freedom as a major problem. Quite the contrary. A 1970 Gallup Poll showed that the general public, the people who pay the bills, thought just the opposite. The survey revealed that lack of discipline—the antithesis of lack of freedom—was the major problem in our schools today. The survey also revealed that the curriculum, eternally under attack by modern critics as not being relevant, was considered to be a major problem in the schools by only one-third of the people surveyed.

Honest Criticism Is Welcomed

Certainly, there is nothing inherently wrong with criticism if it is honest and responsible. A sincere critic of our American educational system should be as welcomed as a music critic is to the opera or the movie critic is to the latest Hollywood premier. Criticism that is honest and open-minded causes people to reexamine assumptions, reconsider goals and objectives, consider possible alternatives, and question current policies and practices; it provides guides to new horizons. Through sincere criticism, education can be improved. The right to criticize is deeply entrenched in the philosophical foundations of American democracy. Our founding fathers, and each generation since, have fought to defend our right to criticize. Indeed, the First Amendment to the United States Constitution guarantees every citizen the right to free speech. Recent books and articles, however, by critics of the educational system have abused this right. In the process they have portrayed themselves as being absurd and ridiculous.

Naturally, there are things wrong in American education. When statistics show that 95 percent of the books are bought by five percent of the American people and that the average American adult reads only a newspaper and a magazine weekly, when we realize that children are not reading up to their potential, and when schools have failed to show a growth in academic achievement concomitant with substantially increased operating costs, there is, of course, room for criticism. Since the largest local expenditure is for education, it is only logical that the schools be under close public supervision.

If education, in general, and teachers, in particular, are slow to respond to new procedures and new methods which are so strongly advocated by modern critics, perhaps it is because they have good memories. Teachers have lived through so many panaceas that promised to solve the problems of education. They remember such programs as "life adjustment education," "team teaching," "i/t/a" "homogeneous grouping" and a host of other programs which promised much, but delivered little if anything.

According to modern critics, if a child fails to learn there is surely something wrong with the school, not with the family, church, community, or the child. If a child refuses to do what is requested, teachers have "failed to motivate" the child. If teachers ask him to do something that he does not want to do, teachers are accused of "stifling the child's creativity." If the students are apathetic, the schools are accused of being "joyless and oppressive." If the teachers do permit freedom of movement and learning, the schools are accused of "lacking discipline." On the other hand, if the students are the least bit regimented, then the schools are accused of "killing the child's spontaneity." Schools are accused of being "godless" and not teaching "moral values." If, however, a teacher attempts to teach anything vaguely resembling morals and values, the teacher is accused of "foisting middle class values" on children or (God forbid) of teaching religion. We have simultaneously been accused of placing too much emphasis on the three R's and not teaching the R's. Thus, the criticism goes on and on.

American Education— Not All That Bad

Our American public schools have attempted to provide what no other society has ever attempted—complete elementary and secondary education for all its children regardless of race, color, creed, talent, desire, or family background. American education is unique in the fact that it is free, compulsory, and universal. The fact that there is room for improvement should not blur this magnificent feat, which has been reasonably successful. Our educational system is the pride of the world.

Furthermore, our schools have been called upon, with monotonous regularity, to combat problems which logically lie outside the realm of education. The schools have been called upon (practically mandated) to arrest drug abuse, reduce highway fatalities, teach sex education, train good drivers, entertain the public with sports and plays, fight venereal disease, reduce racial injustice, conduct charitable drives, ad infinitum. It seems that any problem which comes along is emphatically declared an educational problem and the schools are assigned the task of solving it. In a very significant way this is a tribute to the public schools of America. It highlights the success the schools have had in the past solving such problems.

Unfortunately, because the schools are only a part of society, they can solve only part of the problems. Education is the last bulwark of strength in American society. The family and the church, once powerful influences, are turning more and more of their former problems over to the American public schools. That the schools have accepted many of these challenges is another tribute to our educational system.

Generally speaking, our schools have performed yeoman duty with results that are nothing short of amazing. The American experiment of free, universal, and compulsory education is a paradigm for other nations. Today, our teachers are more dedicated, more knowledgeable, and more involved than ever before. Our children, contrary to popular criticism, are reading better than ever before. They are performing mathematical computations better than ever before, and they are learning more about the world than could have been dreamed of 20 years ago. Finally, our classrooms are more joyful, free, and more flexible than ever before.

Critics Must Not Go Unchallenged

The critics of the educational system must not be permitted to go unchallenged. Their criticism cannot and should not be accepted at face value. Americans must not lose faith in their public schools. To counteract those critics who would have the American public believe that there is a sinister conspiracy taking place behind classroom doors, a parent needs only to ask questions of his child concerning what he is learning, how he enjoys school, and other questions that he as a parent and a taxpayer is interested in knowing. In the final analysis, he is the surest critic of our American educational system. It is my belief that if the child, parents, and taxpayers would examine the educational system closely, they would reach a more rational conclusion than that their children are dying.

31
An Angry Comment from Within

William W. Goetz

Four years ago Charles E. Silberman's *Crisis in the Classroom* appeared amidst rather extraordinary fanfare. *The New York Times* predicted the beginning of a "great debate" on public education in the United States. Since the publication of the Silberman report, I find that the "great debate" has consisted of reviews breathlessly endorsing the report's main arguments, a spate of articles in popular magazines lamenting the sad shape of American public education, and the National Education Association's embracing the report with baffling warmth. On the college and university level, teachers who have made careers of educating teachers are suddenly discovering that the contributions of public schools have been exaggerated. I would like to suggest that there has been no "great debate" since the appearance of *Crisis in the Classroom*; that, instead, there has been a relentless and patently uncritical attack on all public education.

At the inception of this assult I welcomed, as a social studies teacher, outside criticism from social scientists whom I had long admired. But the vehemence and unreasonableness of the criticism and the absence of an effective counterattack has prompted me to express an admittedly angry— but I hope critical—comment on the content and style of this criticism.

An appropriate starting point might be *Crisis in the Classroom*. First, I would suggest that it is, among other things, a remarkable synthesis of much that has occurred in American education since 1960. It could serve as a history of American education for that period, providing an apt sequel to Lawrence Cremin's *The Transformation of the School*. There is, moreover, a critical balance in the report that has gone unnoticed. American schools have failed in many respects, but their successes and accomplishments are dutifully recorded; the English primary schools are seemingly superior to

William W. Goetz, "An Angry Comment from Within the System," originally titled, "The Schools and Their Critics: An Angry comment from Within the System," reprinted by permission from *Phi Delta Kappan,* Dec., 1974, pp. 268-271.

ours, but there are as yet no hard data to support this contention. Finally, there is a chapter on teacher education that is astonishingly incisive and accurate.

Yet, for such a serious study, *Crisis in the Classroom* is extraordinarily impressionistic and derivative. In addition to heavy reliance upon *The New York Times Magazine*, one finds introductions to college anthologies, a letter from a teacher to her former dean, and the author's own intellectual metamorphosis creeping into the data. The primary data seem to be many observations of the schools and what the schools reported, but nowhere is there any indication of how the data were sifted and organized. Many of the observations appear as an "item" to illustrate a generality, but there is no indication of how the generalities were produced.

I make the above observations with some uneasiness, considering the array of authorities amassed in the introduction, and of course I assume there was rigorous analysis that did not appear in the final draft. Yet it was reassuring to note that George R. LaNoue makes the same observation ("The Politics of Education," *Teachers College Record*, December, 1971) when dealing with school critics. He notes that such critics have not taken the failure of the schools "seriously in quantitative terms" and points out the dearth of conceptual models with which to evaluate efficiently the quality of schools. I do not intend to be pedantic about methods of quantification, a field in which I am obviously not an expert, but I think there is ample evidence to suggest that the critics have granted themselves inordinately wide latitude in producing generalizations about what is going on in schools. And what may be more significant, no one seems anxious to challenge this arrogance.

The Silberman report, unlike more radical works, does not advocate dismantling the system but would reform the present one, drawing largely on the experience of the English primary system. The most conspicuous recommendation is the use of the "open classroom" or "informal education" concept, which features greater freedom for children to set their own goals and select their own activities. As an experienced teacher, I have no quarrel with this recommendation. It may indeed be an idea whose time has come in American education. I applaud the attempts of districts and teachers who have initiated such programs. It could be the crowning achievement of the report to have popularized this concept for the American public.

Still, there is an idyllic tone that runs through the chapter on the open classroom (children kissing the bald pates of principals) that makes me just a little skeptical. Given many positive factors such as energetic, competent teachers and supervisors, well-organized curricula and activities—open classroom strategies require much more intensive and sophisticated preparation—and appropriate physical facilities, the concept may work

very well for many students unable to relate to more traditional schooling. I have seen what I consider to be open classrooms in action, and I have been reasonably well impressed by the progress that is being made.

At the same time, I have observed experiments in "informal education" that have bombed out egregiously. At meetings and conventions I am beginning to pick up rumblings that all is not well in districts where open classroom techniques have been adopted. I am not anxious to see this concept fail; I realize the need for different situations in which more people can learn better. I do question whether open classrooms are the universal panacea for elementary and secondary education; I do wonder if infatuation with the concept will not distract many from less exotic instructional problems such as curriculum construction and the development of diverse types of teaching strategies and models; and I do object to its being used as a handy shibboleth to prove (before its merits have been verified) how "bad" and "oppressive" the present system is.

Another theme stressed by the Silberman report, and a recurring dirge of many other school critics, is the schools' obsession with rules and control. Silberman comments:

> These petty rules and regulations are necessary not simply because of the importance schoolmen attach to control—they like to exercise control, it would seem, over what comes out of the bladder as well as the mouth—but also because schools and school systems operate on the assumption of distrust.

A very cute statement and one I would like to examine more closely. Of course schools and schoolmen are concerned over rules and regulations; of course there are many of us who still administer these rules with the finesse of a steam locomotive. But I have a feeling that schools are going to be social organizations for some time, demanding some types of social control. Hall passes and lavatory passes may seem petty and are easily caricatured (especially by those without any responsibility for the social control), but they represent an attempt to deal with hundreds of youngsters of different types and backgrounds interacting with each other and the institutional structure in rather limited space. Is it advisable to tell these students, "Rules reflect distrust. I trust you; therefore, no more rules"? Some students do find rules petty and a source of resentment. Other students find in them a source of security and direction and will admit quite candidly that they need them. I suspect that the rules bother critics of the schools far more than they do the rank and file of secondary students. What bothers students is when the rules are administered unfairly or inconsistently, changed constantly, or ignored by those responsible for their enforcement.

Another aspect of the school debate deserving attention is the constant if ambiguous theme that schools should concern themselves more with moral questions, with fundamental questions of right and wrong, with the quality of life, or with "values." The Silberman report supports this theme; it raises questions that have received scant attention.

One of the questions can be put quite simply: Whose "morality" and whose "quality of life" should be promoted? My impression is that those most anxious about values are individuals and interest groups with a rather definite conception of the values they want youngsters to learn. But how is pluralism protected if public education moves toward specifying moral and value goals? Weren't parochial schools criticized just a short time ago as a divisive influence in American society? If alternative schools are set up, say, under a voucher system, would each school have its own morality and lifestyle?

Edgar Z. Friendenberg has written an engaging and provocative analysis of high school students in *Coming of Age In America*. It is an exceptionally popular book, widely cited in the best journals, placed on the reading lists of foundations courses in schools of education. Despite the sociological framework established in the book, Friedenberg makes it quite clear that he brings "feelings" and "prior judgments" to his study.

These feelings revolve around the "vulgar-minded middle class" that mans the schools and the role it plays in producing students who are essentially anti-intellectual, devoid of self-knowledge, and lacking in concern for human dignity. Friedenberg would resolve this problem by establishing academic and residential schools manned by the upper classes. It is clear that Friedenberg has a certain set of values in mind when he speaks of "self-knowledge" and "human dignity." But few, it seems to me, have asked the questions: From whence has Friedenberg drawn his values? How valid and viable are these values?

Here I would like to engage in a little sociological prying myself, with the aid of David Riesman. (I am indebted to the Silberman report for calling this to my attention.) Riesman comments on the "aristocratic insouciance" that many school critics display when dealing with teachers and schools. Is "aristocratic insouciance" part of the explanation for the considerable interest in values displayed by academic critics? (You know, really you should be like us.) Does it help explain the personal, sometimes emotional, style of critics when dealing with schools? Does it explain why "values" can be presented with the arrogance and self-assurance of an absolutist ontology and encounter such weak resistance?

Thus far I have suggested that the sweeping indictment of the schools has escaped vigorous criticism. At this point, legitimate questions may be posed: Are not schools "bad"? Have they not "failed"? Is there not a school "crisis"? Is there nothing more to the criticism than the words of a few cantankerous writers?

My answer is yes, there is certainly more to be considered—much more, as a matter of fact—than the literary efforts of a few intellectuals. But, although it sounds terribly defensive and small (which could be the reason it is rarely stated), I do not want to minimize the role of critics and their followers in the debate. They have set the tone for debate; their rhetoric prevails; we fight on their conceptual battleground. It is the critics who have sensed the rhythm of the nation's intellectual life and who use it to their advantage. By design or otherwise, they set norms and expectations for others in academic circles. (Aristocratic insouciance again?) Many critics, I suspect, may be embarrassed by this acceptance based on faddishness. But it is a phenomenon which must be taken into consideration if the "debate" is to be analyzed fully.

Let us now deal with the badness and failures of the schools. Consider the statement of the late Columbia University historian, Richard Hofstadter, in *Anti-Intellectualism in American Life*, that there is a "general acceptance" of the fact that schools have been an "educational failure" and a "constant disappointment." Hofstadter came to this conclusion after reviewing the literature of criticism from the nation's colonial beginnings through the school reforms of the late nineteenth century to the school crisis following Sputnik.

But in accepting Hofstadter's statement, I would also like to accept his broad historical framework as a springboard for further analysis. Unlike many contemporary critics, who wrench the concepts of "the schools," "schoolman," and "the system" out of any meaningful historical context, Hofstadter saw the failure as part of the total social and intellectual climate of the nation's history. Given the anti-intellectual tradition of American life, Hofstadter argued that schoolteachers from colonial times would be accorded low salaries and status and that the teaching profession consequently would acquire an image as a haven for the shiftless, the mediocre, and even the eccentric. Schools have failed historically to attract the exceptionally ambitious and the exceptionally competent, Hofstadter suggested, creating a self-perpetuating system of a less than firstclass corps of professional educators.

This image continues to haunt development of the teaching profession, despite the progress made in recent years. Many outstanding young teachers leave the classroom for administrative positions, doctoral studies, or more "challenging" vocations. Classroom teaching is still not viewed as a prestigious final career-goal. (But a pleasant haven in times of economic distress? Yes.) Despite the tons of rhetoric, a system for identifying and rewarding an excellent classroom teacher has not yet been produced. The ideal of a self-correcting, self-improving profession does not come easily to teaching.

But where does one place "blame" for a phenomenon so deeply rooted in the history and culture of society? (As Hofstadter concluded: "The country could not or would not make the massive effort necessary to supply highly trained teachers for this attempt to educate everybody.") Perhaps it is enough to recognize the historical reality and its implications, to be thankful for recent improvements, and to work for additional progress.

Hofstadter was predictably critical of the turn-of-the-century school reforms associated with progressive education, which he treated under the label of "life adjustment." Even here, however, he has a message for those who would like to gain insight into a controversy over-run with rhetorical exuberance and moral fervor. Witness this statement:

> There is an element of moral overstrain and a curious lack of humor among American educationists which will always remain a mystry to those more worldly minds that are locked out of their mental universe. The more humdrum the task the educationists have to undertake, the nobler and more exalted their music grows. When they see a chance to introduce a new course in family living or home economics, they begin to tune the fiddles of their idealism. When they feel they are about to establish the school janitor's right to be treated with respect, they grow starry-eyed and increase their tempo. And when they are trying to assure that the location of the school toilets will be so clearly marked that the dullest child can find them, they grow dizzy with exaltation and launch into wild cadenzas about democracy and self-realization.

Lest one consider the above a historical aberration or collection of clever phrases, I point to the ponderous statements of state education committees, the philosophies of school districts, and even the introductions to courses of study within the schools. In this the silly season of educational criticism, it is well to recall that there have been many silly seasons of educational bombast about what the schools should and could do—a process which, I suggest, has snared the schools in their own rhetoric and made them vulnerable to attack from both the educational and political communities. The lesson should be clear: Institutions that claim they can do almost everything should not be surprised if they are accused of "failing" to do anything.

Despite his overall conclusion regarding the failure of American schools, Hofstadter was too astute a historian and too nuanced a thinker to neglect their obvious achievements or "successes." He commended the common school for forging "a vast and heterogeneous and mobile population" into a nation and for providing "at least the minimum civil competence" essential to the operations of republican institutions. Despite his academic bias, he agreed with Lawrence Cremin that the progressive or life adjustment program, while it did encourage much nonsense in the classroom, made positive contributions in many areas.

> Whatever may be said about the qualitative performance of the American high school, which varies widely from place to place, no one is to deny that the secondary education of youth was a signal

accomplishment in the history of education, a remarkable token of our desire to make schooling an instrument of mass opportunity and social mobility.

How quickly we seem to have forgotten the educational "crisis" created by Sputnik—Admiral Rickover lamenting the level of high school math and science, Arthur Bestor talking of "educational wastelands," the Rockefeller Report calling for excellence in education, Silberman calling for masses of intellectuals, federal money to support university-based curriculum projects, honors courses and advanced placement fever in our high schools. But the frantic drive in this direction was abortive. Toward the end of the sixties a new wave of criticism appeared, proclaiming that the academic reforms had failed or were not meeting existing needs and that the schools had better look elsewhere to justify their existence.

It is understandable that social critics and schools under pressure of social disorganization would move away from preoccupation with academic programs primarily designed to prepare students for college. But it is another thing to write off the curriculum efforts as "failures," or to ignore their accomplishments, or to engage in polemics about the "inhumanity" of the entire endeavor. I suggest that the accomplishments and even the failures of these reform efforts deserve closer study. LaNoue observes: "College Board scores show that the public schools in the sixties *did accomplish their post-Sputnik mandate* of producing students with higher mathematical, scientific, and technological skills." (The italics are mine, to suggest yet another "success" for American schools.) He then places the school debate in a broader context:

> ...the debate has been dominated by the educational romantics whose rhetoric fits the current intellectual mood of condemning all American institutions, the Presidency, the Congress, the judiciary, state and local governments, the military, medicine, business, universities, etc., etc., as failures. Such an undiscriminating mood may be personally cathartic, and many of us indulge in it at times, but no rational public policy can be based on it. Both the achievements and problems of public education should be recognized.

After working closely with the curriculum reforms for close to a decade, I can report that these reforms have produced both achievements and problems. I recall the cry in the middle sixties for a "new" social studies to follow the "new" math and "new" science. I remember the frenzied articles in our professional literature castigating traditional social studies and heralding the university projects as the savior of the field. Then the interminable debates over semantics come to mind. (What does Bruner mean by "structure"? What's a "concept"?) Finally, new materials were made available. Some are outstanding, some mediocre, some miss the mark completely. Some teachers thrive on them, some use them moderately, some ignore them. Some students love them, some tolerate them, some dispise them. Slowly, we all began to realize how really complicated the teaching process is—a process not to be simplified by catchy phrases, publishers' blurbs, or administrators looking for instant success.

Despite the difficulties that must still be worked out, there is a verve and urgency in teaching that was not present in the fifties. Many teachers are able to work with concepts such as "organic curriculum," "inquiry teaching," and even "modulating the cognitional activity." As I have already suggested, it has not been idyllic. There is still a long, hard road ahead to create learning environments where more of our young people can learn better. It would be tragic if the present debate were to distract us from the curriculum reforms started in the sixties. Bruce Joyce of Teachers College, Columbia, noted the challenge in his introduction to *Models of Teaching*, stating that, "despite the fearsome troubles besetting education, there presently exists a really delightful and vigorous array of approaches to schooling which can be used to transform the world of childhood if only we will employ them."

But perhaps the most biting criticism comes from those students who see the school as a "drag," "oppressive," and "boring." This phenomenon is exceedingly intricate and has no easy solution. There are indeed students who are bored for one reason or another with school and who are achieving very little academically. If there is one positive effect of the type of criticism I am counter-criticizing, it is the unique and dramatic way it has portrayed the plight of this type of student.

It should be remembered, however, that many of today's youth grew up very fast in an electronic age; to them, the pacing and atmosphere of most schools seem like a kindergarten existence. Still, there are many who are reasonably content and who make adequate and sometimes outstanding academic and social progress. There are still others who have induced a kind of boredom in themselves and others by constantly talking of "boredom." (Recently I heard a girl remark that she was bored with the talk of boredom.) Unfortunately, the critics, despite the incisiveness of some of their remarks, have given this boredom their blessing, though it is hardly representative of the complex reality of today's students.

How complex this reality is can be appreciated to some extent by examining the results of attempts to end boredom. I have observed some situations where students granted more freedom to study what interests them have grown even more bored with school. (What happens when a student given the privilege to study that which interests him or her decides that he or she is interested in nothing?) I have observed situations where overempathetic teachers caused bored students to become even more bored with the empathetic teacher. I have observed situations where rules have been modified to help students relax but, instead, the atmosphere has become more tense and the students more disgruntled. Of course I have also witnessed individual teachers working with groups of students (many of whom are "dropouts" in other classes), ignoring the rules, and working personal and pedagogical wonders. I have heard of students praising the accomplishments of free school or alternative school experiments. But my main point is that these situations are difficult to analyze; and to draw any meaningful generalizations is as yet a terribly hazardous task. I am convinced that the answer does not lie in peremptorily discarding in word or in fact the existing system of rules and curricula. There is still much to be learned about how the schools, students, and curricula interact.

In a *New Republic* article ("Our Public School Monopoly," September 15, 1973), S. Francis Overlan noted, after some study of public opinion samplings, that most citizens still view the public schools and their curricula as "fine." Obviously I do not find this surprising; but I do not feel like gloating. Could it be that while we are engaged in a tireless and unproductive debate, the taxpayers' revolt and an aloof national administration may do us all in? And this is happening when there seems to be evidence of real progress in the areas of curriculum and pedagogy, when schools are beginning to take education seriously and are developing belatedly a code of professionalism, when more progress can be made with additional study, research, and experimentation. But to accomplish what I think can be accomplished requires a prodigious expenditure of resources, energy, expertise, and commitment. We need help; we even need our critics on our side.

Despite their nastiness, the school critics have the talent and wit to offer keen insights into the teaching process and the total school environment. And, for all their arrogance, they possess the energy and charisma to touch many of us within the system. They could, indeed, touch more if they were to accept the schools, the staff, and the students as they are and not as they wish they would be. Let me make an offer: We will accept them with their nastiness if they will accept us with our inefficiencies. Perhaps then we would have the end of fruitless debate and the beginning of a real one.

32
Can Critics Change the Schools?

Daniel E. Griffiths

American education has never been in better shape or in worse repute. Both situations are due in greater measure to spirited spectators than to members of the education profession. Politicians, announcing that education is too important to be left to the professionals, launched an era of rising expectations with undreamed-of funds for education at all levels, nationally and locally. Other nonprofessionals who worked at pulling down the existing educational establishment have been equally influential, producing a literature that has caught the imagination of the public and catapulted authors from John Holt to Ivan Illich into celebrity.

But where are the professionals? Why have they been silent? Several, hard at work, have incorporated many of the suggestions of the critics into their own programs. In fact some have gone beyond the critics in their zeal for innovation. But professional educators have neither defended defensible positions—like institutionalized public education—nor have they moved to overcome the shortcomings of the critics by developing standards for appropriate and ongoing criticism of educational practices. Not only is criticism a proper role for educators, it is part of their professional obligation.

How the Critics View Educational Issues and Solutions

Although the critics take varying approaches, they generally perceive the public schools in the same way—as institutions that deprive youths of their freedom by imposing a set of values, a social regime, and a rigid curriculum. Seeing the problem in this framework, they proceed to propose either schools in which children are set free or no schools at all. A brief examination of the work of a half-dozen popular critics who span the past

Daniel E. Griffiths, "Can Critics Change the Schools," reprinted by permission from *The New York University Education Quarterly,* Vol. IV, No. 2, Fall, 1972, pp., 1-6, c New York University.

decade and who have written books with a variety of viewpoints must suffice to provide an understanding of the nonprofessional approach in this short space:

> Paulo Freire, *Pedagogy of the Oppressed,* New York: Herder and Herder, 1971.
> Edgar Z. Friedenberg, *Coming of Age in America,* New York: Random House, 1963.
> John Holt, *How Children Fail,* New York: Dell, 1974.
> Ivan Illich, *Deschooling Society,* New York: Harper and Row, 1970.
> Jonathan Kozol, *Death at an Early Age,* New York: Bantam, 1967.
> Charles E. Silberman, *Crisis in the Classroom,* New York: Random House, 1970.*
> * Page numbers cited are in these editions.

If someone thinks a significant critic has been omitted, he may very well be right.

Pedagogy of the Oppressed is important because many see in Freire's work with Brazilian illiterates a criticism of United States education as well as a model for education here to follow in the future. In the foreword to this book, Richard Shaull contends that blacks, Mexican-Americans, and middle-class young people can profit from Freire's discussion of how peasants struggled to become "free subjects" and to participate in the transformation of their society. It must be pointed out that nowhere in the book is there any evidence, only Freire's assertions, that the peasants became free subjects. And certainly there is little external evidence that the peasants of Brazil have participated in the restructuring of their society.

Freire first presents a concept of "banking" education in which the teacher is the depositor and the students depositories. Once this straw man is demolished—and it is not difficult to do so—he moves to a concept of problem-posing pedagogy. This concept should not be news to those who have heard of John Dewey or a host of other educational thinkers, but for Freire it is a brand new idea. In a problem-posing teacher-student relationship the teacher should not impose problems on the student; rather he should discover in the student's environment problems of great consequence to the student. Since "banking" education has been rejected, the teacher cannot tell the student what his problems are, but the student might well wish to work on problems of no consequence to the teacher. What to do? Freire takes his solution from *The Selected Works of Mao-Tse-Tung:*

> It often happens that objectively the masses need a certain change, but subjectively they are not yet conscious of the need . . . In such cases, we should wait patiently. We should not make the change until, *through our work* (author's italics), most of the masses have become conscious of the need and are willing and determined to carry it out. (p.83)

Pedagogy of the Oppressed is not an educational theory; it is a manual for the manipulation of the people. The democratic educator can only learn what *not* to do by reading this book, which is sufficient reason for enduring the turgid prose and the endless dialectics.

Having spent a full year interviewing students in a sample of secondary schools, Friedenberg describes the schools and the students in them and attempts to arrive at relationships in his book *Coming of Age in America.* It is a difficult book to categorize, because even a careful reader cannot separate the evidence of the research study from the author's admitted personal biases.

Friedenberg's general premise is that the school, as a social organization in which youths spend approximately twelve years, must have a substantial effect on their values. He reasons that since teachers are timid, students will become timid, a view still popular today in spite of militant teachers' unions in every city and student activists in many classrooms. Friedenberg's concluding recommendations range from development of educational means for distributing privilege more intelligently, to removal of the compulsory aspect of public education, to creation of new types of publicly supported institutions that will care for the needs of culturally deprived youths, to provision of financial aid to church and other private schools, and finally, to improvement somehow of the quality of school faculties.

Holt's thesis is that children fail because they are afraid, bored, and confused—apparently all at the same time. *How Children Fail* reflects in memo form what Holt perceives as the mechanisms responsible for ineffectual schooling: strategies children devise to meet the demands of adults; the effect of fear and failure on strategy and learning; the difference between what children really learn and what they appear to learn. These are the reasons schools fail, Holt's school among them. This critic's antidote revolves around the notion that schools should be places where children learn what they want to learn, not what adults think they should learn: the school should be a "great smorgasbord of intellectual, artistic, creative, and athletic activities, from which each child could take whatever he wanted, and as much as he wanted, or as little." (p.222)

Whereas the other books being examined deal exclusively with schools, Illich's *Deschooling Society* is concerned with schools only as a paradigm to illustrate "the general question of the mutual definition of man's nature and the nature of modern institutions." (p.2) It is not at all clear how Illich reaches his conclusion that institutionalization results in "physical pollution, social polarization, and psychological impotence," (p.1) for he illustrates the point only with an observation that whereas ten years ago in Mexico it was customary to be born and die in one's own home and to be buried by friends, now doctors and undertakers have interposed themselves. Nevertheless, his basic contention is that the more society institutionalizes services, the less capable people become to organize their own lives around their own experiences in their own communities.

In Illich's view, therefore, the schools are doing their job *too* well. His argument asserts, but certainly does not prove, that universal schooling is economically unfeasible; that because most learning occurs casually, schools are unnecessary; that obligatory schooling polarizes a society; and that if there were no schools, better methods of teaching could be developed. He proposes therefore that schools be disestablished and replaced by an elaborate arrangement of publicly financed, openly listed learning webs, the essential characteristic of which is that people will teach one another, with emphasis on learning practical skills through drill. (pp. 18-19) In the face of his own recommendation for an educational system that would virtually eliminate liberal education, Illich concludes with a further plea for the deinstitutionalization of values and for a society that loves man more than products.

Death at an Early Age is Jonathan Kozol's version of his abbreviated year of teaching in the Boston public schools during 1964-1965. It is difficult to follow what sometimes appear to be Kozol's main themes. For instance, at the outset we find Mr. Kozol teaching in a "segregated classroom" (p. xi) "about thirty-five bewildered-looking children, most of whom were Negro." (p. 29) What is clear, though, is Kozol's assurance that he cares deeply about Negroes, though no one else in the Boston Public Schools does. The story unfolds in fits and starts. Kozol, by his own account, started teaching with no training in education and no experience as a teacher, developed into an excellent teacher in the midst of tremendous adversities, and was fired near the end of the school year for teaching the "Ballad of the Landlord" to a fourth-grade class.

The book is entirely convincing, however, in depicting the tremendous prejudice against Negroes in the Boston schools. Inferior buildings, incompetent, poorly prepared teachers, and outdated materials are the standard, but these are surpassed in their effect on black children by the complete lack of understanding by the professional staff and the outright antagonism of the school system's hierarchy. Kozol's jumbled writing stirred the public's concern for equal treatment for blacks in the public schools.

Silberman's *Crisis in the Classroom* is quite different from the other books. Using a journalist's approach, Silberman attempts to spell out what is wrong with most schools and the teachers in them by reporting "items" that to his mind are bad. By the same device, those practices that strike him as good are recommended as solutions. Thus the "joyless" American elementary school classroom is to be replaced by the "integrated day" of the English primary school, and the "mindless" American teacher is to become the "student of teaching" about whom Silberman was able to say little.

In general, the Silberman book is a perceptive critique of American education, suffereing in lesser degree the faults of the others: a lack of standards that must accompany criticism and scholarship; an overwhelming faith in a single solution for a complex problem; and heedlessness of the realities that affect individuals involved in schooling.

Have the Critics Changed the Schools?

During twenty years of constant attack, the schools have undergone numerous changes. Most likely the critics have not been the cause that has effected change; rather change was on the way when the critics complained. Yet the critics must be given credit—though it be credit by correlation—for creating a public climate that not only supported innovation but demanded it. Friedenberg's outspoken call for alternatives to traditional schools is one example; Silberman's endorsement of open education is another; Kozol's plea for equal opportunity is yet a third.

One cannot read Friedenberg or Kozol and not believe that there is a great deal wrong in the conception of the teacher's role, in regard both to how the teacher lives in the school and to the relationship between teachers and their superintendents, principals, supervisors, and students. Kozol's relationship with supervisors indicated that teachers had no authority to teach what they thought desirable. Considering that Kozol started teaching "with no training in education and no experience as a teacher" (p. xi), this may not have been unreasonable. But the same rules also restricted those who were well-prepared.

Teachers, however, have taken matters into their own hands in the past decade, and the situation is changing, though probably not in a way envisioned by the critics. The emergence of strong local teachers' unions and associations has had a tremendous impact on the way teachers feel, live and work. Salaries have been raised, working conditions improved, and relationships with administrators modified to the point that many principals now lack any authority at all. The hand of the critic in all of this can be discerned, but lightly. It is there, nevertheless.

The prison-like atmosphere of secondary schools has been described and condemned. These judgments now appear to be having an effect. Students in many high schools no longer need passes, can leave the campus when they do not have classes, use the library and lounges without "permission," and exercise a great deal of control over their own behavior. In fact, liberty has gone a bit far in some cases.

In the eight short years since Kozol taught in Boston and the five years since *Death at an Early Age* was published, there has been such a deliberate effort to compensate for and remedy the conditions of blacks in large northern cities that this book, like Friedenberg's, is already dated.

The most obviously successful critic is Charles Silberman, whose *Crisis in the Classroom* has had a tremendous impact on elementary schools in this country. His advocacy of the English "open classroom" has been, if anything, too successful, for many teachers have climbed on the bandwagon without stopping to understand the concept. Silberman should not be blamed for this excess, since he cautions against uncritical acceptance of the idea. Nevertheless, if one wants evidence of the power of the critic, look to Silberman.

How the Critics Fail

The art of criticism is based upon the application of a set of standards to a particular act or set of acts. Thus, the literary critic applies his standards to a book, the drama critic to a play, and the music critic to an operatic performance. Unless there are standards explicitly stated and understood by all, it is difficult to see how there can be criticism in the usual sense of the word. With no clear standards and meager scholarship it is no wonder that the education critics flunk what reasonably should be their first task, namely to demonstrate that schools have failed in some significant way. But they merely assert that the schools are unsuccessful and then sail on.

Because he examined the research on student success or failure in schools, Silberman alone among the six critics cited approached professional standards. But his move from the data to proclaiming that the schools have failed defies reason. He reviews various studies of success in school and apparently accepts Coleman's well-documented conclusion that variations in school inputs seem to have little effect on students' academic achievement. (pp. 53-79) But then he boldly states: "Schools fail, however, less because of maliciousness than because of mindlessness." (p. 81) And later he reviews statements of goals of education advocated by Whitehead, Booth, and others and says: "The schools fail to achieve any of these goals." (p. 115) Outrageous statements of this sort are the result of a lack of standards and poor scholarship.

True scholarship also demands that significant questions be posed. In advocating English education practices, why did Silberman not ask, for instance, how is it that with poorly prepared teachers, low per-pupil expenditures, inferior school buildings, little or no parent or community involvement, and a rather rigid social class system the English have developed an interesting type of elementary education? Attempts to answer this question might have led him to investigate the organizational structure of English schools that makes it possible for teachers and headmasters to be creative and innovative.

As one reads the critics one would never realize that schools exist in cities or towns in real countries and that the people who live in these localities have certain expectations for their schools, build buildings, hire teachers, and, in fact, pay for the schools through elected school boards and taxes. Further, what is taught in the schools is influenced by a vast network of American people: university professors, state and national legislators, publishers, school boards, the media, and pressure groups. Further, schools are staffed—or, more often, understaffed—by real people who have feelings, anxieties, and expectations for their students and for themselves. This basic idea does not come through from the critics and, to the extent that it is missing, the critics are diminished.

Since the critics generally fail to understand the place of schools in the real world, they are addicted to the single-solution syndrome and to educational nonsense. Illich is probably the best case in point, in part because he is so extreme, in part because he is so obsessed with his view of institutions in society.

There are a number of predictable outcomes of deschooling society, none of them discussed by Illich. The public school system, which is the best delivery system yet devised for any of the social services, would be destroyed. Regardless of how one rates the schools, it must be acknowledged that they do deliver educational services. The poor would suffer the most from deschooling, since they would be less familiar and less comfortable with free-enterprise, free-wheeling education. What educational experiences a child would have would depend on what he wants to learn. But how would it occur to him to want to learn to balance an equation, for instance, or even to master the fundamental arithmetic to be able to learn how to balance an equation? The major fallacy of marketplace education is that it would result in no education, and, at its best, just the learning of a few skills from narrow technicians who, in Illich's scheme, would replace broadly trained professionals. Since liberal education will not be rewarded, it will die out, with the result that professionals possessing humane backgrounds, highly developed conceptual ability, and a sense of historical perspective will cease to exist. Education can hardly profit from such a change in personnel.

Jacques Barzun has defined educational nonsense as any plan or proposal or cirtique that plainly disregards the known limits of schooling or teaching as dictated by the common realities of life. Educational nonsense proposes or promotes something else than the prime objective of the school, which is the removal of ignorance. Holt comes remarkably close to pure nonsense when he advocates the smorgasbord school. Such a school would do little to remove ignorance. He touches on nonsense again when he says, "One piece of learning is a good as another." (p. 219) This is absurd on the face of it. Learning to smoke pot is certainly not as good as learning not to smoke it. Any school or teacher who abdicates responsibility for selecting what is to be learned and in what sequence is practicing educational nonsense and is incompetent.

Schools of Education as Critics

The habit of ciriticism is now prevalent in public education, and this has to have some beneficial results over the long haul. Prior to World War II there was little, if any, sustained commentary on the practice of education. Now all aspects of education are under the constant scrutiny of those outside the profession. These critics might have had more success in improving education if they had known more about it. Since this is a condition not easily remedied, an alternative is to get better informed people interested in criticism. The largest reservoir of informed people is in the schools of education and in the public schools. These professionals should, and must, become critics of all aspects of education.

Certainly the central mission of a professional school is the improvement of the profession it serves. It accomplishes this goal in many ways: research, teaching, and service. But it also must serve as critic of what it does as a school of education, of what the practitioners do, and of what the public does. Education is much too important to be left to the outsiders.

The professionals might well start with some unexamined trends: performance-based teacher education, the open classroom, teacher centers, and community control of education. It should be made clear, for example, that performance-based teacher education is a throwback to the thoroughly discredited learning theory of the 1920s, in which all learning tasks were reduced to elements taught one by one. Critical analysis of this movement should be forthcoming from educational psychologists and historians—the professionals especially equipped to do the job.

The obligation of professional self-criticism must be assumed by schools of education in yet another sense. As Professor Henry J. Perkinson of New York University has noted, most education trainees are taught to accommodate themselves to the profession, not to improve it. If the critical approach became a part of the existing training programs, professionals could be produced who would consciously try to improve the profession. This would involve construing the critical approach as both process and product. That is, the training program would not only equip the trainee with requisite skills and knowledge, but it would also deliberately seek to disabuse him of myths, errors, mistakes, and inadequacies. The trainee would also be taught to be self-critical and therefore concerned with the improvement of his won performance. Professors and students would then create a climate of criticism that would be self-reinforcing and would affect the entire profession. A new generation of educator-critics will go far in removing much of the nonsense and irrationality prevalent today, to the benefit of the future of education.

33
The Retreat from Education

Daniel Tanner

Forty years ago, Gunnar Myrdal observed that "the belief in 'education' is a part of, or a principle conclusion from, the American Creed." He went on to note that, in the U.S., "education has always been the great hope for both the individual and society."[1]

Today, some of our social scientists have garnered instant reputations by challenging this premise of the American Creed. Christopher Jencks, a journalist turned Harvard professor, has reinterpolated the data from the massive Coleman report of 1966 and concludes in *Inequality* that "the evidence suggests that equalizing educational opportunity would do very little to make adults more equal." Moreover, "the character of a school's output depends largely on a single input, namely the characteristics of the entering children." Finally, according to Jencks, "everything else—the school budget, its policies, the characteristics of the teachers—is either secondary or completely irrelevant."[2]

Many liberal academicians have been quick to accept this conclusion as valid. "Schools make no difference; families make the difference," observes Seymour Martin Lipset of Harvard's government department in referring to the Jencks study.[3] The same conclusion is reached in a recent report to the President's Commission on School Finance, prepared by the Rand Corporation. After reviewing a number of studies, the report offers this educational policy proposition: *"There seems to be opportunities for significant redirection and in some cases reductions in educational*

Daniel Tanner, "The Retreat from Education—for Other People's Children," (original title), reprinted by permission from *Intellect,* Jan., 1974, pp. 222-225.

1. Gunnar Myrdal, *An American Dilemma* (New York: Harper & Row, 1962), p. 709 [originally published in 1944].

2. Christopher Jencks, *et al., Inequality: A Reassessment of Family and Schooling in America* (New York: Basic Books, 1972), pp. 255, 256.

3. As quoted in Godfrey Hodgson, "Do Schools Make a Difference?," *Atlantic Monthly,* 231:35, March, 1973.

expenditures without deterioration in educational outcomes" (emphasis in the original).[4] Citing this report, Moynihan declares that "a member of the President's Commission would have to be dim indeed to fail to grasp that the Rand Corporation analysts were suggesting that with respect to school finance there is a strong possibility that we may already be spending too much."[5] Moynihan goes on to declare that "after a point school expenditure does not seem to have any notable influence on school achievement . . . (and) this 'discovery' was one of the major events in large-scale social science during the 1960's."[6]

Although Moynihan—a Harvard graduate who served together with Jencks on the Harvard education faculty—contends that we might well reduce educational expenditures for our public elementary and secondary schools, since incremental expenditures do not automatically close the achievement and income gaps between blacks and whites, it would be unthinkable for him to advocate similar reductions in university budgets on the same grounds. Many university academicians, who see themselves as educational policy-makers and theorists, are quick to impose input-output tests on public elementary and secondary schools—tests that they would consider preposterous if imposed on colleges and universities. A new breed of educational analysts has emerged, telling us that schooling is ineffectual as a means of social correction and improvement—as far as disadvantaged children are concerned.[7] They would have us believe that what a child gets out of school is determined solely by what he brings to school. It would seem that, to these analysts, the computer adage of "garbage-in, garbage-out" is analogous to school input-output with regard to disadvantaged children. Although many liberal academicians have been quick to embrace the research of Jencks and others that schools are ineffectual in improving the lives of disadvantaged children, no amount of empirical research will convince these liberal academicians, or even middle-class parents for that matter, that schools do not make a difference for their own children. They demand the very best schools—which means the very best teachers, physical facilities, learning resources, and curricular offerings—for their own children. For other people's children, particularly the disadvantaged, the liberal academicians readily accept Jencks' conclusion that schools make no difference.

In 1899, Dewey wrote: "What the best and wisest parent wants for his

---

4. Rand Corporation, *How Effective is Schooling?* (Santa Monica, Calif.: The Corporation, 1972), p. xiii.

5. Daniel P. Moynihan, "Equalizing Education: In Whose Benefit?," *The Public Interest,* 29:73, Fall, 1972

6. *Ibid.,* p. 71.

7. Michele A. Coakley and Donald Foster-Gross, "Perspectives on Equality," *Harvard Educational Review,* 43:49, February, 1973.

own child, that must the community want for all of its children. Any other ideal for our schools is narrow and unlovely; acted upon, it destroys our democracy."[8] When the liberal academicians declare that schools make no difference for other people's children, while demanding the best schools for their own, they are acting to destroy our democratic ideals. Ironically, virtually all of these critics are educators and, with one or two exceptions, are holders of the Ph.D.. They never say that their own formal education and educational credentials proved to be valueless. Such radical educational critics as Ivan Illich, Edgar Z. Friedenberg, and the late Paul Goodman (Ph.D.'s all) were espousing similarly elitist and anti-democratic views in calling for the elimination of formal schooling for disadvantaged youth, while the advantaged high-achieving youth could continue to be served by our existing schools.[9] It is astonishing how so many educational elitests who, themselves, were of modest social origins, and who owe their present status in society to the opportunities afforded by the most openly accessible educational system in the world, are quick to deprecate the schools as far as other people's children are concerned.

Nevertheless, regardless of the philosophic issues, the Jencks study portends new dangers for the very reason that it represents itself as scientific research based upon empirical data. No less an authority than Arthur L. Stinchcombe, chairman, sociology department, University of California (Berkeley), has declared that the Jencks' assessment of the data "agrees almost exactly with my own" and that "the book represents the best we know about the causes of individual success and about how far inequality in the causes accounts for inequality of success."[10] One of the problems of the social sciences is that the interpretation of empirical data is often influenced markedly by the sociopolitical orientation of the researcher. For example, even in economics—the most empirical of the social sciences—a John Kenneth Galbraith and a Milton Friedman will reach opposing conclusions and come up with opposing "solutions" to such problems as inflation, unemployment, and control of the wage-price spiral, even though they start with the exact same empirical data.

The field of education, or of sociology for that matter, is nowhere near, nor is it likely ever to approach, the empirical paradigms of economics. Yet, politicians, educators, and the general public are expected to alter radically educational and social policies on the basis of a single study that actually is

---

8. John Dewey, *The School and Society* (Chicago: University of Chicago Press, 1899), p. 7.

9. See Ivan Illich, *Deschooling Society* (New York: Harper & Row, 1971), p. 29; Edgar Z. Friedenberg, *Coming of Age in America* (New York: Vintage Books, 1967), p. 26; and Paul Goodman, *New Reformation* (New York: Random House, 1970), p. 88.

10. Arthur L. Stinchcombe, "The Social Determinants of Success," *Science*, 178:6, Nov. 10, 1972.

a reworking of the data from an earlier inquiry which reached quite different conclusions. Whereas the Coleman study of 1966 was a mandate for school integration, the Jencks report tells us that schools make no difference as far as income equality is concerned. From the findings of the Coleman study, the U.S. Civil Rights Commission noted that disadvantaged blacks who attend schools with advantaged whites will show an achievement gain of more than two years over those blacks who attend segregated schools.[11] This is the difference between being a high school dropout and being a youth who completes up to two years of college.

Whereas Jencks and Moynihan have chosen to use the data from the Coleman report to support their contention that added investment in schooling will have virtually no effects on improving educational achievement, Coleman himself reached a contrary conclusion from his findings. According to Coleman, "For those children whose family and neighborhood are educationally disadvantaged, it is important to replace this family environment as much as possible with an educational environment—by starting school at an earlier age, and by having a school which begins very early in the day and ends very late.... This implies new kinds of educational institutions with a vast increase in expenditures for education—not merely for the disadvantaged, but for all children."[12]

A recently completed seven-year study by the International Association for the Evaluation of Educational Achievement, involving the school systems of 19 countries, found that, although the home is the most powerful single influence on educational achievement, schools indeed have significant influences. When the findings of this study were released, some European newsmen were reported to have questioned the wisdom of justifying such an expensive and large-scale research project only to confirm what most laymen already know.[13] Apparently these newsmen were not aware of the current idea in vogue among some leading educational analysts in the U.S. that schools make no difference.

Schooling was never intended to equalize income. The income of a physician, attorney, architect, or accountant who is employed in civil service will not correlate highly with that of a cohort engaged in private practice. Similarly, college graduates in a given field can not be said to have the same working abilities, drives, and commitments for getting ahead in their field. Their incomes are likely to differ widely. Thus, although

---

11. U.S. Civil Rights Commission, *Racial Isolation in the Public Schools,* Vol. 1 (Washington, D.C.: U.S. Government Printing Office, 1967), p. 91.

12. James S. Coleman, "Equal Schools or Equal Students?," *The Public Interest,* 4:70, Summer, 1966.

13. *The New York Times,* May 25, 1973, p. 11.

schooling does not equalize income, it provides individuals with life choices which otherwise would not be open to them, not to mention the countless satisfactions which derive from having the power to exercise such choices. Unlike the factory, the aim of the school, wrote Dewey in 1915, "is not the economic value of the products, but the development of social power and insight."[14]

Contrary to the conclusions reached by Jencks and his associates, the data in the Jencks study nevertheless reveal a not insignificant relationship between education and income. For example, Jencks concedes that college graduates earn at least twice as much income as those who do not attend high school. However, he goes on to claim that 40% of the income difference is attributable to factors other than schooling, such as "varieties of luck and on-the-job competence."[15] Even if we accept Jencks' severe 40% reduction in the relationship between education and income, a strong positive relationship nevertheless persists.

Moreover, in interpreting the data, Jencks virtually ignores the age variable and gives short shrift to the sex variable. The failure to account for age differences and the tendency to lump males and females together in analyzing the relationship between education and income must be regarded as serious weaknesses in the Jencks study. Although the younger adults in our population have significantly more years of schooling than the older working adults, we can not expect the younger age group to enjoy higher incomes than their elders. After all, the latter group is longer—and better—established in their occupations, and the incomes, as well as opportunities for job promotion, of salaried workers are indeed linked to seniority. Recent census data bear this out. For example, adults between the ages of 20 and 29 have completed an average of almost 13 years of schooling, whereas persons between 55 and 64 years of age average slightly more than 11 years of schooling. Yet, family heads under 25 years of age have an average annual income of only $7,354, as compared with $12,920 for those in the 45-to-64-year age group. Only three per cent of family heads under 25 years of age are earning between $15,000 and $25,000 annually, while one out of every four family heads in the 45-to-64-year age group has an income in this range. The percentage differences by age are even more pronounced in higher income ranges.[16]

Nevertheless, despite the age variable, the census data show a clearly positive relationship between education and income. For example, employed males who are earning under $6,000 do not, on the average, have

14. Dewey, *op. cit.,* p. 18.

15. Jencks, *op. cit.,* pp. 8, 222.

16. Bureau of the Census, *Population Characteristics—Educational Attainment: March 1972* (Washington, D.C.: U.S. Department of Commerce, November, 1972), pp. 13, 47.

a high school education, whereas those who are earning $15,000 and over have completed an average of 3.2 years of college.[17] Even if 40% of these income differences is attributed to factors other than schooling, as Jencks contends, the schooling variable is nevertheless significant. It gains even greater significance when the age variable is controlled, as Jencks failed to do in his analysis.

Turning to the sex variable, the relationship between education and income for females should indeed be lower than that for males merely by taking into account the fact that many female workers suffer from loss of seniority and lowered income when they take leaves in order to raise families. They also typically accept lower pay in order to follow their husbands' job opportunities. This applies to a large segment of our college-educated female population. Yet, Jencks confounds the data by lumping these females together with males. Thus, after Jencks reduces the income increases associated with extra years of schooling by 40%, which he maintains is attributed to factors other than schooling, he calculates that four years of college will boost income by some 28%. However, when the sex variable is removed, we find that, even after Jencks' 40% reduction, four years of college will result in an income boost of over 35%.[18] If the age variable is controlled, a college education results in a far more dramatic increase in income.

Jencks also ignores the noncognitive effects of schooling, such as influences on attitudes, aspirations, and values. Obviously, Jencks has misconstrued his own data to support his own sociopolitical biases. As stated earlier, this is not uncommon among social scientists. One's sociopolitical orientation determines whether one sees the glass as half empty or half full.

The world of scholarship is such that instant reputations are to be made by attacking our schools and by proposing and promoting special remedies, or by deriving research results that are designed to shatter the conventional wisdom. The Jencks study neatly satisfies any category of educational criticism while it also appeals to the most cherished biases of elitist educators.

Our public schools have always been the favorite whipping boy of our intelligentsia. When the Soviets launched Sputnik I, our schools were blamed for our nation's failure to beat the Russians in the space race. After the U.S. proved its supremacy in space by being first to land men on the moon, our schools were given no credit. Instead, our schools were attacked for failing to correct the problems of poverty in our society. Soon after

---

17. *Ibid.,* p. 36.

18. Jencks, *op. cit.,* pp. 222-223.

Sputnik I, Harvard's Jerome Bruner attacked the public schools on the grounds that "the top quarter of public school students, from which we must draw intellectual leadership in the next generation, is perhaps the group most neglected by our schools."[19] Ten years later, Bruner turned around and attacked the public schools for concentrating on "the more intelligent kids" while neglecting "the children of the bottom."[20]

Jencks may be perfectly correct in pointing to the shortcomings of our other social institutions, not just our schools, for our failure to eliminate poverty; but he is misleading us when he reports that schools are irrelevant. In examining the penchant for American educators to attack their own schools for every conceivable ill, the Swedish educational researcher, Torsten Husen, has accused American educators of being masochistic.[21] The French publisher-politician, J. J. Servan-Schreiber, has emphasized that America's power to create is attributable in no small measure to its open-access educational system. Servan-Schreiber points to the fact that, in the U.S., from three to five times as many children of workers and farmers have access to higher education as in the Common Market nations.[22] An international study of school achievement revealed in 1967 that the top students in American schools were comparable to those of other nations. Moreover, where 70% of American youngsters were enrolled in the pre-university year of secondary schooling, some 90% of Dutch, German, French, and English youths were out of school at this age. Further, where a large proportion of American youth in the pre-university year of schooling are from working-class families, in European schools the enrollment at this level is heavily weighted toward youngsters from professional-executive families.[23]

In 1962, following a series of longitudinal studies comparing school achievement of Swedish youth attending American-style comprehensive high schools with those attending traditional differentiated schools, the favorable results for the comprehensive high school resulted in the enactment of school-reform legislation by the Swedish Parliament. Not only did the studies find that the highest ability students perform just as well academically in comprehensive high schools as in specialized academic high schools, but that a considerable proportion of youngsters who would

19. Jerome S. Bruner, *The Process of Education* (Cambridge, Mass.: Harvard University Press, 1960), p. 10.

20. Elizabeth Hall, "Bad Education—A Conversation with Jerome Bruner," *Psychology Today,* 4:51, December, 1970.

21. Torsten Husen, "Does Broader Educational Opportunity Mean Lower Standards?," *International Review of Education,* 17:77, 1971.

22. J. J. Servan-Schreiber, *The American Challenge* (New York: Atheneum, 1968), p. 74.

23. Torsten Husen, ed., *International Study of Achievement in Mathematics,* Vol. 1 (New York: Wiley, 1967), pp. 237, 273.

not have qualified for the universities under the traditional differentiated school system were now able to gain university entrance through the comprehensive high school.[24] Today, almost all of the secondary school population in Sweden attends American-style comprehensive high schools. The decision to adopt the comprehensive high school in place of differentiated schools was based not only on the favorable research findings, but also on a philosophic commitment that democracy is enhanced through educational accessibility and when all of the children of all of the people can go to the same schools.

Jencks contends that economic equality in our society is to be gained only by establishing political control over our economic institutions. "This is what other countries usually call socialism," and he argues that "progress will remain glacial" if we "proceed by ingenious manipulations of marginal institutions like the schools."[25] What Jencks overlooks is that Sweden, the most advanced socialistic society, only recently has faced up to the fact that its differentiated educational system was serving as a means of perpetuating class differences. The international study of achievement, discussed earlier, found that, in Sweden, the student population surviving to the pre-university year of secondary schooling was comprised of a higher proportion of youth from professional-executive families than from working-class families, whereas, at the pre-university year in American schools, the proportion from working-class families exceeded those from professional-executive families by almost threefold. Moreover, where 70% of the American age cohort was enrolled in the pre-university year of secondary schooling, only 23% of Swedish youth was enrolled.[26] These differences were even more pronounced when comparing the college populations of the two nations. Sweden realizes that schools do indeed make a critical difference, and has acted to reform its system of secondary schooling by adopting the American-style comprehensive high school. To the Swedes, the schools are hardly "marginal institutions" where equality of socioeconomic opportunity is concerned, as Jencks would have us believe.

To James B. Conant, a staunch advocate of the comprehensive high school, "It is strange that the enthusiasm for an American invention is so limited in this country just at the time when other nations are beginning to explore application of the basic idea." He went on to ask: "Are the high schools of the United States to be so designed as to be effective means of forwarding the idea of a unity based on diversity in a democratic community?" To which he answered: "Far more than the nature of our

24. Nils-Eric Svensson, *Ability Grouping and Scholastic Achievement* (Uppsala: Almqvist & Wiksell, 1962), p. 176.

25. Jencks, *op. cit.,* p. 265.

26. Husen, *International Study of Achievement, op. cit.,* pp. 237, 273.

schools is involved in the answer to this question. The entire structure of our nation may be at stake—possibly even its survival as an open society of free men."[27]

American schools, with all their faults, have accomplished more than any other of our social institutions in generating the expectancy of social opportunity for all the people. In 1897, Dewey wrote: "I believe that education is the fundamental method of social progress and reform."[28] In many other nations, knowledge still remains largely the monopoly of what Dewey described as "a high-priesthood of learning which guards the treasury of truth and doles it out to the masses under severe restrictions."[29] Our nation long ago rejected this elitist monopoly, and chose to see education as the key means of personal and social growth so that each rising generation would surpass the past in having ever greater control over its own destiny. Unfortunately, the contemporary clamor for change and reform is taken too often as proof that our schools have failed society, rather than as evidence of the great expectations that our society has for its schools.

If we, as a people, heed the admonitions of elitist critics, if we want less of the schools for other people's children than for our own children, then American society will not be true to itself and we will have lost all that we have gained through our schools.

---

27. James B. Conant, "The Comprehensive High School," in Alvin C. Eurich, ed., *High School 1980* (New York: Pitman, 1970), pp. 73, 80.

28. John Dewey, "My Pedagogic Creed," in Reginald D. Archambault, ed., *John Dewey on Education: Selected Writings* (New York: Random House, 1964), p. 437.

29. John Dewey, *The School and Society, op. cit.,* p. 25.

34
A View from Within

Philip W. Jackson

Many of us who work in schools, save those situated in urban ghettos, are becoming increasingly reluctant these days to wander outside the shelter of our institutions. And small wonder! Within the classrooms over which we preside and along the corridors through which we pass, the atmosphere is pleasant, if not exactly peaceful. There is the customary confusion that surrounds the processes of teaching and learning, of course, and more than enough discomfort from time to time. But, by and large, a sense of satisfaction and accomplishment accompanies much that goes on within our not-so-ivied walls.

From across the street, however, the view is quite different. At that distance the appearance of internal calm and the business-as-usual attitude on the part of the practitioner cannot help but be interpreted as signs of callous indifference. For outside our schools the air is thick with the cries of critics.

This situation is not exactly new, we know. Schools have long been the favorite targets of critics, both from the outside and from within. And, given the importance of education and the variety of interpretations to be put upon it, such a condition would be surprising if it were otherwise. But, though historically commonplace, attacks upon our schools do vary from time to time in both their magnitude and their substance. At present the volume is unusually high and we find ourselves in the midst of a particularly intensive barrage of catcalls, complaints, diagnoses, and freely proffered remedies for our educational ills. Moreover, in recent months, as the four articles in the first section of this monograph illustrate, the strategy of the critics has taken a new turn.

Until quite recently the desirability of schools and of compulsory attendance by the young were more or less taken for granted by friend and

Philp W. Jackson, "A View from Within," reprinted by permission from *Farewell to Schools???*, Daniel A. Levine and Robert J. Havighurst, eds., Charles A. Jones Publishing Co., Worthington, Ohio, 1971, pp. 59-64 foe alike. The goal of both, even of those who were most unhappy with the status quo, was not to do away with our schools as we now know them, but somehow to improve their operation. Some critics contented themselves with the detection of faults in our present system, leaving their correction in the hands of professional educators. Others went on to spell out in considerable detail their own plans for educational reform. But whether or not they offered specific remedies, most critics, until quite recently, operated on the assumption that our schools, as such, would endure the reformers' zeal. There would be changes, to be sure, but schoolhouses and classrooms and teachers and lessons and some form of compulsory attendance would somehow still be there when the dust settled.

Now, judging from the articles in this monograph, the critic's voice is becoming harsher and his ideas more radical. His tools seem to be changing from hammers and saws to battering rams and bulldozers—from instruments of construction to ones of destruction. Moreover, as these new land-clearance engineers rumble toward the schools, an increasingly large crowd of onlookers seems to be on hand to cheer them along and to enjoy the sport.

Why such radical action is necessary is, of course, the most important question to be asked. The only acceptable answer to that question (aside from acknowledging that some people derive perverse pleasure from the act of destruction for its own sake) is to claim that our schools today are so hopelessly bad that nothing can be done to salvage them. This being so, it follows that no matter what takes their place, the resultant arrangement is bound to be an improvement over what we now have.

Some form of this contention, with various elaborations and qualifications, is advanced by almost all the radical critics of our schools. As Goodman puts it, "Only a small fraction, the 'academically talented'— about 15 percent according to James Conant—thrive in schools without being bored or harmed by them." Reimer takes Goodman's assertion one step further by claiming that, "The school system also fails in part to educate most of its nominally successful students, stultifying, rather than nurturing, their lifetime capacity and desire for learning." Illich is quoted in a national magazine as saying, "Preventive concentration camps for predelinquents would be a logical improvement over the school system." Other critics, though less extreme, echo similar sentiments.

Now such charges are serious indeed. If true, they would certainly justify a battering-ram approach to educational reform. But the seriousness of such a consequence also demands caution. Before taking up the cudgels of attack, we need to understand how Goodman, Reimer, Illich, and others arrive at such a devastating verdict. For, if it should turn out that their verdict is unjustified, we must not hesitate to turn our backs on it, no matter how unfashionable it may be to support the Establishment and no matter how unpopular such a stance may make us at the weekend cocktail party.

If we turn to the search for facts, a disenchantment with the radical critics is quick in coming. For even under the most liberal definition of proof, there is precious little to substantiate the basic premise on which the deschooling argument rests. That is, there is no solid evidence to support the blanket assertion that schools in our society are failing to educate our children, much less that they are actually doing them harm. This is not to say that there are not students—too many, we know—for whom such a charge is true. We hardly need proof, for example, to convince us that life in many of our inner-city high schools is miserable indeed. We are also painfully aware that a sizable number of our middle-class adolescents are being turned off by their school experience. But to move from such knowledge, lamentable as it is, to a general indictment of our entire school system is to take a giant step indeed, totally unwarranted by the evidence at hand.

Not only is there no basis for concluding that public school pupils across the land are gnashing their teeth in despair and rattling their tin cups against the bars of the classroom in protest against the injustices they are suffering but the few scraps of evidence that do exist point to quite the opposite conclusion. From the middle 1930s to the present day, almost every systematic study of educational attitudes that has been undertaken has revealed the vast majority of students, from the middle grades onward, to be surprisingly content with their school experience. Apparently, almost four out of five students, if asked directly, would confess a liking for school, with all its faults.

Such evidence must of course be taken with a grain of salt, for it can always be argued that the majority of students are content with school simply because they have little else with which to compare it (save summer vacation). Nonetheless, even if accepted with great reservation, it is difficult to reconcile the few facts that do exist with the iconoclastic condemnations of the deschoolers.

In addition to basing their arguments on scant evidence concerning the state of our schools today, the proponents of deschooling seem curiously lacking in historical perspective. Though educational progress, like human progress in general, has clearly had its ups and downs throughout history and leaves no reason to believe that future improvement is inevitable, it does seem true that schools in our country, and probably in the entire Western world, are superior in many respects to those that existed a century or two ago. They serve a larger segment of our citizenry, they follow curricula that are more varied and better suited to the future needs of our students than was true in the past, and they are staffed by teachers who, on the whole, are better educated and more humane in their dealings with children than were their predecessors a few generations back. Gone are the hickory stick, the rapped knuckles, and dunce's cap, together with the heavy reliance on rote memory, the rigidity of the recitation method, and the bolted-down desk. Some of the educational practices that have taken their place leave much to be desired, it is true, but with all of our present educational shortcomings, it is difficult to avoid the terribly smug conclusion that our schools are better today than they have ever been before.

Such smugness should not be accompanied by complacency, however, for whatever progress has been made has required hard work, and there is much yet to be done. Moreover, we have no guarantee that things will not get worse rather than better. Nonetheless, the overall impression of progress, unstable though it may be, does not sit well with the assertion that our present system is one great failure. Faced with such a charge, one is tempted to say to the critic, "If you think our schools are bad now, you should have seen them in your grandfather's day!"

Much as it might dampen the critic's flame, a calm look at what goes on in our classrooms reveals them to be neither Dickensian nor Orwellian horrors. They are neither prisons, presided over by modern-day Fagins who take delight in twisting ears and otherwise torturing children, nor are they gigantic Skinner boxes, designed to produce well-conditioned automatons who will uncritically serve the state. Anyone who believes in the truth of such fictions should take a few days off to visit his local schools. Should he find the fiction to be matched by reality, he would indeed have reason to seek change by whatever means are available. But anyone who, with or without such personal experience, proceeds to argue that such is the state of all or even most of our schools, must either be misinformed or irresponsible.

Even if we overlook available evidence, both contemporary and historical, and accept the conclusion that our schools are in such a sorry state as to warrant abolishing them, we must ask what will happen when their doors are closed for good. What, in other words, will our youth be doing during the hours normally spent in school?

The answer to that question is a bit vague, to say the least, in the writings of most critics, but usually it is assumed that school age children, free from the artificial demands of the classroom, will be enthusiastically engaged in learning (Goodman calls it "incidental learning") through contact with real-life situations. Guided by nothing more than natural curiosity and an instinctual love for learning, our children will presumably wander over the streets and fields of our land, gathering rosebuds of wisdom along the way. Adults, gladdened by the sight of these wandering scholars, will hail them as they pass and will invite them into the shops and factories and offices and hospitals, where they will become apprentices and learn at the feet of their elders those skills and trades that will equip them to take a productive place within our society.

Of course, no self-respecting critic would accept this caricature of the postschool era, but the romantic idealism contained in such an image is strongly evident in the imagination of many who criticize our current educational scene. However, when they begin to muse on how this Whitmanesque ideal might be achieved, something very much like the structure of our present schools, or at least the best of them, begins to emerge.

The chief difficulty with many advocates of the incidental-learning position is their failure to distinguish between learning and education. For most of us, incidental learning of one sort or another is indeed occurring all the time. As I glance up from my desk at this very moment, for example, I have just "learned" that my neighbor is about to mow his lawn! But education obviously involves much more than the accumulation of such fortuitous bits of information. It involves learning that is prescribed and planned and guided. Humans can indeed educate themselves, but experience seems to show that the process occurs more effectively with outside help. It was with this realization that the idea of a teacher was born. When our forebearers began to come to grips with the fact that not all adults could spend their time at such a pursuit, the notion of a school was in the offing.

Doubtlessly, there *are* children who, freed from the formal demands of schools and with a minimum of adult guidance, would set about the laborious task of educating themselves. But whether all or most children, if pressed to do so, would turn out to be such self-motivated learners is indeed doubtful. Moreover, there is at least some reason to believe that those who would suffer most from the absence of classroom constraints and teacher guidance would be those children who already exhibit signs of educational impoverishment. Thus, left largely to their own devices, our out-of-school learners would likely behave in ways that would result in exaggerating the cleavages that already separate social class groups within our society.

Finally, even if educators or their critics wanted to set children free to learn on their own without the confines of a school and all the restrictions it implies, there is ample reason to believe that parents and other adults in our society would not stand for it. Like it or not, our schools presently perform a custodial function as well as an educational one. Parents, particularly those of young children, simply do not want their offspring to be unsupervised during much of the day. We could, of course, substitute compulsory day-care centers or neighborhood clubs for compulsory schools, but, when we consider such alternatives, they begin to look not all that different from what used to go on in the empty schoolhouse down the block.

In summary, the arguments of the deschoolers suffer from two serious flaws. They begin with a false picture of how bad things are in our schools today, and they end with a highly romanticized notion of what might be substituted for our present educational system.

Meanwhile, back in the classroom, there is a lot of work to be done. Our inner-city schools, particulary high schools, *are* disaster areas; too many of our students, particularly our adolescents, *are* being turned off by their school experience; the bureaucratic structure of our schools, particularly our larger ones, *is* more abrasive than it needs to be; our graded system *is* too rigid and requires loosening up; our teacher certification laws *are* shamefully archaic and prevent many good people from taking their place in the classroom; our schools *do* need to be linked more imaginatively to the communities they serve.

These *are* serious problems, badly in need of solution. The crucial question is whether their solution requires the abandonment or the overthrow of the entire system. To answer that question, we must consider what is *right* about our schools as well as what is wrong with them. In balance, at least seen from the inside, the pros clearly outweigh the cons.

35
The Unfinished Promise

Fred M. and Grace Hechinger

Education has been America's invisible frontier. It has enticed generation after generation of young people to move forward into territory that had been strange and forbidding to their parents. The promise of that open frontier liberated the young from the confinement of their past, but in the process it also often severed them from their roots. For some, the frontier was temporarily shut down by prejudice and politics; but, as soon as those barriers were lifted, those who had been held back surged forward by taking full, often almost compulsive, advantage of education.

Jefferson's ideal of an "aristocracy of talent" may have seemed an impossible dream in his time, but it remains crucial to self-government. The "diffusion of knowledge" cannot be said to have failed when the diffusion of contemporary American leadership is compared to the narrow base from which such leadership used to emerge, and still does in many other nations. Public schools and the great network of state universities have responded to the technological society's insatiable demand for managers, executives, and planners. Graduates of this vast public education system have long since joined the earlier cozily homogeneous cadre of leaders until today they outnumber them. Whatever might once have been considered the American equivalent of the playing fields of Eton as the training ground for policy-makers has long since been replaced by the public high school. Even the elite colleges themselves—the only remaining bastion of the Old Boy Network—now draw the majority of their students from that egalitarian pool and contribute directly to the diffusion of status and leadership.

Social critics and radical reformers have not had to look far to be able to focus on American education's specific flaws and failures. Many historians, and virtually all history textbooks, have ignored the pervasive influence of education on the shaping of American thought and the

Fred M. and Grace Hechinger, "The Unfinished Promise," reprinted by permission from *Growing Up in America*, McGraw-Hill Book Co., 1975, pp. 406-411.

ordering of American society. Thus, the field was wide open for revisionist critics to evolve a succession of devil theories—tales of conspiracies enlisting the schools in evil purposes. In this distorted view, education becomes a tool to enslave; schools are an instrument of oppression; the colleges, an assembly line that produces a standard-model ruling class; universities, blind servants of the military-industrial complex. The entire educational enterprise thus emerges as a giant, efficient machine created to assure conformity to an approved political scenario and servility to capitalist technocracy.

Such theories are seductive. They gain support because they single out some real weaknesses which, at a particular moment, are of serious and justified concern. For example, schools have indeed allowed themselves, time and again, to be used by conservative establishment forces to impose unthinking obedience to a special brand of Americanism; the ruling elite has sought to perpetuate itself by trying to turn some colleges into finishing schools for its brand of gentlemen; the universities have, at times, done the government's bidding without sufficient concern for the morality and wisdom of the government's policies. Public school educationists have, on many occasions, been guilty of some of the follies of which they have been accused. American pedagogues have espoused theories that failed to teach; condoned policies of exclusion and neglect which, by shutting out large groups of children, violated public education's own basic principles. At other times, they have embraced vapid academic standards which temporarily jeopardized the nation's intellectual stamina.

It is not difficult to show that, at one point or another, American educators have been smug (rejecting all criticism with the standard reply that the schools were better than ever), or arrogant (insisting that, if only the lay public kept hands off, the professional pedagogues could cure all of society's ills), or defensive (attributing the children's failure exclusively to circumstances beyond the schools' control).

It is not that the critics are wrong about any specific observation; it is rather that they train their telescope on an isolated part of the landscape and, on discovering a patch of dry rot, conclude that they have seen a panoramic vision of doom. Insularity compounds these distortions. Measured against a utopian ideal, for example, the American school is indeed often autocratic and oppressive; compared to existing models, say, in France or Germany, the same schools are oases of liberation.

American education has often been under severe stress. Whenever it ignored its own prinicples and goals, as it did in condoning the "separate but equal" doctrine that violated both the spirit and the letter of the Constitution, the educational leadership undermined the foundations on which the public school pioneers wanted to build a new interdependence between school and society.

But the major strands of education's fabric have stood the test of time remarkably well. Faith in education remains a unifying force. It is as strong in today's urban ghettoes as it was among a different population of similar ghettoes throughout the nation's history. It is a faith that even slavery could not erase; it remains the faith that still transcends all lines of color and national origins. Black militants, who charged that schools which failed to teach their children were guilty of "educational genocide" expressed the Black parents' traditional American belief that the difference between educational success and failure is the difference between life and death.

Such grass-roots faith in the magic of education placed a heavy burden on schools, which had no magic answers to the problems they were expected to solve. But, despite its flaws and setbacks, American education has been remarkably successful in giving a high measure of social and political cohesion to a diverse population without any common ethnic or historic heritage. If schools have failed to wipe out poverty and to eliminate conflicts of wealth and status, they nevertheless prevented those social and economic strata from becoming frozen. Education may not have emerged as the great equalizer envisioned by Horace Mann; but American education more than any other force has kept society fluid and upwardly mobile. The rise, within one generation, from unskilled labor to the professional class, for example, is still commonplace. For each new group of first-generation collegians, the campus remains the staging area for economic achievement and social elevation.

While reality belies the myth of a classless America, education continues to be an effective escape hatch that reduces the danger of explosive class warfare. Radical leaders, including those of the 1960s student rebellion, have repeatedly failed to rally the poor and the deprived to their cause, in large measure because of the continuing faith in the evolutionary power of education. The promise to improve the schools and colleges, or to remove barriers to educational opportunity, proved highly magnetic; but those who threatened to bring the educational institutions to a halt, or to tear them down as part of a revolutionary strategy, soon found themselves without followers. In July 1974, only two years short of the Revolution's bicentennial, James Alexander Harris, one of six children of a welfare family, was elected president of the National Education Association which, he recalled, twenty years ago had still conducted much of its business in two separate compartments—"For Whites" and "For Colored."

America's educational origins were elitist and restrictive. To give the poor any schooling at all was a matter of charity. But the founders instinctively sensed the inevitability of conflict between an elitist social order and the egalitarian politics of a self-governing republic. Jefferson's proposal to make available free schooling from first grade through the university to a few of the ablest youngsters, regardless of family background, was a small beginning; but it started a trend that eventually made one fourth of the nation either learners or teachers.

Over the years, support for mass education became overwhelming. The demand by each new generation of parents was irresistable. What often remained vague was the strategy to accomplish those goals or an understanding of education's limitations. The debate over what constitues the most effective curriculum, begun by Jefferson and Franklin, still continues. The conflict between the advocates of utilitarian training and the supporters of broad, general knowledge has never been resolved, with the result—probably essentially beneficial—that the two streams continue to mingle and modify each other. When James B. Conant appealed for the comprehensive high school in which vocational training could coexist with intellectual studies, he was actually pleading for the retention of the kind of republican egalitarianism in which youths are not separated at an early age into those who work with their hands and those who work with their heads.

This view of schooling contains a vital political safeguard. It lowers the barriers between blue- and white-collar workers; it reduces the likelihood that an excessively specialized education will, at times of economic recession, give birth to an alienated intellectual proletariat ready to seek totalitarian solutions simply because there are no jobs for its narrow competence.

The American decision not to sort children at an early age for different types of schooling which would in turn predetermine their future economic status in society was a sharp break with a tradition that in many European countries still remains dominant. Readiness to keep options open is more than a pedagogical tactic; it is an ideological commitment. Some have scorned the commitment as an anti-intellectual threat to academic standards; but experience has shown that those nations which established academic hurdles between elementary and secondary school find themselves trapped in a selection process that is more responsive to economic and social class than to talent and potential.

Although American education has instinctively opted for the open access, it has found no perfect solution for the attending problem: how to sort children for the purpose of giving them the most suitable instruction, without shunting them into "tracks" which would subtly recreate elitism and divisions. This danger has been underscored by some consequences of school integration, when deprived children were transferred to schools with a predominantly affluent, middle-class clientele.

Such examples show the complexity of an ideal that seeemed so simple when Horace Mann predicted that rich and poor would send their children to the same public schools, thus wiping out all differences of class. The goal has remained both unchanged and elusive. Reflecting a deeper change in the nation's mood, the earlier easy optimism has been dimmed.